CAMBRIDGE STUDIES IN
CRIMINOLOGY XLIX
General Editor: Sir Leon Radzinowicz

BURGLARY
IN A DWELLING

THE HEINEMANN LIBRARY OF CRIMINOLOGY
AND PENAL REFORM

CAMBRIDGE STUDIES IN CRIMINOLOGY

BURGLARY
IN A DWELLING
*The offence, the offender
and the victim*

Mike Maguire
in collaboration with
Trevor Bennett

HEINEMANN LONDON

Heinemann Educational Books Ltd
22 Bedford Square, London WC1B 3HH

LONDON EDINBURGH MELBOURNE AUCKLAND
HONG KONG SINGAPORE KUALA LUMPUR NEW DELHI
IBADAN NAIROBI JOHANNESBURG
EXETER(NH) KINGSTON PORT OF SPAIN

British Library Cataloguing in Publication Data

Maguire, Mike
    Burglary in a dwelling.—(Cambridge studies in criminology; 49)
    1. Burglary—England—Thames Valley
    I. Title II. Bennett, Trevor III. Series 364. 1'62   HV6665.G7

    ISBN 0-435-82567-4

Phototypesetting by Georgia Origination, Liverpool
Printed in England by Biddles Limited, Guildford, Surrey.

Contents

List of Figures

List of Tables

Acknowledgements

Sincere thanks are due to many people without whom neither the research nor the book would have been possible. It is impossible to name them all and we hope that those we miss will forgive us. A large debt of gratitude is owed to the Home Office who provided the research funds, and in particular to the members of the Home Office Research Unit who acted as both formal and informal consultants. Here we are particularly grateful to Dr. R. W. G. Clarke, Mrs. P. Mayhew and S. W. C. Winchester. We also thank the Prison Department and several prison governors for allowing us to visit penal establishments, prison staff for their tolerance of long interviews, and inmates for co-operating in the study.

The Thames Valley Police gave us ungrudging help and free access to information. In the Force Headquarters we would especially like to thank the Chief Constable, Assistant Chief Constable Leslie Emment, Chief Inspector Ware, the members of Statistics branch and those in the records office, all of whom we put to some trouble. The heads of the three Divisions in which we carried out fieldwork were also extremely co-operative, and junior officers acted as invaluable guides and liaison officers.

The members of the Bristol Victims Support Scheme were kind enough to allow us to visit them for a day, and Chris Holtom generously lent us some of his research data.

We are indebted for advice and encouragement to our colleagues in Oxford, to the Reader in Criminology Dr. Roger Hood, and to the series editor, Sir Leon Radzinowicz. Particularly warm thanks are due to Mrs. Sarah McCabe who read the manuscript and offered detailed criticism, and to Mrs. Hilary Prior and Mrs. Nancy Bartrum who undertook, without complaint, a great deal of typing from badly written scripts.

Finally, we would like to thank all the burglary victims who invited us into their homes and the forty convicted burglars who agreed to co-operate in the study. All gave considerable time and thought to answering our questions.

I. Introduction

British criminology is surprisingly lacking in detailed studies of specific forms of criminal behaviour. The physical reality of offences—how, when and where they are carried out, how much is stolen, how much damage is done—and the significance they assume in the lives of both offender and victim are factors often omitted from discussions about penal policy, while information about the operational methods, lifestyles and inter-relationships of people who regularly commit particular types of crime is, to say the least, fragmentary.

This book represents a modest attempt to shed more light on an important property crime which most people experience at least once during their lifetime. Burglary in a dwelling is one of the most common serious offences recorded by the police, but also one which retains a certain air of mystery and stirs up intense emotional responses. The idea of a criminal penetrating one of the most private places of a person's world—his or her own home— is unpleasant and upsetting, and can produce psychological effects which last long beyond the loss or inconvenience suffered at the time. These are caused partly by the symbolic violation of the 'sanctity' of the home—a common result being the feeling that the house has been 'tainted' or 'polluted' by the intrusion—and partly by fear of the unknown. In the majority of cases the victim has no idea who was responsible for the offence and the imagination is allowed full rein. The burglar may be imagined as a dangerous and violent stranger, or victims may begin to suspect acquaintances of holding grudges against them. Such thoughts can poison social relationships and lead to constant worry that the event will be repeated. If the house is entered during the night while the victims are asleep, feelings of helplessness may be magnified and childhood fears of the dark and of 'noises in the night' re-awakened in a vivid manner. Daytime burglary is often associated in people's minds with a different fear, that of vandalism. Many have exaggerated notions of the frequency with which burglars ransack the houses they steal from, a belief fuelled by stories and articles in magazines and the popular press. *Woman*, for example, published a typical article about burglary in November 1978, in which it was stated:

If they do no more than strew your possessions around, you've come off lightly. Teenage burglars tend to do rather more—mixing flour and jam on the kitchen floor, spreading treacle around the lounge, ripping up photographs, or worst of all, treating your home as if it is a toilet.

Although, as we shall show, such behaviour is relatively uncommon, the mere thought that it *might* have happened is often sufficient to intensify the experience of victimisation. Finally, for many women the offence carries connotations of a sexual assault and open parallels have been made with rape. As a senior policeman stated in a newspaper article (*Daily Telegraph*, June 1978):

> Women, particularly, whose houses are burgled find it almost like a sexual offence to have every part of their private lives exposed to some dirty-fingered villain.

The tendency for discussion to dwell excessively upon the most serious cases may not only worsen the impact of burglary upon new victims, but may also increase the general fear or concern in the community about the prospect of being burgled. Both British and American research has suggested that such anxiety affects a considerable proportion of the population. Ennis (1967:75), for example, found that 14 per cent of interviewees in a random sample of households were 'very much or much concerned' about the possibility of having their home broken into, and subsequent surveys in Washington DC (Scarr 1973:250) and Toronto (Waller and Okihiro 1978:81) produced figures of 21 per cent and 13 per cent respectively in answer to similar questions. In England, a *New Society* survey in November 1966 found that more people 'worried a great deal' about burglary than about violence outside the home, and Sparks *et al.* (1977:207) found in 1973 that 18 per cent of residents in three areas of inner London agreed with the statement that 'people are not safe in their own homes'. Although answers to survey questions have to be treated with some scepticism, there is little doubt that burglary comes high upon the list of crimes that cause public anxiety.[1]

While we would in no way wish to understate the seriousness of the offence, it is hoped that by dispelling exaggerated notions and misconceptions our research will contribute to the reduction of excessive fears, which can be extremely harmful, and to the increase in interest in ways of softening the blow experienced by victims. We also hope to stimulate more informed discussion about the possibilities of preventing or discouraging burglary by means of an analysis of patterns of offending at a local level, and of an interview-based account of the habits of persistent offenders. It has to be admitted that the offence is one of the most difficult to prevent and to detect, but more knowledge of and understanding about its frequency and distribution, and about the attitudes and behaviour of those who carry it out are essential prerequisites for any practical policy. One of the most striking features of burglary is the variation in rates and patterns of victimisation to be found between different areas. To a large extent it appears to be a 'local' problem, and efforts to combat burglary in one area may be totally unsuited to an area only a few miles away. In looking at three contrasting areas of the Thames Valley we stress the wide differences to be found between the characteristics and practices of burglars active in each, and the consequences that these have for policing.

The overall plan of the book is to build up a picture of burglary from a series of different viewpoints. In the remainder of this chapter we briefly mention some previous studies, describe the scope of our own research and discuss some legal aspects of the offence. In chapter II we first examine what is known about the incidence and distribution of burglary across the country as a whole, then look at patterns of offending within the three areas in which we conducted fieldwork. Questions are raised about the relationship between different categories of offender and the types of housing that they are most likely to burgle. This is followed by an analysis of the times of day at which burglaries occur and the most common *modi operandi*. In chapter III we look at the lifestyles, attitudes and practices of known persistent burglars. Our account is based upon interviews with a number of adults and young adults who admit to frequent involvement in house burglary as a method of supplementing their income or indeed as their main source of income. In chapter IV we trace the 'career' of a man who regards himself as a professional burglar and who gives an account of his progress from petty theft to a series of country house burglaries that resulted in losses thought to be in excess of half a million pounds. In chapter V we consider the impact of burglary upon victims and the manner in which they are handled by the police. Finally, in chapter VI we examine current approaches of the courts, the police and others to the phenomenon of burglary, and look at the possibilities and limitations of policies aimed at preventing, containing or simply helping people to 'live with' the problem.

Until 1980 almost no published work in England had examined burglary specifically. In that year two books appeared in close succession: those by Peter Burden and Dermot Walsh. The first, a somewhat sensationalised account by a *Daily Mail* reporter, concentrates upon the most serious aspects of the offence. It describes mainly cases in which violence, vandalism or thefts of high value were involved, and depicts burglary as a multi-million pound 'business' in which offenders plunder the rest of society with relative impunity. The police are seen as helpless witnesses to a 'boom' in burglary, the courts are castigated for passing lenient sentences, and successive Home Secretaries blamed for a failure to build new prisons or to increase the strength of the police. Walsh, a sociologist, takes a more detached look at the problem. He emphasises the long history of the offence as a central occupation of criminal groups, and recognises that such groups will always take advantage of weak points in the way in which property is protected. His study is aimed mainly at understanding the psychology of the individual burglar, as well as the relationship of burglary to other forms of crime and to the wider structure of society. Although he makes many interesting points, the study is highly speculative and weak in both its presentation and its use of empirical data. He bases most of his findings upon conversations with a small number of convicted burglars and a survey of the characteristics of 67 victims compared with 33 'non-victims'.

The only other full-length study of burglary in England appears to be an unpublished thesis by Chappell (1965). This provides an excellent history of the development of the laws against breaking and entering, and also contains an analysis of the characteristics of offences committed in a largely rural county. Unfortunately, it is again based on a very small sample of cases and, although carried out in a thorough and professional manner, the study has only limited value for our purposes. The writer provides little information about the areal distribution of offences, and did not interview either burglars or victims.

North American research into burglary is developed to a much greater degree and has produced several empirical studies which provide excellent comparative material. The two most comprehensive are by Reppetto (1974), a wide-ranging survey of residential crime in Boston, Massachusetts, and by Waller and Okihiro (1978), which looks at burglary rates and the problems of victims in Toronto, concluding with some interesting and controversial policy recommendations. There are studies of burglars' lifestyles and behaviour (Shover 1971, David 1974), sophisticated analyses of patterns of offending (Scarr 1973, Pope 1977), and evaluations of preventive measures (for example, White *et al.* 1975). The subject has also interested architects, planners and psychologists concerned with the effects of environment upon criminal behaviour (Newman 1972, Jeffrey 1971).

Sources of information

Apart from surveying previous literature on burglary, drawing on published statistics, and engaging in informal conversation with as many interested parties as possible, we gathered our data from four main sources. We first analysed information held by the police about every burglary in a dwelling recorded in the Thames Valley Police Authority area in 1975, a total of 6,484 offences. This was stored on computer cards in the Thames Valley Police headquarters at Kidlington, Oxford, and included a record of the area, date, time, method of report, nature and value of property stolen, and type of search carried out, so far as these were known, for each offence. Detected offences were also identified and brief information recorded about the age, sex and number of the offenders arrested. Although incomplete in some aspects, the data were useful as a background to the local studies, enabling us to compare basic patterns in each area with those across the Thames Valley as a whole.

The three areas we selected for close attention were deliberately chosen to illustrate and to allow discussion about the different forms that burglary can take in areas of different social character. They displayed widely varying offence rates and significant differences in the type and value of property stolen and the characteristics of offenders arrested. The areas, which will be described in more detail later, were police sectors or sub-divisions covering (a) Banbury and surrounding villages, (b) most of the town of Reading, and (c) part of the wealthy 'commuter belt' centred on Gerrards Cross. In each we noted, from written police reports, as much information as possible about every burglary in a dwelling recorded over a one-year period, and constructed a map of their location. If an offender was arrested within a period of six months for any of these burglaries, we collected information about his or her age, place of residence and previous record, and any statements made to the police or used in court about the circumstances in which the offence took place. Wherever possible we spoke to the police officer investigating the case and, once convicted, to the offender in question, in order to discover more about what had happened. Unfortunately, mainly because of delays in bringing people to trial, we were successful in seeing only a minority of the alleged offenders.

The third major source of data was from interviews with victims. In Banbury and Gerrards Cross ('Gerrards Cross' was taken to include its near-neighbour, Chalfont St Peter; the two towns virtually merge into one another) we tried to interview the victim of every burglary known to the police over the one-year period chosen, while in Reading, which produced almost 800 offences, we set out to see the victim of every third case recorded. The final response rate was 62 per cent. Altogether 322 victims were interviewed in their own homes, the majority at a point between four and ten weeks after the event. During the interviews, which lasted on average for about one hour, further information was gathered about the circumstances of the offence, and people were asked in some detail about their reactions to the event. Other subjects covered included the police handling of the case, questions about crime prevention and insurance, and the victim's perceptions of and attitudes towards the offender.

The final source of information was a series of extended interviews with self-confessed persistent burglars. Forty people who defined themselves as burglars (or at least as thieves with a preference for burglary) were interviewed in custodial institutions, some more than once and one many times. Fifteen of these had been convicted for offences falling into our samples in Gerrards Cross and Reading. The remainder were inmates with a history of burglary who were willing to talk to us when we let it be known in a local prison that we were interested in the subject. No attempt was made at formal sampling. The burglars selected were either identified by prison officers as frequent practitioners of the art or else recommended to us by earlier interviewees as people 'worth talking to'. A small number of others thus contacted denied that they were or had been persistent burglars and their contribution was discounted. The 40 on which we base our discussion in Chapter III all admitted to having burgled at least 20 houses, and the majority well over 100.

The law against burglary

Before embarking upon our analysis, it is important to clarify the status of terms such as 'burglary', 'burglary in a dwelling' and 'housebreaking', all of which one hears used somewhat loosely to describe the phenomenon we are interested in. 'Burglary' is an offence defined under Section 9 of the Theft Act 1968, which covers all forms of illegal entry into buildings with intent to steal or to commit other named offences (see p. 8–9). 'Burglary in a dwelling', a sub-category of burglary, is not a separate offence in law, although it is a Home Office classification (No. 28), used in the recording and counting of offences to distinguish burglaries committed in dwellings from those committed in other buildings. 'Housebreaking' was an offence until 1968, when it was absorbed under the new definition of burglary laid down in the Theft Act. It is still used colloquially, but has no legal meaning.

The history of the development of the law concerning illegal entry into buildings is complex, but it may be helpful to provide a brief outline. A much fuller account can be found in Chappell (1965), and Walsh (1980:17–38) has added a more sociological flavour. Our purpose here is mainly to emphasise how, while definitions have changed considerably, both legislators and the judiciary have striven to maintain violation of the privacy of a dwelling-place as the most serious form of illegal entry into buildings.

The origins of the offence and indeed of the word 'burglary' are obscure. It has been suggested that it was a compound of 'burgh' (house) and 'laron' (thief), but this is not accepted by all scholars. 'Burgaria', the Latin form used in written records, may have been simply an arbitrary term coined by medieval lawyers. One of the earliest known definitions, recorded by Britton in about 1300, referred not only to housebreaking but also to the breaking of churches and the walls or gates of cities. Chappell (1965:3–9) argues convincingly that it was attacks upon the security of a building or settlement, and not theft of the contents, that the law was principally designed to punish.

Before 1500 there was little consistency in the definition or application of the capital charge of burglary. In some parts of the country it was brought for breaking into any kind of building in the furtherance of theft. In others, on the other hand, it seems to have been used more sparingly, mainly as a replacement for the Anglo-Saxon crime of 'hamsocn', defined by Hume as 'the felonious seeking and invasion of a man in his dwelling-place'. However, during the early 16th century the common law underwent more rigorous codification, and burglary acquired a relatively stable definition that remained unchanged in essence until 1968. One of the most frequently cited versions is that of Sir Edward Coke, which dates from the early 17th century (Coke 1797, vol. 3:63):

> A burglar is by common law a felon that, in the night, breaketh and entereth into a mansion house of another, of intent to kill some reasonable creature, or to commit some felony within the same, whether his felonious intent be executed or not.

Offences committed in buildings other than dwellings, those committed in daylight and those in which entry was not obtained by force were considered less serious, and remained for some time as common law misdemeanours. During the 17th and early 18th centuries the death penalty was extended by a complicated series of statutes to cover most forms of breaking and entering and theft from buildings (Radzinowicz 1948:41–9), but when the tide of opinion turned against hanging in the early 19th century, capital punishment was relatively quickly abolished for these offences, leaving burglary once again on its own as a capital crime. Aggravated burglary

remained punishable by death until the Larceny Act of 1861. For the
next century, too, the maximum sentence for burglary was life
imprisonment while that for other offences in the 'breaking' family
(except sacrilege) ranged from seven to fourteen years.

Two main arguments were repeated by legislators and lawyers on
numerous occasions to justify the existence of a separate law with
particularly heavy penalties to protect dwellings. These were (a) that
the inhabitants of a house are likely to be put in fear, and (b) that
forced entry into a dwelling constitutes a violation of a person's
natural right to privacy and peace within his own home. Hale (1682)
wrote that 'every man by the law hath a special protection in refer-
ence to his house and dwelling', and the 18th-century jurist Sir
William Blackstone explained the gravity of the crime as follows
(Blackstone 1830:4, 223):

> Burglary has always been looked upon as a very heinous offence,
> not only because of abundant terror that it naturally carries with it,
> but also as it is a forcible invasion and disturbance of that right of
> habitation which every individual might acquire even in a state of
> nature.

The importance placed upon the time of the offence—the hours of
darkness—stemmed from the notion that the sleeping householder
was in no position to protect himself by force of arms (*ibid.*:224):

> The malignity of the offences does not so properly arise from its
> being done in the dark as at the dead of night, when all creation,
> except beasts of prey, are at rest; when sleep has disarmed the
> owner and rendered his castle defenceless.

However, during the 1960s the Criminal Law Revision Committee
(CLRC) recommended fundamental changes in the definition of
burglary. These changes blurred traditional distinctions and brought
together under one umbrella all the old breaking offences as well as
offences of non-forced entry into any kind of building. The outcome
was Section 9 of the Theft Act 1968, by which a person is now guilty
of burglary if:

(1)   (a)   he enters any building or part of a building as a trespasser
            and with intent to commit any such offence as is
            mentioned in subsection (2) below; or
      (b)   having entered any building or part of a building as a tres-
            passer he steals or attempts to steal anything in the
            building or that part of it or inflicts or attempts to inflict
            on any person therein any grievous bodily harm

(2)   The offences referred to in subsection (1a) above are

offences of stealing anything in the building or part of a
building in question, of inflicting on any person therein
any grievous bodily harm or raping any woman therein,
and of doing unlawful damage to the building or anything
therein.

The maximum sentence was set at 14 years' imprisonment. The
new law was justified by its architects not only as a simplification of
unnecessarily complex legislation for the benefit of the police and the
courts, but by the assertion that social changes had long since
rendered some of the traditional distinctions obsolete. For example,
the development of police forces, street lighting and the telephone had
made the difference between daylight and night-time offences less
important, and the old concept of 'breaking' had become artificial
when applied to modern house designs. They also decided that
magistrates should be allowed to deal summarily with cases involving
non-forced entry into dwellings, a right that was later extended by the
James Committee to include break-ins. The argument used is further
illustration of the CLRC's willingness to break with tradition (CLRC
8th Report:85):

> The fact that the place burgled is a dwelling is only one of the
> possible aggravating features of burglary. Others are the fact that
> an offence is pre-meditated or carefully planned, the method of
> entry, the behaviour of the burglar in the building, and the amount
> which he steals or attempts to steal . . . To isolate one feature
> would not only be illogical but harmful.

The flexibility of the new law gave sentencers a free hand to
develop a system of penalties for a wide range of offences under one
heading, and, if they so chose, to treat house burglary as a straightforward crime against property. Burden (1980:145), who is highly
critical of what he regards as 'a blurring of the edges' of the law, states
unequivocally that

> burglary law has been devalued . . . and offences which ten or
> fifteen years ago were regarded as very serious and were tried at an
> Assize Court or Quarter Sessions are now being dealt with by
> magistrates. Offenders who only five years ago merited terms of
> imprisonment are now being given suspended sentences and
> probation orders.

Yet, as we shall see in chapter VI, the majority of cases of burglary in
a dwelling are still dealt with in Crown Courts, and the offence has
continued to be punished more severely than other forms of burglary
and theft. Indeed, the proportion of adult offenders imprisoned for
burglary in a dwelling has increased slightly since 1969.

II. Patterns of Burglary

In this chapter we tackle some basic questions about where, when and in what manner burglaries take place, and what kinds of offenders are responsible. We hope to distinguish certain general patterns but also to emphasise the extent to which these vary according to the social characteristics of different areas. The chapter is divided into three parts. The first two are concerned with what might be called the 'demography' of burglary, that is, how often do burglaries occur, who is most likely to be burgled, and by whom? Part 1 considers these questions on a broad level, using national statistics and previous academic research to build up a background picture of the size and shape of the problem. Part 2, which is based upon data gathered from three contrasting areas of the Thames Valley, demonstrates important variations at a local level, both in the distribution of offences and in the characteristics of the offenders responsible. Part 3 is concerned with the physical circumstances of burglary, that is, the times at which offences are most likely to be committed, the methods by which houses are entered, and the extent of disarrangement and damage to property that is caused. Our main sources of data here will be an analysis of all offences of burglary in a dwelling recorded in the Thames Valley in 1975, and the results of interviews with 322 victims.

Of course, 'facts and figures' about crime and criminals are notoriously unreliable, riddled with methodological and definitional difficulties. Throughout the chapter we shall repeatedly examine the status and limitations of the numerical data upon which findings are based. Although some serious doubts will inevitably remain, it will be suggested that problems of measurement are less destructive to conclusions about patterns of burglary than is the case with most other types of offence.

1. The broad picture

Numbers of burglaries identified, reported and recorded
We are immediately faced with the criminologist's perennial bugbear—the problem of the so-called 'dark figure'. It has to be

conceded at the outset that the question: 'how ...actually take place?' is unanswerable. 'Victims' may that they have been burgled: they may fail to notice missing or think that items have simply been mis. practical purposes, however, knowledge about s unimportant. Incidents take on meaning as burglari identified as such by somebody apart from the perpetrato. They may then become socially significant either as unpleasant events in the lives of members of the victimised household and their acquaintances, or if reported and recorded, as crimes to be investigated by the police.

Events in the latter category are easily counted and analysed. Each police division returns monthly figures for burglaries recorded in its area. These are aggregated to produce the annual totals for England and Wales published in *Criminal Statistics*. On the other hand, such figures represent only the final outcome of a complex filtering process and, if they are to be used as a guide to the extent and patterning of burglary actually affecting the community, it is essential to examine the process of reporting and recording in order to estimate roughly how many offences and of what kind fail to reach the official records.

Although the number of offences recorded in any category of crime is subject to a certain amount of police discretion, this seems to play a relatively minor part in the recording of burglary. The majority of eligible incidents are brought to police notice through reports from victims. Unlike some 'street' offences, where individual officers come across potential breaches of the law and can use discretion as to whether or not to record a crime, it is relatively rare for a police patrol to observe a burglary in progress. Eighty-nine per cent of burglaries recorded by the Thames Valley police in 1975 stemmed from unsolicited complaints by members of the public. (Similar findings have emerged from studies by Mawby 1979, and Bottomley and Coleman 1981:46.) The remainder were discovered mainly in the course of 'other inquiries', for example on the confession of somebody being questioned about his recent behaviour. Most of the reports received are clear-cut cases of burglary, described as such by the victim and leaving the officer concerned no option but to record a crime. McCabe and Sutcliffe (1978:55–6) found that 71 per cent of reports of breaking and entering received by the police in Oxford and Salford resulted in an official crime report compared with 37 per cent of complaints about 'assaults', 40 per cent about 'damage', and nine per cent about 'disturbances' of various kinds (cf. also Schneider 1978:104).

McCabe remarks that, in contrast to some of these other categories, burglary is perceived by the police as 'real' crime.

...nough the 'gatekeepers' of police stations—the desk serge-
ants—may deflect many complaints which contain potential crimes
on the grounds of ambiguity, triviality or mischief-making by the
complainant, reports of break-ins are treated seriously and are
normally referred immediately to the CID. Certainly, as Bottomley
and Coleman (1981: Chapters 2 and 4) stress, a proportion of such
reports are eventually discounted (for example, 'no-crimed') or re-
categorised (for example, as theft in a dwelling or theft from a meter),
but this proportion is relatively small and represents in many cases an
entirely sensible assessment of the circumstances of the case. The
main grounds for rejection are a belief that the complainant is
dishonest (for example, has broken into his own pre-payment meter
or has 'faked' a burglary in order to make an insurance claim) or
mistaken (for example, has mislaid what he thought had been stolen),
or that there is insufficient evidence that the house has been entered
illegally. Bottomley and Coleman provide some examples of policemen 'cuffing' crimes (deliberately failing to record trivial offences in
order to avoid paperwork or to maintain clear-up rates at an
acceptable level), but there is little to suggest that this occurs on a
large scale in the case of burglary. Officers face disciplinary action if
such practices are discovered, and the risk is high with burglary since
insurance companies will request confirmation that offences have
been reported. The only serious ammunition for arguing that
burglaries are frequently cuffed comes from Sparks *et al*. (1977:154),
who deduced from indirect evidence that the Metropolitan Police
Department had recorded under half the cases reported, ignoring
most incidents in which there was no loss or damage. However, the
authors stress not only that this is a crude estimate, but that if correct
it may be a result of the exceptional problems of high crime loads and
understaffing which afflict the MPD (*ibid*.:164, note 3).

Probably more important than the filter of police discretion is that
of the failure of victims to report burglaries. The most ambitious
attempt to measure the number of offences known to victims and the
proportion that they report has come from the regular National
Crime Survey carried out in the United States for the Law
Enforcement Assistance Administration (LEAA) and published by
the Department of Justice. Similar surveys have also been conducted
on a smaller scale, notably in Canada, Holland and West Germany,
and questions about burglary have been included on four occasions in
the British General Household Survey (1972, 1973, 1979, 1980).
Representative samples of households are interviewed and their
members are asked to report criminal offences committed against
them during the course of the previous six or twelve months. The

results are usually expressed in terms of rates of victimisation per 1,000 households, and are put forward as a more realistic measure of the incidence of crime than is provided by police statistics. Victims are also asked whether or not they reported the offence to the police, which provides a 'reporting rate' for the crime in question.

Some of the initial claims made for the accuracy of this method of measurement were grossly exaggerated, and Sparks *et al.* (1977) have illustrated the serious methodological problems involved in the way questions are worded and in the limited ability of interviewees to remember incidents and to place them in time. Nevertheless 'forward record checks' (for example, Schneider 1978) have found that burglary is one of the offences most easily remembered and most often placed correctly in time, as well as causing relatively few problems of definition. The findings with regard to reporting rates for burglary have also been reasonably consistent. They indicate that people report to the police between 45 and 75 per cent of all cases in which they have reason to believe that their house has been entered illegally (see Appendix 1, Table A1). Where entry is forced the reporting rate is even higher: the major United States surveys put it at over 70 per cent (cf. Department of Justice 1977: Table 95) and a British survey at 90 per cent (Durant *el al.* 1972:241).[1]

The overall message from research into the relationships between police-recorded and victim-defined burglary is that the official figures represent somewhere between one-quarter and one-half of all cases in which residents think or know that they have been burgled. The lowest estimate is that of Sparks *et al.* (1977:154), who calculated that little more than one in five incidents perceived as burglaries reached the records of three police sub-divisions in London. As already pointed out, there are doubts about these results, but even if Sparks is right, his study underlines more than any other the second major survey-finding to which attention should be drawn: whatever their numbers, unrecorded burglaries as a group are markedly less serious in terms of loss or damage than recorded burglaries, and a high proportion of unrecorded cases are 'walk-ins' and unsuccessful attempts at entry. One of the most common reasons given for failure to report an offence is that the victim considered the matter 'not important enough' (Durant 1972:243, Department of Justice 1977:78, Reynolds 1973, Sparks *et al.* 1977:120). It is almost certain that the great majority of cases in which houses are ransacked or valuable property is stolen do in fact appear in the official statistics.

In the light of these remarks, the incidence of burglary in England and Wales as reflected in the annual *Criminal Statistics* may now be considered. No direct comparison can be made between figures produced before and those produced after 1968 because of the changes in definition created by the Theft Act. In addition, the Perks Committee report (1967) drew attention to several inconsistencies in the compilation of statistics which were subsequently rectified, and any conclusions about 'trends' earlier in the century must therefore be treated sceptically. With these cautions it is still interesting to note two main points. The first is that up to 1968 there was a continuing rise in the proportion of breaking offences (of all kinds) among all indictable offences recorded. In round figures, this increased as follows:

1900:	11 per cent
1930:	16 per cent
1950:	19 per cent
1968:	22 per cent

Secondly, Chappell (1965) remarks that before the Second World War offences of shopbreaking accounted for the largest part of the increase, but that the pattern changed noticeably as overall crime rates began to 'soar' from the latter half of the 1950s. Between 1955 and 1968 the total number of breaking offences recorded rose from 75,000 to 287,000, and it was housebreaking that increased at much the fastest rate.

If this trend reflected a real shift in the behaviour of thieves, it was probably accounted for by two main factors. On the one hand, insurance companies were insisting upon increased security in commercial premises, and radical improvements in the design of safes made businesses harder and less attractive targets. On the other, the period saw a boom in household goods, with valuable consumer durables such as televisions and record players finding their way into even the poorest homes. This offered thieves an easily accessible source of items that were readily saleable and could rarely be individually identified.

Official figures produced since 1968, which are almost certainly more reliable, indicate a significant reduction in the rate of increase in residential burglary. Table 1 shows the number of offences of burglary recorded as known to the police in England and Wales each year between 1969 and 1979. It can be seen that although the totals grew appreciably, with residential burglaries passing a quarter of a million in 1977, they rose at a considerably slower than average rate: over this period, burglaries in dwellings increased by 39 per cent, other burglaries by 25 per cent and all indictable offences by 59 per cent. (The recorded total for 1980 was 294,933, an increase of 16 per cent on 1979, but *Criminal Statistics* notes that this figure is not

Table 1   Offences of burglary in a dwelling and in a building other than a dwelling (including aggravated burglary) recorded as known to the police, England and Wales, 1969–79

	Burglary in a dwelling (thousands)	Percentage variation on previous year	Burglary in a building other than a dwelling (thousands)	Percentage variation on previous year	All indictable offences: percentage variation on previous year
1969	181.8		233.1		
1970	190.7	+ 4.9	233.0	0.0	+ 4.7
1971	204.6	+ 7.3	237.7	+ 2.0	+ 6.2
1972	201.9	− 1.3	226.1	− 4.9	+ 1.5
1973	178.4	− 11.6	205.6	− 9.1	− 1.9
1974	214.2	+ 20.1	259.2	+ 26.5	+ 18.4
1975	237.8	+ 11.0	277.7	+ 7.1	+ 7.2
1976	230.6	− 3.0	279.4	+ 0.6	+ 1.4
1977	262.6	+ 13.9	335.8	+ 20.2	+ 15.3
1978	257.2	− 2.1	302.8	− 9.8	− 2.7
1979	252.8	− 1.7	291.3	− 3.8	− 0.7

Source: *Criminal Statistics*

comparable with earlier years owing to changes in police recording procedures).

Furthermore, there is evidence that much of the apparent increase may be due to a high proportion of offences reaching the published statistics. Estimates based on the results of four General Household Surveys suggest that the ratio of victim-recalled to police-recorded burglaries and thefts in dwellings fell from 1.99 in 1972 to 1.62 in 1980 (*Criminal Statistics* 1980:28–9). Over this period, while police-recorded figures rose by 68,000 (from 249,000 to 317,000), the estimated number of offences known to victims rose by only 18,000 (from 495,000 to 513,000).

The general trends in the recorded frequency of burglary outlined above are closely paralleled in many other western industrialised countries. In the United States the number of residential burglaries recorded almost trebled during the 1960s, but the rate of increase slowed markedly during the next decade. Italy and the Scandinavian countries, which see the highest proportions of insurance claims for burglary (Clinard 1978:80), are among several European countries which also noted substantial increases during the 1960s. Even in Switzerland, where for reasons that are difficult to ascertain crime rates are strikingly low, burglary figures more than doubled between 1960 and 1970 (*ibid.*:49, 148). Victimisation surveys can tell us nothing about this period of rapid increases, but indicate that the widespread crime explosion, if it was as dramatic as police figures have suggested, has lost its initial impetus. The LEAA surveys even point to a slight decrease in household burglary rates during the 1970s, and Dutch surveys show only a slow rate of increase, considerably below the official rate (Department of Justice 1979, Van Dijk and Steinmetz 1980).

Direct comparison of rates of burglary between countries (that is, relative to population or to number of households) is highly problematical owing to differences in the law and in recording methods. However, it is worth noting that police-recorded rates of residential burglary in the United States are over 50 per cent higher than those recorded in Great Britain. Standardised victimisation surveys might provide a more reliable means of comparison but, as already pointed out, only the United States has so far been prepared to invest the considerable sums needed to conduct these surveys on a large scale.[2] In 1976 the United States National Crime Survey found a rate of 90 burglaries per 1,000 households. In Toronto, a small victimisation survey (Waller and Okihiro 1978:20) calculated the rate at 26 per 1,000 households, which is several times lower than that found in any major city in the United States. The authors can only suggest that Canada is historically a more law-abiding country than the United States and that 'a residue of respect for law and order may still remain in Canadian society'. Thus far, the only British study comparable in any way is that by Sparks *et al.* (1977), which found rates in three districts of inner London which were apparently approaching American city proportions. Unfortunately, all the above surveys were carried out in different manners, and the authors of the London study in particular present their results with caution.

Type and value of property stolen

The overall increase in recorded burglaries during the 1970s was much less striking than the sharp rise in the number and proportion of cases involving the theft of valuable property such as antiques, silver and jewellery. As the latter are very likely to be reported there is little doubt that the figures reflect a real upward trend in lucrative burglaries. Between 1973 and 1979 insurance payments in respect of burglary rose from £9 million to almost £49 million, and in the latter year the total recorded as stolen reached £71 million.[3] In 1979 there were more cases in which property worth £500 or more was stolen than there had been in 1973 for property worth £100 or more (see Appendix 1, Table A2). Even with the most generous allowances for inflation, thefts of property worth £1,000 or more at 1979 prices more than doubled during this six-year period. This trend coincided with a growth in markets for articles which keep their value in times of inflation, and it seems that thieves took advantage of the boom in antiques in particular. The proliferation of small antiques businesses in the mid-70s provided many more opportunities for selling stolen articles of high value than had previously been the case. The problem became especially serious in the London area, the centre of the antiques trade. In 1975, for example, 42 per cent of all home burglaries involving £1,000 or more took place within the Metropolitan Police District, and the rate of such burglaries was 37 per 100,000 population in London, compared with 13 in the Thames Valley.

What might be called 'middle-range' burglaries—those involving property such as colour televisions, stereo systems, cassette players and less valuable silverware or jewellery—have also increased at a faster rate than recorded petty burglaries. In 1979, 24 per cent of all burglaries recorded resulted in losses of between £100 and £500, the typical range of values for such items. These kinds of goods, which have become commonplace in ordinary homes over the last few years, provide an attractive target for thieves, even for those without the expertise or 'contacts' to dispose of expensive jewellery or antiques. They are relatively difficult to identify individually and there is a strong second-hand market for them.

Nevertheless, increases at the middle and higher ends of the scale should not be allowed to obscure the fact that the majority of cases still involve thefts of fairly low value. Although the mean amount stolen per burglary is well over £200, this is inflated by a relatively small number of extremely profitable crimes. The median, a much better indicator of the 'typical' burglary, stood at below £50 in 1979. Sixty-three per cent of recorded cases resulted in a loss of less than £100, and 25 per cent in less than £5. Of course, value tables based on the results of victimisation surveys produce even larger percentages of cases with minor losses. The General Household Survey 1979 found that 32 per cent of cases uncovered had involved a loss of under £5.[4] [Personal communication from the Office of Population Censuses and Surveys.]

Aggregated figures cannot reveal the extent to which value stolen varies by area. Not surprisingly, victims in Banbury lost considerably less per head during the period 1977–1979 than their wealthier counterparts in Gerrards Cross (see Appendix 1, Table A3). Further variations over smaller geographical areas will be discussed later in the chapter. Similarly, the type of property stolen depends very much upon the character of the district. In 1975 over the Thames Valley as a whole, the items most frequently stolen were cash (45 per cent of cases), goods such as television sets, radios, stereo equipment (17 per cent), jewellery and silver (14 per cent), and cigarettes, alcohol and food (13 per cent) (see Appendix 1, Table A4). Walsh (1980:93) also noted that the main item stolen in Exeter was cash (in 'at least' 37 per cent of cases), and found 'portable electrical devices, TV sets, cassette recorders, shavers and so forth' to be 'the burglars' second favourite choice'. Broadly similar patterns emerge in Scarr (1973:132) and Waller and Okihiro (1978:28). However, in our three study areas the proportion of cash thefts varied between 51 per cent in Reading and 23 per cent in Gerrards Cross, and thefts of jewellery between 9 per cent in Banbury and 54 per cent in Gerrards Cross.

A major source of cash was from pre-payment meters, which were 'broken' in 19 per cent of the 6,484 cases recorded in the Thames Valley in 1975. A further 770 offences were recorded as 'theft from an automatic machine or meter' rather than burglary, so it is likely that the true proportion of burglaries which involve 'meter-breaks' is well above one in five, a situation that calls into question the wisdom of this method of payment for gas or electricity.

Generally speaking, burglars seemed either to take cash only (this was the case in one-third of all Thames Valley offences) or else to select a variety of items within a certain broad type. Some seemed to concentrate upon small but valuable items such as watches, jewellery and silverware, others on television sets or record-players. People who stole cigarettes and food usually left more valuable property alone. On the other hand, a substantial minority of cases, notably in Reading, involved very large 'mixed bags' of property, where the offenders seemed to have loaded everything they could into a car or van (see p. 39).

Finally, very little property stolen in burglaries is recovered. Only 12 per cent of Thames Valley victims who lost property saw any of it again. Despite a lower clear-up rate in cases where the value amounts to more than £10 (see Appendix 1, Table A8), the chances of recovery are greater here than in less serious cases. (Appendix 1, Table A5). This is because the former usually involve durable items which are more easily identifiable and cannot be spent or consumed, unlike cash, food or drink, which are the most common targets in petty burglaries. Naturally, the apprehension of the offender provides the best chance of retrieving property. Some property was recovered in 34 per cent of detected cases. The police also recapture from offenders many stolen goods which are never claimed by victims: there have been several 'Aladdin's Cave' cases in the Thames Valley area recently, where a roomful of valuables has been found but only a handful of the previous owners identified—a good argument for some system of marking property (see chapter VI).

The distribution of offences

Since 1969 the residential burglary rate recorded by the police in England and Wales has varied between 10 and 15 offences per 1,000 dwellings or, roughly speaking, one offence for every 70 to 100 homes. Allowing for non-reporting, this might be taken to imply that the 'average British citizen' can expect to be burgled twice or three times during his lifetime, and call the police perhaps once. However, offences are by no means evenly distributed throughout the country, and even within small areas there are wide variations in rates of victimisation.

It has been shown several times that there is a close relationship between burglary rates and urbanisation. For example, McClintock and Avison (1968:80–1) measured the incidence of breaking offences relative to population in a sample of police force areas in 1965 in England and Wales. They found not only that urban forces recorded rates well in excess of county forces, but that rates increased progressively from small towns (229 offences per 100,000 population), to medium-sized towns (302), to large towns (358), to large cities (473). (See also White *et al.* 1975:4.) The differences appear to have grown even greater since their study was completed. In 1978 the Metropolitan Police District recorded over 69,000 offences of burglary in a dwelling, approximately one for every 40 dwellings. At the other end of the scale Suffolk police annually record no more than one burglary per 200 dwellings. Victimisation surveys have found similar variations in the United States, a good indication that the pattern is not produced artifically by differences in recording practice.

The Thames Valley police area contains three towns with a population of over 100,000: Reading, Oxford and Slough. Our analysis of records from 1975 showed that over one-third of the burglaries recorded in the whole area occurred within these three towns, although they jointly contained only 20 per cent of the population. Small country towns such as Thame, Chipping Norton and Witney recorded only a handful of offences each month, showing rates three to four times lower than that of Reading, the major contributor. However, there are certain interesting exceptions to the general rule. The most striking was Gerrards Cross, one of the wealthiest towns in the Thames Valley and part of the 'stockbroker belt' surrounding London. Despite a population of under 8,000, it was burgled at a rate in excess of that of London as a whole. A number of other wealthy small towns situated within easy driving distance of London, for example, Ascot and Sunningdale, also recorded exceptionally high rates.

Burglary rates based upon high levels of aggregation conceal important patterns at a more local level. Within large and medium-sized towns the distribution of offences has usually been found to conform to one general rule: the highest concentrations of burglaries appear in or close to socially disadvantaged housing areas. North American studies have found positive correlations between high burglary rates and census tracts containing a high percentage of over-crowded housing units (Scarr 1973:105), tracts with a low average income (Reppetto 1974:38–9), tracts with a high percentage of single males or of households with lodgers (Waller and Okihiro 1978: 51–3) and tracts with a high proportion of black residents (Boggs:1970). Research into areal patterns of crime is relatively sparse in Britain, although studies in Sheffield (Baldwin and Bottoms 1976, Mawby 1979) have provided some valuable material. Here social class and tenure-type have been found to be the most important factors associated with crime rates. The highest burglary rates were discovered in an area in which about 70 per cent of the population lived in privately-rented dwellings, mainly run-down terraced housing which was sub-let. Council estates—particularly a pre-war estate to the north of the city with a local reputation as a 'problem area'—were also prominent, although there was considerable variation among them. Middle-class suburban housing areas escaped comparatively lightly. Generally speaking, areal studies have given support to the well-known Chicago Model (Shaw and McKay 1969) of decreasing crime rates from city centres outwards, although Mawby notes that in Sheffield the pattern is disrupted by peripheral council estates with high burglary rates.

Paradoxically, these findings do not necessarily mean that individual householders in low income groups have a higher risk of being burgled than the better-off. Findings on this question are contradictory. Several studies based either on police figures or on victim surveys have found a significant increase in risk with level of income (Waller and Okihiro 1978, Van Dijk and Vianen 1978:17) and with rateable value (Chappell 1965:212, Baldwin and Bottoms 1976:63, Winchester and Jackson, in preparation). However, the survey by Ennis (1967:31) produced a directly opposite result, while LEAA surveys have found that people at either extreme of income scales are more likely to be burgled than those in the middle range. Finally Walsh (1980:126) and Sparks (1977:86) found no statistically significant relationship between wealth and burglary. The apparently illogical finding of the majority—that poor areas, but not poor individuals, suffer the highest rates—has been explained by the assertion that offenders tend to select the most affluent targets within any given area (Reppetto 1974:39), although once again this has not always been shown to be the case. For example, Waller and Okihiro (1978:63) found that the way individual targets are chosen varies considerably between different kinds of housing area. In housing situated in or near the poorer areas of Toronto, the only significant factor distinguishing victims from non-victims was the length of time that the house was normally left unoccupied, while in housing away from such areas the level of income of the householder was a highly significant predictor of victimisation. The implication is that in districts close to areas which contain a large number of 'potential burglars', targets are selected in a relatively indiscriminate and opportunistic manner, while in the predominantly middle-class suburbs a smaller number of more discriminating offenders deliberately seek out the wealthiest residents. Clearly, there are many confusing issues yet to be satisfactorily resolved and there is no simple answer to Walsh's question whether burglars are 'Robin Hood-like figures' or whether the offence is primarily an example of 'the poor stealing from the poor'.

Apart from the general nature of the area in which a house is located, the relative wealth of its occupants and the frequency with which it is left unoccupied, there are many other factors which may affect its statistical chances of being burgled. Two obvious candidates for consideration are the level of protection by crime prevention devices and the degree of care taken in locking up. However, as we shall see in chapter VI, it is by no means certain that by increasing the physical 'security' of his house a man significantly reduces his risk of victimisation. More important factors may be the precise siting of a house in relation to local streets and footpaths, neighbouring houses, fences, hedges, and so on. For example, Walsh among others has noted a preponderance of offences near main roads; corner properties are often said to be particularly vulnerable; houses without ready access to the rear seem to run less risk of attack. Of some relevance here is Newman's theory of 'defensible space' (1972), in which it is postulated that burglary is much less likely to occur in situations where groups of neighbours overlook common areas commanding the entrances to their houses.

Although Reppetto (1974), Waller and Okihiro (1978) and Mayhew *et al.* (1979) have all cast some doubts on this theory, a recent attempt to measure risk factors (Winchester and Jackson, in preparation) gives it some indirect support by suggesting that surveillability and access are highly significant factors in determining a house's risk of being burgled. The authors, who surveyed 846 houses in Kent, found the best predictor of victimisation to be what they called 'environmental risk'. They define this by a combination of features which affect the ease with which an offender can approach potential entry points to houses without being seen. These features include proximity to major roads, visibility from the street or from other houses, ease of access to the rear, and whether or not the house is adjoined by private open space. In a discriminant analysis they found that environmental risk was almost twice as important as occupancy and four times as important as rateable value in distinguishing between victims and non-victims.

Winchester and Jackson's preliminary analysis showed that the two categories of house at highest risk were: (a) the large high-rateable-value house in its own grounds in the country, distant from most other houses, not easily visible from public areas and frequently left unoccupied, and (b) the high-rateable-value house situated on a busy through road in town, with a fairly large private garden so that the house is not easily overlooked and not easily visible from public areas. Other interesting calculations they made were that small detached houses had an annual risk of being burgled of one in 20, large detached houses of one in 42, and bungalows of one in 68, whereas, at the other end of the scale, semi-detached houses and houses in short terraces had a risk of one in 209, and those in long terraces of only one in 540.

It must of course be remembered that these kinds of calculation are based upon samples drawn across a wide and varied county. It is likely that the risk to, for example, semi-detached houses is vastly different in different parts of Kent, and even in different parts of one town. This is due not so much to areal variations in siting, rateable value or occupancy as to the facts that people who are likely to commit burglaries are unevenly distributed among the population and, as we shall see, tend on the whole to steal close to home.

The 'burglar population'

Patterns of offences hold little meaning if not explained in terms of offender behaviour. Waller and Okihiro's remarks (1978) above about 'potential burglars' and target selection raise a series of important questions about who makes up the bulk of the 'burglar population', how far offenders travel to steal, and what categories of offender select what kind of target. Here research is hamstrung by yet another 'dark figure' problem—that of undetected offenders. The clear-up rate for burglary in a dwelling rarely rises above 30 per cent, and in large cities it can be as low as 10 per cent. If non-recorded burglaries are included, it would be a conservative estimate to say that in at least five out of six cases the identity of the offender remains unknown. In 1978, for example, 260,000 burglaries were recorded, of which 75,000 were cleared up (in round figures). For this total of offences 25,000 offenders were either convicted or cautioned, each being held responsible on average for three cases. Assuming a 50 per cent reporting rate and the same average of three offences per person, during 1978 over 450,000 burglaries went unpunished and some 150,000 individuals escaped detection. Of course, many of these apparently 'hidden' offenders may in fact be found among the 25,000 who were convicted. As we shall show in chapter III, it is not unusual for persistent offenders to commit very large numbers of burglaries within a short period. When arrested they may admit to only a few, or, even if willing to make a full confession, they often cannot remember the location of the bulk of their offences.

This being so, it is worth considering the proposition that a relatively small group of persistent offenders account for the majority of burglaries carried out. This contention would be much easier to support if burglary were committed only by adults. The records of both adults and young adults convicted of the offence reveal an exceptionally high level of recidivism. For example, calculations based upon tables published in *Criminal Statistics* (1978:183–90) indicate that only about 11 per cent of males aged 21 and over found guilty of burglary are first offenders, compared with 35 per cent of those found guilty of standard list offences. The majority have five or more previous convictions, and most court cases incorporate more than one charge or include other cases 'taken into consideration'. From a 're-arrest crime switch matrix', prepared for the US President's Crime Commission, Hood and Sparks (1970:137) calculated that 35 per cent of adults convicted of burglary would be subsequently re-arrested for the same type of offence, and that only 23 per cent would not come before the courts again. (The equivalent figures for larceny of $50 and above were 16 per cent and 41 per cent respectively). Blumstein and Larson (in Szabo ed. 1970:407–9) have produced various versions of such matrices which show that if a burglar is re-arrested there is a 46 to 63 per cent chance that it is again for burglary. A Home Office study based upon a sample of offenders convicted in January 1971 (Phillpotts and Lancucki 1979) found that 68 per cent of burglars and robbers were reconvicted within six years, and that on their first re-appearance 38 per cent of these reconvictions were for burglary or robbery. Of those with five or more previous convictions, 88 per cent offended again. No other broad class of offender exceeded a 50 per cent reconviction rate. Much of the above applies equally well to young adult offenders (aged 17–21) who display similar patterns of recidivism and whose court appearances frequently include high numbers of 'TIC's.

It is theoretically possible that the persistent offenders who pass through the courts with such regularity give a totally unrepresentative picture of adults who commit burglaries. Once known to the police as a thief, a man's chances of being caught increase considerably. There could be a vast army of 'occasional' burglars who escape detection, or even of exceptionally clever persistent burglars who are completely unknown to the police. These, however, are extremely unlikely propositions when one considers both the nature of the offence and public attitudes towards it. (See also Smith and Marshall 1981.) Respect for the privacy of others within their own home is deeply embedded in British culture and the vast majority of the adult population rarely even contemplate breaking such a strong 'taboo'. While several studies indicate the readiness of wide sections of the community to break the law by shoplifting or pilfering (Hood and Sparks 1970:46 ff., Henry 1978), such activities occur in a setting where the offender is legitimately present. The extra element of trespass involved in burglary, as well as the fact that it concerns theft from individuals rather than from an impersonal institution, provide barriers which comparatively few mature people will cross. Moreover, as we shall later emphasise, burglars often depend upon the support of ostensibly criminal groups, entry to which is usually the outcome of a long process of learning and socialisation as a thief. Adults without such 'connections' would normally find it difficult to sell articles of any real value that they stole, even supposing they had overcome the psychological and practical barriers against breaking into a stranger's home.

Unfortunately this neat picture is complicated by the activities of juveniles. In 1978, 49 per cent of all persons convicted or cautioned for burglary were under the age of 17. Although juvenile burglars also display recidivist patterns to a greater extent than those convicted of other offences, well over half are first offenders and the majority are not re-convicted. Self-report studies show in contrast to adults (cf. Tittle 1980), a surprisingly high proportion of young teenagers from all backgrounds will admit to having stolen property from houses. Belson's study of 1,400 London boys (1968) found that 17 per cent had 'got into a place and stolen' and that 31 per cent had 'stolen something out of a garden or yard of a house'. West and Farrington (1977:27) found that 11 per cent of a sample of juveniles admitted to breaking and entering within the previous three years. Scandinavian research (Christie *et al.* 1965) based on a survey of entrants to military service obtained similar results. In the latter study the important point was also made that criminal behaviour was most likely to occur between the ages of ten and fourteen, falling off steeply as the boys grew up. Finally, all self-report research agrees that whereas many children have committed serious offences, only a tiny minority admit to *persistent* criminal behaviour. For example, the Scandinavian studies found that only two per cent claimed to have broken into buildings 'several times'. The obvious implication is that, for most, burglary constitutes simply a form of adolescent experimentation which is taken no further.

Taking all the evidence together, it seems a reasonable guess that a significant proportion—perhaps as high as 40 per cent—of all burglaries are committed by juveniles, many of whom are passing through a 'phase' of delinquency, while most of the remainder are committed by adult or young adult persistent offenders known to the police and arrested on several occasions during their 'careers'. Detected cases suggest that children are involved in over half of burglaries which involve thefts of minor value. For example, in the Thames Valley area in 1975, 52 per cent of detected cases with a loss of under £50 produced a juvenile offender. The fact that children, who are less sophisticated than adults and tend to break into houses very near their own homes (see p. 27), are easier to catch than older burglars perhaps exaggerates their contribution in recorded cases, but this is counteracted by their probable involvement in a higher proportion of unrecorded burglaries, which generally involve thefts of low value.

The addresses of convicted burglars of all ages show that they come overwhelmingly from disadvantaged backgrounds. Baldwin and Bottoms (1976:132–4) found that Sheffield offenders were concentrated in 'difficult' housing estates and 'twilight' areas of the city, made up primarily of council and privately rented property respectively. In fact there was a fairly strong association between offender rates and offence rates: those areas where proportionately most burglaries occurred also produced the highest number of offenders in relation to population. It is of course possible that the police devote more resources to investigating the activities of individuals resident in lower-class areas than elsewhere, thus distorting the true distribution of burglars. Some self-report studies (cf. Dentler and Monroe 1961, Hoods and Sparks 1970) have indicated that middle-class children privately admit to as many offences as working-class children but are much less likely to be arrested or prosecuted. However, it has been argued that this result is a misleading product of the questionnaire method and that interview studies usually show a clear class difference. Mawby's studies of policing (Mawby 1979, and in Brantingham and Brantingham eds. 1981) also conclude that differences in the amount of police attention given to different kinds of area are not as great as some commentators have suggested, and anyway, owing to the crucial role of the victim in solving crime, have comparatively little effect upon detection. Although we are not entirely convinced by this argument (many burglaries are also detected through information from known criminals), there is certainly not sufficient contrary evidence to damage seriously the claim that burglary is predominantly a crime of the lowest socio-economic groups.

Who burgles whom?

There have been few systematic attempts to investigate the relationships between different categories of offender and the areas in which they choose to burgle. This question was considered briefly by Reppetto (1974) in his discussion of patterns of burglary in Boston. Like Waller and Okihiro (1978) he noted the fact that while inner-city rates of burglary were higher overall than suburban rates, there were heavy concentrations of attacks in some particularly affluent outlying parts of the city. In the former case, he argued, the high rates were due to the presence of the large, predominantly young and relatively static 'criminal population' to be found in most disadvantaged inner-city areas, while in the latter case the affluent areas acted as an attraction to older and more experienced offenders who were ready to travel in search of worthwhile targets. Indeed, he concluded from interviews with a range of burglars that age was the most important factor in deciding where an offender operated. While juveniles tended to steal in a largely haphazard manner within their own neighbourhood, the '18–25-year-old moved outside his own neighbourhood for at least half his hits' and 'the first consideration' for the man of over 25 'was the neighbourhood should be affluent and therefore he spent most of his time working in single-family suburban houses' (Reppetto 1974:23–4).

Research in England gives only limited support to this model. Both Chappell (1965:373), and Baldwin and Bottoms (1976:83) concluded from samples of detected offences that adult burglars travel further than juveniles to burgle, but that the differences were by no means as clear-cut as Reppetto's work suggests. Furthermore, Baldwin's study found no significant differences between offenders aged 16–20 and those of 21–25.

What seems most interesting and surprising about the results of investigations into the distances travelled by burglars is not the differences by age, but the fact that even in cases involving adults the majority of detected burglaries take place within two miles of the offender's home. In nearly 70 per cent of those committed in Sheffield by people aged 26 or over, the burglar had travelled less than two miles (Baldwin and Bottoms *op. cit.*), and in over half of all detected cases monitored by both Baldwin and Chappell the offender lived within one mile of his victim. Such findings underline the general truth of the statement by McClintock and Avison (1968:247) that, 'on the basis of the known criminal population . . . the primary problem of maintaining law and order and dealing with offenders—whether first offenders or recidivists—remains predominantly a local one'.

Of course, one mile can be an important distance within a town or city, leading into a totally different type of housing area. Baldwin and Bottoms (*op. cit.* p. 97–8) emphasise that although crime is committed 'locally' to a large extent, it does not follow that offence and offender areas should be regarded as synonymous. Even for juvenile offenders, 'three quarters of whom operated within a mile of their homes', the small distances travelled were 'sufficient to affect quite markedly the location of the offence and offender areas'. Mawby (1979), too, points out that although areas with high offender rates normally produce high offence rates, this does not automatically mean that the local offenders commit the crimes. There may be a certain amount of interchange between offenders living in high-crime areas situated close together. Some evidence for this comes from Brantingham and Brantingham (1975) who suggest that many offenders break into houses on the 'borders' of their own residential areas. They found a disproportionate number of cases occurring in 'zones of transition between distinct natural areas or neighbourhoods'. Finally, it must once again be stressed that the above studies are based upon caught offenders and detected offences. It may be that those who burgle close to home are easier to catch than those who travel from where they are known, thus exaggerating the extent of 'local' burglary.

2. Local patterns

We now turn our attention to our own research. Several of the questions raised in Part 1 will be reconsidered in the light of an examination of burglary patterns in three police sectors of the Thames Valley. The analysis provided does not pretend to be mathematically sophisticated. One of our main aims was to describe and contrast the dominant features of the offences committed in each area, and to relate these to the characteristics and behaviour of the very different kinds of offender who appeared to be at work. We were also interested in the thoughts and feelings of both offenders and victims, which entailed a heavy workload of interviewing. Reluctantly, we had to abandon ideas of conducting local victimisation surveys or of interviewing a sample of 'non-victims'. We were therefore unable to undertake a systematic study of factors which may affect an individual's chances of being burgled, and much of what we say on that subject remains speculative. (Nevertheless, the study by Winchester and Jackson referred to on pp. 21–22 has brought welcome support to several of our tentative conclusions.)

More importantly, we were dependent upon police records for our information about the spatial patterning of burglaries in the three areas. Fortunately, there is some evidence that this is not as severe a handicap as it might at first appear. For example, Mawby (in Brantingham and Brantingham eds. 1981) reports that the distributional patterns of crime in Sheffield that emerged from a local victim survey coincided surprisingly closely with those gleaned from police data. Waller and Okihiro (1978) found likewise for burglary in Toronto. In other words, it does not appear too unreasonable to assume that, in terms of their location on the map and the social class of their victims, the burglaries recorded by the Thames Valley police are fairly representative of all burglary incidents in the area, reported or not.

One way in which we tried to go further than other studies was in tackling the problem of cases that are not solved. Our mode of collecting information was to map offences week by week as they were reported, to interview as many of the victims as possible, and to obtain information from them and from local policemen which would give us some scope for 'informed guesses' as to what kinds of offender had been responsible for at least some of the undetected cases. It was quite common, for example, for three or four similar burglaries to occur in one small area during a particular afternoon or evening, leaving little doubt that one offender or group of offenders had committed all of them. The police might have a definite suspect, or a witness may have seen somebody behaving suspiciously near one of the houses. Some victims also had fairly strong suspicions about the identity of the offender but had no firm evidence to prove it. Again, interviews with burglars convicted of some of the offences recorded revealed that they had committed other burglaries in the area with which they had not been charged. Although information from all these sources has to be treated with caution, taken together and combined with general knowledge about crime in each area obtained from the police and from local persistent offenders, it contributes much to the construction of an overall picture of what is occurring.

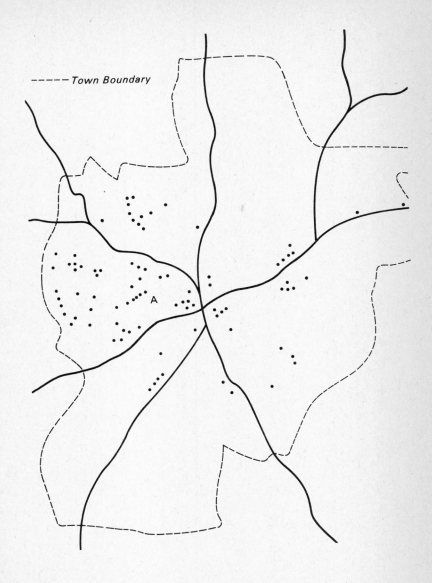

*Figure 1   Distribution of recorded offences of burglary in a dwelling, Banbury,
April 1977–March 1978*

Banbury

The first area, the police sub-division GD, includes the town of
Banbury and a wide area of countryside and villages surrounding it,
up to a fifteen-mile radius in places. Banbury is an old market-town
set in the heart of a prosperous farming area. It has a population of
about 30,000 which has expanded considerably since the war, mainly
through the development of light industry. It has taken some 'over-
spill' of workers and their families, in particular from London and
Birmingham, but nonetheless there is not a heavy turnover in
population and the community is held together by many old family
networks. The town is relatively isolated from other urban areas of
any size.

We examined all cases of burglary in a dwelling recorded by the
police in this sub-division between April 1977 and March 1978,
excluding a small number which took place in houses under construction, guest houses and unoccupied holiday cottages. (A similar
policy was followed in the other areas, it being our view that these do
not constitute genuine dwellings.) The total recorded was exactly
150, 88 of these occurring within the town boundary. This represents
a rate of approximately one offence per 120 dwellings, well below
average for the Thames Valley as a whole.

Examination of the map (Fig. 1) on which we plotted the sites of
burglaries recorded in Banbury reveals that offences were clustered
mainly in an area to the west of the town (marked 'A'). Further
clustering was evident around the town centre, and apart from a
group of offences in a new housing estate to the north, most of the
remainder took place on or close to main roads leading out of the
town. The main grouping will be considered first, then offences
committed elsewhere in the town, and finally burglaries that occurred
outside the town limits.

Council-estate burglary

Forty-five (51 per cent) of the 88 offences recorded in Banbury
occurred within a triangular area 'A' to the west of the town. This
contains under 40 per cent of the total households but the greater part
of the town's local authority housing. Seventy-five per cent of the
dwellings in this area are owned by the council. The quality of the
housing varies considerably and one or two streets have gained a bad
reputation for vandalism and juvenile crime while other parts of the
large estates are regarded as quiet and respectable. There are also
small enclaves of private housing with fairly high rateable values.

Despite the proximity of these apparently more attractive targets,
the private housing was not burgled disproportionately. There were

three definite little 'bursts' of burglary in which four or five offences were reported in a small area within a short period, and the targets in these were mainly gas or electricity pre-payment meters in council houses. The remaining cases were scattered apparently haphazardly across the district, the only notable feature being that over 90 per cent of houses were entered from the rear. Many rows of houses had alleys running along behind them and it was our impression from visiting the area—although we did not test it statistically—that such streets were more likely to have been victimised than those with less easy access to the back. (Some support for this contention is to be found in Winchester and Jackson, in preparation; see chapter VI).

Nine of the 45 cases in Area 'A' were cleared up within six months, although in two cases the defendant was found not guilty. All nine convicted offenders (there were two 'pairs' and five convicted alone) came from Banbury, and in every case but one the offender was either known to the victim or lived within half a mile of the house burgled. Two were relatives of their victims, two were near-neighbours and one (also responsible for at least two other offences nearby) was eventually charged with stealing from his own meter. None of these offenders could be described as professional burglars by any stretch of the imagination. Three were female and one was a very young child, the remaining five being males between the ages of 18 and 44. All the men had criminal records, but these were mainly a hotchpotch of petty thefts and occasionally drunkenness or assault.

In a further 14 cases in this area, either the police had a name or description of a suspect or the victim had a strong idea of the identity of the offender. Such suspicions are often based on someone being seen near the house or on personal quarrels, and must therefore themselves be treated with suspicion. However, there were good reasons for believing that young local teenagers had been the culprits in four of these cases and that up to six others involved relatives or acquaintances who had been in the house before, including in at least two cases the estranged husband of the victim. Whatever the truth in individual cases, it seems probable that in as many as a quarter of all those reported the offender was previously known to the victim.

Police response to burglaries in these housing estates, particularly to 'meter-breaks', was often cynical. One officer took an extreme view:

> They treat the meters like money boxes. They break them open when they're short of money and then try to make it look like burglary.

Asked to put a percentage figure on this happening, he replied that 'eighty to ninety per cent' of meter-breaks were 'inside jobs'. From our interviews with victims we are certain that this is a gross exaggeration, as several were still palpably upset by the event, but the comment illustrates the general feeling of the police that crime in the area is mainly a product of local problems and not caused by strangers from outside. This at least appears to be a correct assessment from the evidence we have. The overall picture that emerges is one of petty offending aimed principally at thefts of cash from near-neighbours. Thirty-three per cent of the burglaries recorded involved meter-breaks (there were also a roughly equal number of meter-breaks recorded as theft rather than burglary), and the value stolen exceeded £100 in only two of the 45 cases. The total amount recorded as stolen in burglaries in the area was £1,145, an average of only £25 per case.

Despite the fact that it contributes a relatively high proportion of the criminal offences recorded in Banbury, it must be stressed that the area in question has only a minor 'crime problem' compared with many other council-housing estates in larger urban areas. A fairly similar area of Reading (see p. 38) is burgled at least twice as frequently, and this in turn has minor problems compared with the estates in Sheffield described by Baldwin and Bottoms (1976) or with the deprived area of Widnes surveyed by Hedges *et al.* (1980). The latter found that as many as 18 per cent of houses on the Cunningham Road estate had been burgled in the year prior to the improvement scheme carried out there. Even so, the example from Banbury illustrates the point that in local authority housing estates, which generally suffer relatively high rates of victimisation within any given town, burglary can be regarded very much as a local problem, and any attempt to tackle it should be based upon an understanding of local conditions and relationships. Elsewhere, as we shall see, burglaries are much more likely to be the work of 'outsiders'.

Other burglaries in Banbury

Burglaries in other parts of Banbury were less easy to classify. There was a much wider range of property stolen and fewer cases of previous links between offender and victim. Eleven of the 43 burglaries recorded were cleared up, producing a 'mixed bag' of offenders. One was an experienced travelling thief from the north of England who 'stopped off' when passing through the town to burgle a detached house a few yards from the main trunk road. A similar kind of offender was suspected of responsibility for four other cases involving thefts of valuable silver which occured in quick succession on another main road, and for another group of burglaries a few miles out of town. The other offenders arrested within six months came from Banbury. They were made up of two children, a 50-year-old woman with mental problems (who committed a variety of offences against neighbours), an older teenager who burgled a house in which he had been a guest, an alcoholic vagrant, and two well-known local persistent property-offenders in their twenties. Descriptions of people seen leaving two properties burgled in the town centre suggested that they were middle-aged men, probably under the influence of alcohol; and local children were strongly suspected of some of the offences in a new housing estate to the north of the town.

On the evidence presented, one has to conclude that Banbury does not suffer a serious burglary problem. Even if several of the undetected offences were committed by 'professional' burglars—which is unlikely, considering the generally low value of property stolen—the dominant pattern would still be one of offences committed in sporadic fashion by a variety of people from the town, few of whom would describe themselves as 'burglars'. The cases outside Area 'A' seemed to include a higher proportion of 'stranger-to-stranger' burglaries, but, with the exception of those committed in middle-class housing on or very near main roads (which appeared to be the work of a very small number of offenders), there was little evidence of careful selection of targets. Several of the town-centre burglaries were of modest houses which, it is assumed by the police, simply happened to have caught the eye of someone who found himself in town without much money—or, in at least three cases, of someone who was intoxicated.

Country burglary

Sixty-two burglaries were recorded in the Banbury police sub-division outside the town limits. Broadly speaking, these seemed to fall into three categories. At one extreme were cases where children from a village entered houses of people they knew and stole food or small amounts of cash. At the other were burglaries in which valuable property such as silver and jewellery were stolen by apparently 'professional' travelling thieves (some thought to be from outside the county) who selected wealthy targets including an historic country house. The former type were identifiable because a large proportion of minor cases were cleared up and in others there were very strong local suspicions as to the identity of the culprits. The latter type were recognisable by the skill with which they were committed, the type of property that was selected (much of which would have needed a specialist receiver to dispose of it), and the fact that on four occasions two or three high-value burglaries were reported within a short period in villages a few miles apart. Between the two extremes were a mixture of cases, including burglaries by persistent thieves from Banbury or one of the larger villages who drove a few miles from their homes in order to avoid the attentions of the local police, generally selecting ordinary village houses and stealing perhaps cash or electrical goods rather than identifiable silverware or jewellery. In other 'middle-range' cases it was impossible to guess what kind of offender had been responsible.

The first of the above categories, although apparently trivial, caused a great deal of disturbance in some small communities where crime and even the sight of a policeman was unusual. In one case a woman reported a minor burglary, then on discovering that her young nephew was responsible tried to withdraw her complaint. The police refused to comply and he was taken to court. Conversely, another woman in a remote village personally confronted some children whom she thought responsible for burgling her home and made them confess, yet had great difficulty in persuading the police to follow up her initiative. Generally speaking, the town police are outsiders in such communities and, we were assured by several victims, not as sensitive as 'the old village bobby' to ways of solving problems with local children without recourse to the courts. The main damage that burglaries of this type causes is the souring of relationships between neighbours and relatives, as well as, in some cases, the acquisition of a police record by children never likely to become involved in serious crime.

Eight of the 11 'country' burglaries cleared up involved children (one pair of boys were responsible for four cases), and in seven undetected cases children were strongly suspected. On the other hand, at least 20 burglaries appeared to be the work of experienced mobile criminals. In most of these cases wealthy properties were tidily searched and a few selected pieces of silver or other valuables stolen. In ten of them the value stolen was recorded at over £300 and in five it exceeded £1,000. As few as four or five burglars may have been responsible for all these offences, which tended to occur in small groups at widely spaced intervals. Two examples are cited.

In the first, a large isolated farmhouse and a country mansion situated about half a mile away were both burgled, probably around dusk on a winter weekday. The family from the farm were absent for two days and on their return found silver worth about £2,000 missing from their dining-room. They had no idea how the thief had entered the house, which had apparently been well locked, although he had climbed out through a window which he left open behind him. Otherwise nothing had been moved and it took several minutes for them to realise that anything was amiss. The nearby country house was entered while the alarms were switched off, through the one window with a broken lock. It is thought that the thief had been in the gardens (which are open to the public) earlier in the day, noticed the broken catch and returned as it was getting dark. Once again he selected only some valuable silver and disturbed nothing else. The owner noticed nothing missing until two days later, but when he did a number of people remembered small incidents which fixed the time of the burglary and helped in the reconstruction of what must have happened.

The second example was a particularly skilful burglary which occurred about 2 a.m. in a cottage backing on to fields near the edge of a village. The burglar entered the house a few days before Christmas, and had to move Christmas cards and decorations in order to get in through the window. He forced the lock on the silver cabinet, which he emptied, closed the cabinet carefully, and on leaving through the same window replaced all the Christmas cards on the sill. The victim was in bed at the time, and there was a dog in the house, which barked once or twice. The victim heard this, but did not pay much attention to it or get up to investigate. She did not discover the offence until the next afternoon when opening the cabinet. When we interviewed her, a rumour was circulating in the area that the burglar was a man who left his car a considerable distance from the scene of his intended crime and ran across country wearing a track-suit in order to avoid being followed or stopped in his car near the scene of the burglary.

Such offences pose great problems of detection for local police forces since the burglars tend to be active in the area for only a day or two, committing perhaps three or four lucrative offences before disappearing completely. Unless they are caught in the act or stopped in a random traffic check, there is little possibility of an arrest by divisional police officers. Only one of the 20 offences mentioned above had been officially cleared up after six months, although names were associated with a number of others and it is possible that if these offenders are arrested elsewhere some Banbury area offences will be (or, by now, have been) cleared up at the same time.

With the failure of the police to make any prompt arrests, we were unable to interview any of the burglars responsible for these high-value cases. (The one serious offence cleared up became a 'TIC'—offence taken into consideration—in a big case involving a network of burglars and receivers over a wide area of southern England. The man charged did not come to court until after our field-work was completed.) However, we did interview in depth a man who had specialised in country-house burglaries (some in the Thames Valley area) during the year prior to our study, and who was serving a long prison sentence for similar crimes to those described. He had supplied a stream of stolen porcelain, silver, carriage clocks and jewellery through local receivers to a number of big buyers in London and on the Continent for a period of more than two years. He rarely committed more than one or two burglaries a week, and generally took only property of high value. He stressed *mobility* as his most important weapon against the police: 'The secret is to keep moving, keep putting miles on the clock.' We have called the man 'Peter Hudson' and in chapter IV an extended account will be given of his development as a professional thief.

Burglaries of the two extreme kinds so far described are relatively easy to recognise and classify. About one-third of the country burglaries recorded did not appear to fall into either category, and there was often no indication of who might have been responsible. There were, however, some examples of the work of people whom we classified as 'middle-range' persistent thieves. Unlike Reading (see next section), Banbury does not contain a large 'criminal community' of persistent offenders who adopt a consciously criminal lifestyle, using the language and learning the craft of thieves in a continuing co-operative effort to obtain a significant income from crime. Nevertheless, there are small networks of such people, some of whom include residential burglary in their criminal 'repertoire'. Two were arrested during our period of study for burglaries involving property of medium value within the town, and two more for country cases. In one of the latter, a 30-year-old man with twelve previous convictions for theft and burglary simply cycled about three miles out of town one morning until he found an isolated cottage to burgle. In the other, two 25-year-old men with seven previous convictions for burglary between them visited a village pub at lunchtime and then broke into a nearby house, stealing property worth about £50.

Several other cases, both on the outskirts of the town and in surrounding villages[4], may well have been the work of these or other similar persistent offenders. The type of property stolen—radios, record players, cassette recorders, television sets—suggests offenders who have a market for consumer goods that are not easily identifiable individually, but who (unlike the 'higher class' of mobile criminals described earlier) do not have access to receivers who will take more valuable, and recognisable, items such as silver and jewellery.

Of course, this distinction between 'upper' and 'middle' levels of persistent thief remains at this stage somewhat speculative, and may not be as clear-cut as we imply. It may be that thieves who stole valuable items from large country properties also burgled at the 'middle' level, and *vice-versa*. However, the fact that burglaries which took place within one area over a short period usually involved thefts of similar items suggests that different types of burglar with specific preferences were at work. This theme will be returned to in the next chapter, where the target-selection of the persistent burglars we interviewed will be discussed.

Reading: 'middle-range' burglary
The second area we looked at was delineated by police sector EA, which covers most of the town of Reading apart from the suburban area of Tilehurst to the west. Reading is the largest town in the Thames Valley, with a population of 130,000. About 100,000 people live within the police sector studied. The town has extensive light industry and frequently-used motorway and rail-commuter links with London. To the north there are relatively prosperous residential areas characterised by large detached houses, while in parts of the centre and in the area immediately south of the centre living standards are generally lower and the housing can be of poor quality. We noted details of all cases of burglary in a dwelling recorded by the police during 1978, which, when uninhabited buildings were excluded, came to a total of 797. The burglary rate for the year was roughly one offence per 44 dwellings, only marginally below that for the Metropolitan Police District.

Fig. 2 shows the distribution of burglaries recorded in this police sector. The greatest concentrations occurred in residential areas close to the town centre and in the large council-housing estate to the south (area 8). The middle-class areas to the north escaped comparatively lightly. Yet, although the parts of the town most heavily victimised were those that contained the poorest housing, the situation differed from Banbury in that in the centre of town Reading burglars selected a disproportionate number of high-value properties. For example, in area 7, in which wealthy and poor homes are situated in close proximity, large detached houses were a clearly preferred target. One particularly prosperous street here was subjected to nine separate visits in the twelve month period.

Over the sector as a whole, the highest and the lowest socio-economic groups were burgled more frequently (in proportion to their numbers) than those in intermediate categories.[5] Where the upper end of the scale was concerned, the location of the house seemed to be an important factor in deciding an individual's risk of victimisation. Middle-class housing adjacent to poorer areas such as in areas 7, 5 and 9) was much more likely to be burgled than similar

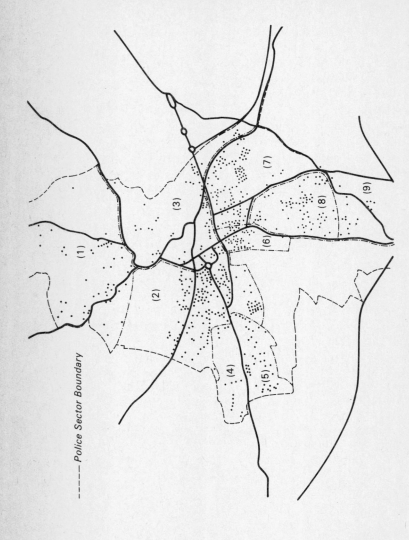

------ Police Sector Boundary

Figure 2   Distribution of recorded offences of burglary in a dwelling, Police Sector EA, Reading 1978

housing further away (such as in areas 1 and 3). The patterning also suggests that offenders were unwilling to penetrate too deeply into exclusively middle-class areas on the outskirts of the town, concentrating chiefly on houses close to the main roads. This is especially striking in area 1.

According to police records the average value stolen in Reading burglaries was £155. (Our interviews produced a mean of £240; see Appendix 1, Table A3.) Jewellery was stolen in 17 per cent of cases and electrical goods in 14 per cent. While in Banbury offenders tended to take only cash or relatively small items, in Reading there were many cases in which large 'mixed bags' were collected, including bulky electrical equipment and television sets. We interviewed offenders from Reading who spoke of piling up property in a convenient place to be loaded into the boot of a car, a process that might involve walking back and forth into the house a number of times. All this suggests a higher level of ambition among burglars in Reading than in Banbury and the presence of easier outlets for stolen goods. The high burglary rate also indicates either a much greater number of people who are prepared to engage in fairly substantial thefts or a tendency for offenders to repeat the act at frequent intervals.

A glance at the characteristics of offenders arrested for burglary in Reading shows that they were considerably different from their counterparts in Banbury. Seventy (27 per cent) of the 259 cases in our interview sample were officially 'cleared up' within a period of six months, although by the time we ceased fieldwork only 45 had reached the final stage of conviction or caution. These 45 completed cases produced a total of 33 offenders. Twenty-one of these were arrested alone and there were four 'pairs' and one 'foursome'.) Only seven were under the age of 17. Of the remaining 26 (who were all male), 24 had previous convictions and 18 of these had been convicted previously for offences of burglary in a dwelling. Indeed, 15 had been convicted previously five or more times. We are thus talking mainly about a criminally active group of young adult offenders who come before the courts on frequent occasions. (Twelve were aged between 17 and 21, and 14 were aged 21 or over.)

Although most had previous convictions for burglary, these were usually scattered among a variety of other offences, mainly theft, but also fraud, minor assault and taking of vehicles. The majority were unemployed at the time of their arrest, and few had ever retained any one job for more than a year. Twenty-four of the 26 aged 17 or over lived in the town of Reading and hence had travelled no more than a few miles to the target in question. However, the Reading offenders were much less likely than those in Banbury to have had any previous connection with the victim: in only five of the 45 burglaries were the two definitely acquainted. Moreover, 47 per cent of them also admitted five or more other burglaries to be taken into consideration by the court, and 40 per cent of these 'TIC's were for offences committed outside the police sector. In other words, although there is no evidence that many burglars come into Reading from elsewhere to commit offences, those living in the town often travel out into surrounding villages or nearby smaller towns in search of houses to burgle.

The question arises of how representative these offenders were of all those who committed burglaries in Reading that year. Unfortunately, unlike Banbury victims, few of those interviewed in Reading had any idea as to who might have been responsible for their burglary. Nevertheless, this very fact, taken together with the findings that there were only a small number of detected cases in which offender and victim were acquainted, that the amounts stolen were generally higher, and that 'better-class' houses were more often selected for attack, strongly suggests that Reading burglary is on the whole a more impersonal and 'business-like' affair than it is in Banbury, committed by people who engage in crime more often and who regard it as an integral part of making a living. The type of property taken, too, points in many cases towards offenders who have access to receivers and are therefore in touch with some kind of 'criminal subculture'.

Indeed, all the indications are that the bulk of undetected burglaries in Reading, with the possible exception of those committed in area 8 (which produced more juvenile offenders than adults among those arrested, and which displayed many of the features of 'council-estate burglary' described in the section on Banbury[6]) are the work of persistent adult or young adult offenders who form part of a well-established 'criminal network' in the town. This was certainly the view of the local police, and is further supported by the statements of the convicted offenders we interviewed. We interviewed 10 of the 33 convicted burglars described above, and all admitted that they had recently committed burglaries in the town apart from those for which they had been officially held responsible. Moreover, all but two admitted that they had burgled substantial numbers of houses over a period of years and said that they knew others who, as one put it, were 'at it all the time'.

Our analysis of burglaries in Reading did not point so clearly to a distinction between 'upper' and 'middle' levels of persistent thieves as did the analysis of burglaries in the country area around Banbury.

Certainly, some of those arrested in Reading had a reputation with the police and among their peers as being 'good villains', but an examination of the offences for which they were convicted revealed a surprising lack of discrimination in the type of housing they attacked. For example, a man of 34 who was generally regarded as a competent thief had what had originally appeared to be both 'good-class' and 'petty' burglaries in almost equal numbers among 15 offences 'taken into consideration'. He had committed several offences in one day near the town centre, in some cases stealing jewellery from wealthy homes and in others forcing the doors of terraced houses in a poor area in order to steal a few pounds in cash. Others admitted burglaries scattered wide apart in contrasting areas of the town.

We also found no strong support for Reppetto's contentions (1974; and see p. 26) that young adults travel shorter distances to commit offences and steal less valuable property than adults. The average value stolen in detected cases involving young adults was £120, and in those involving adults over 21 it was £190. Neither group had travelled significantly further from home to steal, nor did they each attack different kinds of area. We had to conclude that in Reading one cannot assume that high-value burglaries or burglaries in middle-class areas are the work either of older men or of the 'best' or 'most professional' thieves. In a town with a substantial self-defined criminal population, even the youngest and least competent members of the 'criminal fraternity' will quite often try their luck at breaking into more expensive housing in unfamiliar areas.

This does not of course mean that there are no major burglars operating from Reading. On the contrary, the police were able to name four or five men recently arrested who had been involved in large-scale criminal enterprises. However, it does suggest that such people tend to go elsewhere to carry out their crimes. The above remarks raise some difficult questions about the classification of offenders, which will be considered in chapter III.

Gerrards Cross: commuter-belt burglary

The third area we examined was the police sector BC, which encompasses the small towns and villages of Beaconsfield, Chalfont St Giles, Chalfont St Peter, Denham and Gerrards Cross in south-east Buckinghamshire, on the very outskirts of London. Gerrards Cross, in which (with Chalfont St Peter) we concentrated our interviewing of victims, has a population of under 8,000 and is one of the smallest towns in the Thames Valley. It is a very affluent commuter area, again with easy motorway- and rail-access to London. A high proportion of its properties are large detached family houses laid well back from the road. Many have their own driveways and are hidden by trees, bushes and shrubs. The rest of the sector is also dominated by high-value housing, although not quite to the same extent as Gerrards Cross itself. Between March 1978 and February 1979, 357 offences of burglary in a dwelling were recorded in the sector as a whole, 134 of these in Gerrards Cross and Chalfont St Peter. In Gerrards Cross itself, the recorded burglary rate was the highest in the Thames Valley, showing one offence for every 25 households.

In contrast to the other two areas, burglaries in Gerrards Cross were scattered right across the town, the only immediately noticeable feature of their distribution being a concentration on properties near the junctions of roads. Indeed, nearly 20 per cent of all cases involved the last house in a street. This finding is not quite as dramatic as it sounds, as many of the streets are short and contain only a few residences, but even so the preference was a clear one. It was confirmed by all five offenders we interviewed who had been convicted of burglaries in Gerrards Cross. They pointed out that corner properties afford at least three alternative escape routes in an emergency. These interviewees also mentioned the plentiful cover provided by trees and bushes as a particular 'bonus' of the area, and visual inspection gave us the impression that houses not immediately visible from the road were chosen more frequently than those with less cover surrounding them. (See also Winchester and Jackson, in preparation).

One other feature that may have affected the selection of targets was the presence or absence of a burglar alarm. Although we were told by the police that a very high proportion of properties in the area were fitted with alarms, under a quarter of the 82 victims interviewed were so protected. The five burglars interviewed said that they were capable of defeating alarm systems, but unless there were strong attractions in a particular property they usually chose houses without alarms.

As one would expect in so affluent an area, the majority of burglaries netted valuable property. From police figures, the mean value stolen in cases in which we interviewed the victims was £536, and the median value was £200, while the equivalent figures from our interviews were £869 and £500 respectively (see Appendix 1, Table A3). Jewellery, stolen in 54 per cent of cases, was the most 'popular' item, cash being taken in less than a quarter of cases. Altogether, allowing for cases in which the value had not been established at the time the report was filed, it appears that well over £90,000 worth of property was stolen during our year of observation in Gerrards Cross and Chalfont St Peter.

Although the average value of property stolen in Gerrards Cross burglaries greatly exceeded that in our other areas, this alone does not necessarily mean that the offenders were of a different 'class' of burglar. We obtained details of 16 people arrested for offences committed there during the year, all of whom were over 18. Four or five of these had made clumsy mistakes, and not all were in a position to dispose of what they stole in a quick and profitable manner. One man who had stolen silver worth over £10,000 could only sell it by weight for £400. On the other hand, the majority were clearly highly competent and 'well-connected', and were considered by the police to be 'professional criminals'. The group as a whole had fewer previous convictions than adult offenders in Reading, and these tended to be spaced wider apart in time. Ignoring juvenile offences, their records were made up mainly of commercial and residential burglaries. Some also included robberies and major thefts, but there was a notable dearth of offences such as taking of vehicles, minor assaults and shoplifting, which typified the records of Reading and (to a lesser extent) Banbury burglars. They had also been convicted in a wider range of areas, showing their greater mobility as thieves.

All sixteen had travelled several miles to commit their burglaries in Gerrards Cross. They had all used cars, a situation quite different to that in Reading where the majority had been on foot. Indeed, the local police are certain that almost every burglary in their area is committed by people from outside the district. They name 'West London' as the main source of their problem. (One officer described Gerrards Cross as 'London's piggy bank'.) This appears to be a fairly accurate assessment according to the addresses of those arrested. Nine of the 16 lived in Greater London, the remainder coming from other towns in the Thames Valley area.

We interviewed five of the above offenders, one of whom stood out as exceptionally shrewd and businesslike in his approach. 'Denis', was a Londoner in his late thirties who had been breaking into houses since the age of 13. He claimed that the proceeds had been his main and regular source of income and that he had committed virtually no other kind of theft for 20 years. These claims were made more believable by his almost obsessional calculation of risks and his desire to avoid detection at all costs. (He had been fairly successful in this, being convicted only three times as an adult.) He was convinced that house burglary entailed less risk of arrest than any other major crime and that it was also extremely lucrative if one 'knew where to go'. He took the minutest precautions to limit the suspicions of passers-by or neighbours near the scenes of his crimes. He took care over the way he dressed and even selected the type of vehicle he used for a particular offence in terms of how well it fitted the area. He was one of the few we interviewed who sized up targets days in advance, making trips solely to familiarise himself with the most promising houses and the area surrounding them. If possible he found out the names of the occupants, and telephoned the house in preference to knocking on the door to establish whether there was anybody at home. He had also developed a series of specialist buyers, for example one who would take gold, and another dealing in antiques.

The others interviewed were less meticulous in their preparations, but all claimed to have made a 'good living' from burglary. Gerrards Cross was only one of a number of wealthy areas they visited, attracted by the certainty that almost any house they chose would contain items of considerable value. Unlike Denis, they usually worked with other people who helped them by driving the car, loading property or acting as look-out. These partners quite often changed according to who was available, although one claimed that he had a regular 'assistant' whom he was 'training' as a thief. We shall describe their methods of operation more fully in chapter III.

3.   The physical circumstances of burglary

The above outline of patterns of burglary in three areas has illustrated considerable variations in householders' chances of being burgled, in the type and value of property stolen and in the sophistication of offenders. There was also a certain amount of variation between areas in the physical circumstances of the offences—the times at which they were most often committed, the method of entry and the extent of disarrangement or damage to property—but not usually to a significant degree. Although we shall point out differences between areas where appropriate, the major interest here is in the overall rather than the local picture. To describe it we shall draw mainly upon police figures for the whole of the Thames Valley and upon the results of our 322 interviews with victims.

Times offences are committed
It is difficult to put a time to most burglaries, as they are rarely witnessed by the victim. A large proportion take place when the house is empty and are not discovered until hours later; others occur overnight without waking the occupants. In still others, no signs of entry or disturbance are apparent and victims may remain unaware of the burglary until a particular item is missed or perhaps an offender confesses.

In analysing times of offence, it has to be accepted that the more precise one wishes to be the more 'unknowns' there will be in the sample. Thus in the Thames Valley in 1975 one can be sure of the month of commission in 97 per cent of recorded cases, the day of commission in 53 per cent of cases (or 75 per cent if 'overnight' offences are included), and the hour of commission in only eight per cent. Unfortunately, the unknowns cannot always be assumed to be distributed in the same manner as the knowns, as the times at which people discover burglaries are not randomly distributed. The latter are related to patterns of social life, including the times most people get up in the morning or return home from shopping, work, an evening out, or a weekend away.

Despite this handicap we are confident that we have identified a clear pattern in the timing of offences. This has emerged in different ways from all our data. We pressed victims for their best estimate of the time of the burglary, and the results are close to those of calculations based on police records.

Before more precise estimation, two features were already clear: daytime burglaries outnumbered those committed at night and the number of burglaries committed on Sundays was much lower than on other days. It also appeared from the times that were known to within a few hours that the afternoon was the peak time for burglary. These findings held for every month of the year, although, overall, the mid-winter months, notably December, produced more burglaries than the summer months, and the proportion of night-time burglaries was higher in the summer (see Appendix 1, Table A10).

In an effort to obtain a more detailed picture, we performed a statistical exercise on the 1975 Thames Valley data, redistributing offences evenly over the periods within which they were known to have occurred. For example, if there were 20 cases in which the earliest possible time of commission was 6 p.m. on a Monday and the latest possible time was 1 a.m. the next morning, each hour between these two hours inclusive was allocated 20 ÷ 8 (i.e. 2.50) offences. This operation was performed for every combination of less than 24 hours' duration throughout the week, so that eventually each hour of the week had an estimated annual total of offences. Although the method used tends to 'flatten' any unusually high concentrations (if most of the overnight offences took place at 2 a.m. but were not dis-covered until morning, they would appear as distributed equally throughout the night), the resulting pattern at least gives some idea of the 'ebb and flow' of burglary from hour to hour throughout the week. This is shown in graph form in Fig. 3. (Monday, Tuesday and Wednesday produced patterns so similar to Thursday that the latter can be taken as a representative weekday.)

It is clear that on Mondays to Thursdays burglary is primarily a daytime phenomenon. We estimate that on these days over 50 per

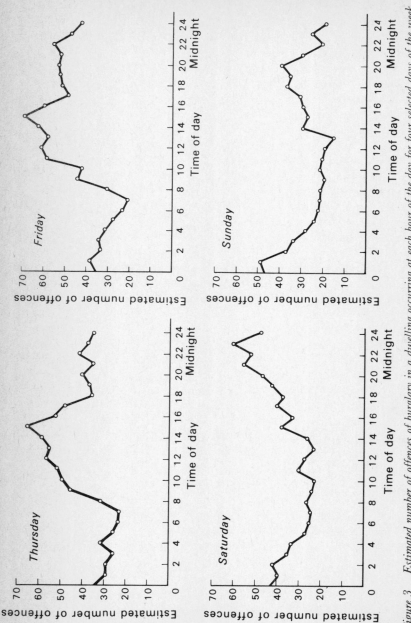

Figure 3   Estimated number of offences of burglary in a dwelling occurring at each hour of the day for four selected days of the week Thames Valley, 1975 (totals for year)

cent of offences take place between 9 a.m. and 5 p.m. The basic weekday pattern seems to be a steady rise through the day from 7 a.m. to a peak at 3 p.m., followed by a sharp drop to 6 p.m., a minor revival during the evening, then a decline from 10 p.m. through the night. Fridays differ from other weekdays in that they maintain high rates throughout the evening. (Indeed, Friday appears to be the peak day for burglary, a feature confirmed by Reppetto (1974:106), Scarr (1973:142) and Hampshire Constabulary (1978:10), although not by all researchers.)

The patterns for Saturdays and Sundays present a quite different picture. On Saturdays the evening brings the highest risk with a peak period between 9 p.m. and 11 p.m. Comparatively few offences occur in the late morning or early afternoon, and the daytime total is only half that of any weekday. Sundays are similar in pattern to Saturdays up to 6 p.m. with a low number of daytime offences, but unlike Saturdays their evenings do not see an increase.

Where possible, we calculated whether the offence had occurred in daylight or darkness (see Appendix 1, Table A10). The overall ratio was about 2:1 for daylight, but on Saturdays alone the known 'darkness' offences outnumbered those known to have been committed in daylight. This is due mainly to the proliferation of burglaries on Saturday evenings. (The number of 'overnight' offences—defined as those taking place after 10 p.m. but not discovered until the next morning—did not vary so greatly throughout the week, although, again, Saturday nights produced the highest total). In all we estimated that a maximum of one in four burglaries occurred during the hours when most people are asleep, and from discovery times it is likely that no more than one in five of all burglaries took place with people actually asleep in the house. Only 51 (16 per cent) of the 322 victims we interviewed had been in bed at night when burgled.

There was a certain degree of variation in times of attack between our three study areas, although the overall findings were not contradicted. Banbury showed the highest proportion of evening offences, Reading the highest of night-time burglaries and Gerrards Cross, the area attracting the most professional offenders, the highest proportion of daytime offences. The most striking feature was the figure of 23 per cent 'overnight' cases in Reading, well in excess of the other two areas (see Appendix 1, Table A9). The explanation given by burglars was that Reading contains a number of late-night clubs and cafés and that many thieves meet in these before going on to commit offences. By contrast, the five offenders interviewed who had been convicted of burglaries in Gerrards Cross all expressed a preference for daytime, pointing out that Gerrards Cross was a dormitory town and a high percentage of houses were unoccupied particularly during the early afternoon. Sixty-six per cent of offences here for which the period of day was known occurred between 8 a.m. and 5 p.m.

Our findings can be compared with figures from a number of other studies. They are quite different to those of Chappell (1965:223), who found that 48 per cent of his 116 cases of breaking and entering involved entry while people were asleep. Whether his sample was unrepresentative, or the changes in definition of 1968 make comparison questionable, or burglars have changed their behaviour over 15 years[7] is not clear. But most other more recent studies in which house-breaking is analysed give a considerably lower night-time rate.

Reppetto's interviews with Boston burglars (1974:17), supported by police data, led him to the conclusion that burglary is primarily a daytime offence, although he is alone in specifying *mornings* as the peak period: 'Most interviewees worked in the morning (between 6 a.m. and 12 noon) and few worked after midnight, when people were most likely to be at home in bed.'

Scarr (1973: Table 22) presents the figures (for Prince George's County, Washington DC) which are closest to our own. He found that nearly 50 per cent of reported burglaries for which times were estimable took place between 10 a.m. and 4 p.m., compared with 13 per cent between midnight and 7 a.m. For him, too, residential burglary is a daytime, weekday phenomenon.

All the above findings are based on or confirmed by police data. An exception is the study by Waller and Okihiro (1978:25), who found that while Toronto police records yielded a low night-time burglary rate, 24 per cent of offences occurring between 10 p.m. and 7 a.m., their own victimisation survey produced a figure of 42 per cent. Also, in direct contrast to Reppetto, their survey showed the morning to be the *least* active period for burglars. Once again, however, we are discussing a small sample: a total of 124 victims. The most authoritative study not based on police data is the Dayton-San José Pilot Survey (Department of Justice 1974), which was one of the early mass victimisation surveys carried out in the United States, and covered 92,000 burglaries (the majority of which took place at night) and residential burglaries (for which evening, followed closely by day-time) showed the highest rates.

The problems of obtaining accurate information and the lack of careful definition by some writers of terms such as 'night' necessitate caution in making precise statements about temporal patterns of burglary, or comparisons between different studies. Yet despite a certain amount of variation in findings, most writers are agreed that above all the timing of burglary is related to *occupancy*. Mid-afternoon on a weekday, the time our research indicates as the peak period, is one of the times that houses are most likely to be unoccupied. Conversely, the low point on the graph (6–8 a.m.) is the time at which people are most likely to be at home but not asleep. The dip at 6 p.m. in the evening could also be accounted for by the fact that people tend to be in for their evening meal. The secondary peak later in the evening, particularly on Saturday evenings, comes at a time when many people have gone out for entertainment. The task of the burglar is made easier when the absence of lights advertises which houses are empty. Finally, the period after midnight, when nearly all houses are occupied, shows a low rate, although not as low as 6–8 a.m. because the effectiveness of occupancy is reduced when people are asleep.

Table 2 shows the proportions of houses occupied and unoccupied at the time of burglary, as far as could be deduced from police reports, and based on the 1,304 cases recorded in our three study areas. At least three-quarters were empty at the time. Reppetto (1974:17) found that the even higher proportion of 92 per cent were unoccupied during burglaries in Boston. These figures clearly underline the fact that burglary is a surreptitious crime in which as far as possible the offender avoids the risk of contact with the victim.

Table 2   Occupancy of houses burgled, three selected police sectors, Thames Valley: covering in each a one-year period between 1977 and 1979

	Number	Percentage
Occupied overnight	231	17.7
Occupied day or evening	61	4.7
Unoccupied	978	75.0
Not known	34	2.6
Total	1,304	100.0

Methods of entry

A popular image of a burglar as portrayed in films or on television is of a silent, careful figure, skilfully prising open a window or picking a lock. The reality is often quite different. In many cases, doors and windows are left unlocked or open, and entry is child's play. Smashing a window or shouldering through a weak door are other common means of entry, and if an instrument is used it is normally an ordinary long screwdriver (hence the term 'screwing houses').

The language used by the police to record method of entry is sometimes ambiguous. For example, 'entered through insecure window' covers a range of 'insecurity' from an open window to one where the catch had to be expertly jiggled until it opened. The victim in the first case might be called careless, but in the second he understandably may not have realised how simple it is for an experienced burglar to get in. Even so, the fact that over one-quarter of the crime reports we examined specifically referred to insecure doors and windows is one indication of how inadequately houses are protected in general (see chapter VI).

The methods of entry recorded in Thames Valley cases in 1975 are classified in Table 3.

Table 3   Method of entry, all cases of burglary in a dwelling recorded by Thames Valley police, 1975

Method of entry	Number	Percentage
Glass smashed or removed	1,776	27.4
Bodily pressure	1,630	25.1
Instrument used	725	11.2
Structure of house attacked	59	0.9
No force or instrument recorded	2,294	35.4
Total	6,484	100.0

As these figures demonstrate, burglars normally either take advantage of an unlocked door or window, or else simply push or smash their way in. There is rarely any need to resort to more sophisticated methods such as glass-cutting or picking locks. American research has produced a similar picture. Scarr's Washington DC figures showed glass broken in about one-quarter of all cases (1973:139). Reppetto in Boston found that 38 per cent of entries through windows were made by breaking glass, and 40 per cent of these through doors by 'direct impact' (1974:20). Even his offender interviewees—most of them experienced burglars—admitted the crudity of their methods, and he was able to apply the description 'skilled' to only 11 per cent.

The place of entry is not included in the 1975 Thames Valley data, but we manage to ascertain this information in most of the cases recorded in our three study areas in 1977–9. Table 4 shows both the method and place of entry for all dwellings excluding flats and rooms in lodgings.

Windows were more often the entry point than doors, and were smashed, forced and opened without force in roughly equal proportions. Over one third of the doors entered were unlocked, and one in four were entered by breaking a glass panel.

Table 4   Method and place of entry, burglary in a dwelling (flats and lodgings excluded), Reading, Gerrards Cross and Banbury: covering in each a one-year period between 1977 and 1979   (N = 1,085)

	Forced %	Pane smashed %	Open/ insecure %	Other/ not known %	Total %
Window	21.8	21.7	15.5	2.1	61.1
Door	10.2	7.4	11.3	3.9	32.8
Not known/other	—	—	—	6.1	6.1
Total	32.0	29.1	26.8	12.1	100.0

Chappell (1965:236) found windows to be the entry point in 70 per cent of cases, and the vast majority of these were rear windows.[8] However, American experience seems to differ from British. Figures quoted by Waller and Okihiro (1978) (77 per cent), Reppetto (1974) (68 per cent) and Scarr (1973) (61 per cent) show doors in a clear majority, and most of these were front doors. Of course, a higher proportion of Americans live in high-rise apartments and the door is often the only practical way in. Indeed, 69 per cent of the flats and lodging rooms burgled in Reading and Banbury 1977–78 were entered through a door.

With the exception of flats, most dwellings are entered from the rear of the building. Of the 902 properties (excluding flats) burgled in our 1977–79 sample for which this information is known, 65 per cent were entered from the rear and 27 per cent from the front. 73 per cent of entries made at the front were through a door, 76 per cent of those at the rear through a window. All but a handful were made at ground level. In all, a *rear downstairs window was the entry point in 48 per cent of cases for which information is available* (see Appendix 1, Table 11).

Searches and damage

One of the main fears people have about being burgled is that their house may be ransacked or 'vandalised'. Crime prevention advertisements use the image of a ransacked room to discourage carelessness in locking up, and, as mentioned in chapter I, articles about burglary in the popular press tend to emphasise this aspect. It was also notable that about a quarter of the victims we interviewed made unprompted references to vandalism, expressing relief that no serious damage had been committed in their cases. Many believed that such behaviour was the norm rather than the exception.

In fact, our evidence indicates that wilful damage to property occurs in only a small minority of cases. Only 53 (0.8 per cent) of the 6,484 Thames Valley cases analysed included the entry 'damage incidental to main offence', and only five of the 322 victims we interviewed had suffered clearly gratuitous damage to their property. Scarr (1973:28) found few cases of serious damage in Washington DC, and Walsh (1980:91) states that 'pointless destruction was not common in Exeter burglaries'.

On the other hand, Walsh (*ibid.*:89), without giving any figures, claims that burglars 'frequently' indulge in the much more unpleasant practice of defecating or urinating in the house. We have found no evidence at all to support this statement. Only 22 (0.3 per cent) of Thames Valley cases referred to 'nuisance committed (excreted, masturbated, urinated, vomited)' and Hampshire Constabulary (1978:19) reported 'house fouled by burglar' in one per cent of cases in that county in 1977. Among the 322 victims interviewed, we found only one case of defecation. Rare as it is, this phenomenon requires some explanation. Friedman (1968) puts forward the somewhat dubious suggestion that burglars do it to bring good luck. The suggestion made by Walsh (1980b) is even more unlikely. He proposes that burglars urinate because they have been drinking to get their courage up, and that they do so on towels, carpets or beds in order to cut down the level of noise. ('If the burglar were to urinate on to a hard surface, as in a normal lavatory, his hearing would be cut off by the sound.') The burglars we spoke to said simply that it was a deliberately malicious act committed by a small proportion of young criminals. Only one admitted to having defecated at the scene of some of his crimes, and he explained it as a result of the tension he felt, comparing the urge with the natural instinct of an animal in danger preparing to run away.

Police descriptions of the type of search carried out by burglars are usually limited to 'tidy', 'untidy' or 'very untidy', and in many cases no information is recorded. For what it is worth, among the 1,304 burglaries we monitored in 1977–79, 17 per cent were recorded as untidy and three per cent as very untidy. To obtain a more helpful picture of the degree of disarrangement caused, we asked victims to describe in detail what had been moved and classified their replies as in Table 5.

This clearly indicates that 'ransacking' of houses is a comparatively infrequent feature of burglary.[9] In the vast majority of cases the burglar's intention is to steal what he can as quickly as possible and any disarrangement of property is brought about only by his haste. Surprisingly often it took victims several minutes after entering the house to realise that anything was amiss: 47 per cent said that the first

Table 5 *Type of search: information from victims in three areas of Thames Valley, 1977–79*

	Number of cases	Percentage
Nothing noticeably moved (except property stolen or damage at entry point)	174	54.0
A few items moved or knocked over	55	17.1
Drawers, cupboards left open, clear signs of a search	43	13.4
Drawers tipped out, property scattered on floor	38	11.8
Items thrown around, full-scale ransacking of rooms	7	2.2
Serious damage to property	5	1.5
Total	322	100.0

sign of the burglary that they had noticed was an open or broken window or door; 28 per cent first noticed that items were missing; only 12 per cent were first struck by the disturbance of property within the house.

Although internal damage is comparatively rare, many victims are faced with a broken window or other damage caused by the burglar's method of entry to the house. Crime reports have a space for the cost of damage, but this is rarely filled in as people do not immediately know the cost of replacing a lock or a window pane. To obtain such information we asked victims how much they had spent, or still needed to spend, on repairing damage of any kind. The results are shown in Table 6.

Table 6 *Cost of damage caused by burglaries: interviewed victims in Reading, Gerrards Cross and Banbury, 1977–79*

Cost of damage	No damage	Damage on entry only	Damage inside house (excluding meters)	Damage to meters	Total
Nil	135	—	—	—	135
Under £15	—	106	10	8	124
£15 and under £60	—	28	13	10	51
£60 and over	—	—	12	—	12
Total	135	134	35	18	322

In 42 per cent of cases there was no damage at all, and in another 39 per cent the cost of repairing the damage was less than £15.[10] Excluding prepayment meters, damage to property within the house occurred in 11 per cent of cases, and the repair bill exceeded £60 in less than four per cent. Even among these 12 serious cases, the damage was committed more often in furtherance of theft, for example, by breaking down internal doors or breaking open expensive cabinets, than in acts of gratuitous vandalism.

Gerrards Cross victims reported a considerably larger proportion of cases involving damage on entry. Many residents are conscious of the high burglary rates in the town, and the level of security measures taken appears to be higher than in the other areas. Only eight per cent of entries were through insecure doors or windows compared with 40 per cent in Reading. Unfortunately, the extra force needed to break better locks results in more damage. In addition, it was interesting that the burglars operating in this area, who are generally considered more 'professional' than average, also produced a higher proportion of untidy searches than those in either Reading or Banbury. This spoiled our preconceived notion of the professional as an 'artist' taking a pride in a 'neat job'. As one very competent thief pointed out, if the house is empty and there are no close neighbours there is no reason to waste time in replacing everything as it was.

Contact between offender and victim

One of the most disturbing features of residential burglary is the possibility that the victim may stumble upon the offender in the act of stealing and that such a confrontation may result in violence. In fact, it is relatively unusual for victim and offender to meet face to face and, even then, most intruders will attempt to escape rather than offer violence.

The worst possible consequence – murder by a burglar who has been disturbed – is thankfully an extremely rare occurrence. Walsh (1980:41) calculated that an average of three to four such cases occurred annually between 1957 and 1962. *Criminal Statistics* notes that 49 of the total of 571 homicides recorded in 1979 took place in the furtherance of theft or gain. It is unlikely that more than a handful of these resulted from house burglary: many arose from street robberies or attacks on commercial property. Similarly, although it is obviously unknown how often burglars carry weapons, the number of aggravated burglaries recorded is low (0.01 per cent of all recorded burglaries), and has not increased dramatically since the mid-seventies. In 1980, there were fewer than 70 burglaries (of all kinds) in which the offender was known to have carried firearms, and at least half of these involved air weapons.

Precise information about the frequency of violence is scarce, although Scarr (1973:11) and Reppetto (1974:17) use indirect evidence to show the reluctance of burglars to risk potential confrontations. More helpfully, Chappell (1965) found four cases of (relatively minor) violence among his sample of 125 victims and Waller and Okihiro (1978:32)

Table 7 Visibility of burglars at the scene of the crime: interviewed victims, Banbury, Reading and Gerrards Cross, 1977–79 (N = 322)

House not occupied (N = 252)

House occupied (N = 70)

	House occupied	House not occupied
Nothing seen or heard (261)	(38)	(223)
Noises heard or person seen near house, but not investigated (24)	(11)	(13)
Offender disturbed but not seen (16)	(8)	(8)
Offender seen escaping (8)	(1)	(7)
Offender confronted (13)	(12)	(1)

found two among their sample of 116. One of our 322 cases involved a particularly unpleasant sexual assault upon an old lady by a mentally-retarded 15 year old boy. The only other assault occurred when a woman returned home and accidentally trapped a burglar in her flat: he pushed her roughly aside as he ran off. There were also two cases of threats. In one of these a woman was made to reveal where a sum of money was hidden, and in the other a householder was threatened by a previous acquaintance following an argument over business. All other cases in which the offender was disturbed passed off without serious incident.

Of the 322 victims we interviewed 251 (78 per cent) were out when the burglary occurred. Most of these discovered the offence themselves on their return, although in 16 cases neighbours reported it while the victim was away. Only ten (four per cent) of those returning home disturbed the burglar at his work, and even then in eight of these cases they simply heard him running away or saw a light switched on or off. In six other cases neighbours disturbed offenders and saw them escaping, but were not involved in confrontations. Fifty-one victims (16 per cent) were asleep in bed at the time the burglar entered the house: 39 of these remained unaware of his presence, and of the 12 who were woken up, only five came face to face with the offender. The remaining 19 victims were in the house during the day or evening when the burglar entered and six of these confronted him.

Altogether, offenders were disturbed in 37 (11 per cent) of the 322 burglaries, seen in 21 of these cases, and confronted in 13 of the 21. In another 16 the victim told us that a suspicious person had been seen near the house, although not associated with the crime until later, and in eight others noises were heard but not investigated. This leaves more than 80 per cent in which the event passed (as far as the victim knows) without the offender being seen or heard (see Table 7).

The 'confrontations' were, for the most part, brief and non violent. Five occurred at night when the burglar entered a bedroom, three during the day when the offender had mistakenly thought the house unoccupied, two involved deception of elderly people in order to gain access to the house, and two occurred when the offender pushed his way into an acquantance's house as a result of a previous quarrel.

Surprisingly, all those who awoke to find an intruder in the bedroom reported remaining calm during the confrontation. Two challenged the burglar (who in each case was under 20), causing him to run away. One, a male pensioner, made an inebriated man wait while he telephoned the police and even the two victims of night-time threat and assault acted coolly. Finally, the daytime confrontations generally resulted in the offender fleeing as soon as he realised that the house was occupied. Nobody was physically hurt in any of these.

III. Persistent Burglars

'We have heard that you are amateurs, but really you are professionals who happen to do things in a very amateurish way'
Magistrate quoted in *Bicester Advertiser*, 30 September 1981

The main purpose of chapter II was to describe the physical consequences of the activities of burglars in different areas: the spatial and temporal patterning of offences, the costs and damage caused, and the salient characteristics of those convicted. However, by itself, knowledge of when or where burglary most often occurs, and of the categories of people who are most likely to be arrested, neither explains how offenders behave nor gives sufficient ammunition to policy-makers for the design of strategies in crime control. To understand better why such patterns occur, it is necessary to gain some insight into the thought processes, motivations, attitudes and lifestyles of people who commit the offences. In this chapter we attempt to undertake this difficult task.

Of course, as already indicated, offenders vary widely in commitment, skill and experience, in the kinds of property they steal and in the frequency with which they commit burglaries. To obtain anything like a full picture we would have had to interview juveniles as well as adults, and 'one-off' as well as persistent offenders. Unfortunately, the time and resources at our disposal precluded such a comprehensive account and we decided to limit ourselves to a discussion of persistent adult and young adult burglars, people who have broken into houses on a more or less regular basis over a period of years. Although unsatisfactory in terms of completeness, this choice of persistent offenders is particularly suitable in the case of burglary, where the problem of recidivism is more acute than in virtually any other kind of offence.

The central plank of our approach will be to examine the phenomenon from persistent offenders' points of view, outlining the goals they are trying to achieve and the hurdles they have to overcome. The main areas considered are burglars' perceptions of crime and the criminal world, their interactions with fellow criminals and receivers, their methods of organization and operation, and their chances, both real and imagined, of 'making crime pay'.

Although those under discussion are referred to as 'burglars', this does not mean that burglary is the only crime they commit. Hood and Sparks (1970:134-40) have collected evidence to show that homogeneous criminal careers are comparatively rare. This was confirmed in our interviews with 40 men in custodial institutions. Fifteen of these had been convicted of offences falling within our samples of cases in Reading and Gerrards Cross and the remainder were prisoners willing to be interviewed when we let it be known in a local prison that we wished to talk to house burglars. All those interviewed admitted to having broken into numerous houses over the years. When asked to estimate the total number of burglaries they had committed to date, about half were unable to make an estimate more precise than 'hundreds'. Those who produced a specific figure gave answers ranging from 20 to 2,000, the most common estimate being between 100 and 500. Nevertheless, all but five also had convictions for other kinds of property offence, notably for taking motor vehicles, burglary of commercial premises and forgery of cheques. Although most accepted the label 'burglar' as a fair description, it was not necessarily the term they would have chosen themselves. A number suggested instead the police slang term 'villain' or plain 'thief'. Perhaps the most accurate way of describing them would be as thieves whose 'main line' is burglary.

As most interviewees were selected by a process akin to the 'snowball' method, through recommendation by prison officers or other offenders, or by volunteering themselves, they cannot be said to constitute a representative sample of incarcerated burglars, let alone of persistent burglars as a whole. On the other hand, they came from several different areas (ranging from London to small towns in the Thames Valley), their ages varied between 18 and 44, and they displayed considerable variations in their degrees of specialisation, their levels of 'earnings' and their successes in evading the law. We are confident that their combined experience was sufficient to give us a good insight into the range of lifestyles and operational methods of persistent burglars active in the Thames Valley region. We are also satisfied that, apart from some obvious exaggeration and self-aggrandisement, our questions were answered sufficiently honestly to produce a valid overall picture. The interviews were conducted in a friendly and informal manner, structured only by a number of themes which were explored in some detail with each man. Most interviews lasted for more than an hour, and some men were seen more than once, so that there was ample opportunity to spot inconsistencies in their accounts. We established relationships of trust in many cases, and pride ourselves on the fact that the prison grapevine passed on the verdict that we were 'alright' to talk to and would not reveal any information given in confidence.[1]

We begin with an assessment of how our interviewees perceived the 'world of crime' in which they had become involved. In particular, the image of crime as a 'business' or a 'career', the attitudes towards victims, and ideas about the attainment of 'class' as a thief are considered: it is argued that the images do not always conform to reality and can be used to disguise some unwanted truths about the burglars' own endeavours. We discuss a common tendency to divide persistent thieves into two opposing categories ('amateurs'—'professionals'; 'good thieves'—'mugs'), arguing that the majority can be regarded as falling into an intermediate group which we call 'middle range'. Many acquire considerable skills and have visions of becoming successful professional criminals, but their successes tend to be of a temporary nature as they are thwarted by problems and conflicts inherent in the adoption of a criminal lifestyle. These problems manifest themselves mainly in the relationships among participants in criminal enterprises, and we investigate themes such as status, secrecy, social organisation, 'grassing' and the disposal of stolen property. We attempt to isolate factors which affect the scale and frequency of operation in which burglars become involved and their capacity to avoid arrest and conviction. Finally, the attitudes of offenders towards the possibility of 'going straight' or escaping from a criminal lifestyle are considered.

Crime as 'work'

We were continually struck in interviews with offenders by the frequency of use of terms implying that there are close parallels between regular participation in criminal activity and earning a living in a legitimate manner. Thefts are referred to as 'jobs' from which one can 'earn well'. Burglars 'work' particular areas. There is a 'market' for stolen property, with regular 'dealers' or 'buyers'. There are 'pros', 'experts' and 'specialists' in various areas who gain status from their skill or earning ability. Those who no longer steal are sometimes referred to as 'retired'. Above all, most of the offenders interviewed were keen to convey the impression that their way of life involved a rational form of behaviour geared to financial profit, and that they were members of an old-established and fairly well-organised 'profession' in which those who reached the top could expect substantial rewards. Few saw burglary primarily as an aberrant activity expressing personal problems or as 'caused' by alcohol, depression or illness of any kind.

Of course, actors' explanations of their own conduct do not always coincide with those of observers, and closer examination of burglars' lives throws up inconsistencies and contradictions which do not seem to fit the picture they project. To some extent, the notion of 'crime as work' may be regarded as a (perhaps unconscious) device for covering up some unpalatable truths.

First, the use of euphemisms such as 'earning' helps to hide the basic fact that stealing from other people's houses is regarded by the mass of the population, and indeed by some people who are fully prepared to steal in other ways, as a despicable offence which shows gross disregard for the privacy of others and frightens and upsets victims. Burglars go to some lengths to try to neutralise this aspect of their behaviour and to present it as a necessary evil which they do their best to minimise. Nearly all insisted that in their everyday lives they were as trustworthy as anyone else, and that they would not steal from friends or from vulnerable members of society such as the aged. They claimed that mentally they separated the sphere of crime off from the rest of their lives as 'business': a world in which ordinary moral principles are suspended or made subordinate to the universally understandable aim of 'making a decent living'.

> No. 5:   It's totally commercial.
> No. 17:   Yeah, it's a trade, isn't it?
> No. 31:   I only do burglaries for the money.
> No. 18:   I just want to earn as much money as possible as quickly as possible.

In such a world, the distress caused to victims, although recognised, is treated as unfortunate but unavoidable, and pushed to the back of the mind:

> No. 2:   I never think about the victim. I don't particularly enjoy it, it's just money for me when I'm broke.
> No. 24:   I don't care about the victim, although I've never wanted to smash their place up—I've never smashed a place up in my life. I tend to feel that he has his job and I have mine.

However, many felt uncomfortable enough to introduce a further 'neutralisation technique' (cf. Sykes and Matza 1957), asserting that they stole only from people who could afford the loss:

> No. 1:   Now I do richer houses. I don't feel sorry for the people in them.
> No. 25:   I always do rich places, so they can always afford it. I'll never do a working man's place because they've had to work hard for their money—I know what it's like.
> No. 22:   As I said, I only like to do rich people's houses. Once when I was working with someone else we did a house which we found was a crippled bloke's house, he was an old boy and

obviously not very well off, and we just stopped what we were doing and left. I never do council houses or old people's houses for that reason. One reason of course is that I'm not going to get very much out of it so there's not much point. If I do a big house or a business they're all insured and they can afford it and it's not going to affect them very much. I wouldn't like to do someone's place and take all the money they had. But it's not like that with big places. They don't really care about it.

This argument was sometimes stretched into an active justification rather than simply a passive excuse. Some expressed resentment against the unequal distribution of wealth in the country and others claimed that richer victims often profited from being burgled:

No. 9:   What niggles me is that other people have money and I haven't. I hate kids with posh parents who give them cars and everything they want.

No. 6:   I make money out of it and so do a lot of them I steal off. Some of them claim more than a thousand pounds more than their jewellery's worth. Nobody loses really.

We found only two who consciously recognised that even wealthy people may have feelings:

No. 38:   Quite often I do feel sorry for the people. What annoys me is the way that women lock up their jewellery boxes. I know what I'm looking for. If the box is open I just take what I want and leave the rest. If it's locked I get it home and find clasps and lockets and bits of hair—I don't want that sort of stuff. We put all that in what we call the 'rubbish bin' and chuck it in the river. I get quite upset sometimes seeing these personal things which obviously have a high sentimental value. If it wasn't so risky I would like to drive back there sometimes and throw them over the hedge or something. Other times I don't feel sorry for the victim. They are all rich round Gerrards Cross and I'm sure they can cover anything I take.

No. 26:   The worst thing I have done conscience-wise was to break the house of an old lady who the local paper announced was in hospital. She was quite a wealthy lady who had a safe in her house full of jewellery. I did feel bad about it, but of course I eased my mind in the pub.

Of course, despite their protestations to the contrary, the fact remains that many burglars do attack poorer housing. On several occasions we pointed out to those who claimed that they stole only from the rich that their current list of offences contained thefts from council houses. This was usually met by claims that such offences had occurred in exceptional circumstances—for example, that they had not had a car at the time or that the properties in question were 'better class' council houses occupied by people earning more money than most. Despite such attemps to retain their moral armour, our impression was that the following answer, given by a 19-year-old, was more honest.

> No. 10:   I'll do any sort of house. Most people have tellies and they're worth 50 pounds. I don't have any principles about ripping off poor people or anything—you've got to push that aside and be ruthless. (For the further discussion of the theme of self-justification, see Ericson, 1975:29-38)

Secondly, the 'career' or 'profession' analogy can disguise the realities of criminal behaviour since it implies some sort of linear progress, such as a steady increase in income, status or experience. Certainly, most interviewees said that, with age, they had become more adept at dealing with the police, at learning whom and whom not to trust, at cutting down risks and disposing of stolen property—all of which could be regarded as 'learning the trade'. Such experience helped to improve their standing among other thieves and brought them better financial rewards.

On the other hand, there was also a strong circular element always threatening to negate any upward progress. The career could become a 'roller-coaster', or 'a game of snakes and ladders' in which one was regularly thrown back to 'square one'. As one man explained, every time he came out of prison he had to 'start from nothing', finding new accommodation, re-establishing contacts, sometimes deciding half-heartedly to 'go straight' but gradually drifting back into crime in order to 'get a decent standard of living'. Another told us that two months before we saw him he had held £8,000 in cash in his hands, had lived in a well-furnished flat and had owned a new car. Within the intervening period he had lost everything and now faced at least eighteen months in prison. In such a precarious world success and failure are judged largely over the short term. If a comparison is to be made with legitimate professions, it is sensible only with regard to high-risk, individualistic occupations such as pop-singing, motor-racing or playing the stock market.

Thirdly, the use of language associated with the business world can give a false impression of the extent to which thieves behave in a rational-economic manner, calculating profit and loss and adapting their behaviour to changes in 'market forces'. Although many spoke in such terms, their actual behaviour often belied their words. As we shall show later, it would be wrong to suggest that the majority had reached a full and objective assessment of the profitability of the criminal enterprises they had been engaged in, and altered their subsequent behaviour in accordance with their 'findings'. Like anybody else, a thief can easily develop a selective memory, exaggerating the number and size of past rewards and forgetting negative experiences; or he may admit that in the past he has made an overall 'loss' but convince himself that with a little more luck his tactics will pay off in the future. Equally, he may resolve to give up crime altogether but lose his resolve as time passes and temptations arise.

For this reason, a more suitable analogy may be that of gambling. Regular gamblers are notorious for remembering the wins while explaining away the losses, and are eternal optimists about a new tip or a new system. They have before them the image of the successful 'professional' gambler who beats the odds through skill and judicious bets, and from time to time have a run of good fortune which encourages them to believe that they are making gambling pay. However, remarkably few have the dedication, skill and application to win over the long term.

Classifying burglars: villains or mugs?

The last-mentioned point introduces the subject of relative abilities and achievements among thieves. As in any other 'trade', some people are recognised as better burglars than others and hence acquire extra respect from their fellows. Indeed, judgements about the 'calibre' or 'class' of individuals are a frequent feature of con-versations among thieves. We noticed a tendency to polarise such judgements, so that people were either described on the one hand as 'professionals', 'good thieves', 'class operators' or 'real villains', or on the other as 'losers', 'mugs', 'wankers', 'idiots', 'paperweights', 'doughnuts' or 'baby burglars'. These distinctions, however, often seemed to be used by the speaker less as an objective description of the person concerned than as means of achieving some form of reflected glory. Burglars were anxious to let it be known that they associated only with a 'better class of criminal' and thus by impli-cation fell into that category themselves. Two consequences of this were that some named individuals were accorded totally opposite qualities by different interviewees, and that several who were given enthusiastic references by their acquaintances turned out on closer inspection to have had palpably unsuccessful careers.

This habit of dividing offenders into two contrasting groups is by no means limited to thieves themselves. Detectives earn more esteem from their colleagues by arresting someone considered to be a worth-while prize and will emphasise what a 'clever villain' they have managed to catch. They will also complain about the time they have to waste on chasing 'toe-rags' or 'cowboys'. Although much of this can be seen simply as competitive banter, it has been accepted by several criminologists, particularly those interested in the higher levels of criminal activity, as a realistic means of classifying persistent offenders.

Irwin (1970:8-26), for example, contrasts the 'thief', who possesses 'solidness' and 'character', with the 'disorganised criminal' whose main characteristics are 'self-defeatism' and 'fucking up'. The latter criminals, he claims, 'who make up the bulk of convicted felons, pursue a chaotic, purposeless life, filled with unskilled, careless and variegated criminal activity.' Jackson (1969:23), having chosen the term 'career thief' to describe his subject, Sam, distinguishes him from 'the rums, the incompetents, the career convicts, the amateurs, the impetuous'. Letkemann (1973:20-3) makes a primary distinction between the 'true criminal' or 'rounder', who is 'committed to the il-legitimate lifestyle as demonstrated in reliable and consistent behaviour patterns' and the 'bum' who does not possess 'the dedication and stability of the true criminal'. He accepts the verdict of a prison inmate that: 'In this place you've got only thirty thieves—the rest are misfits, nuisances.' Finally, Waller (1978b), referring to burglars specifically, distinguishes the 'break-in artist' from 'the more typical amateur'.[2]

There is considerable disagreement among such writers about both the best term to use to describe the 'superior' group and the precise qualities which distinguish them from other criminals. The classic work is that by Sutherland (1937), which describes the life of a 'professional thief'. The author defines professionalism mainly in terms of the characteristics of the man he has selected: specialisation, skill, wit and tutelage from and recognition by other professionals. Others have expanded this early definition by incorporating different qualities they discovered in other high-class criminals, the overall result being a confusing array of what McIntosh (1975:9) criticises as 'rather arbitrary dimensions applied simultaneously in such a way that the types defined correspond roughly to common-sense cate-gories.' Among the attributes considered relevant have been character (reliability, courage), status (respect from others), ability (technical skills, intelligence), motivation (commitment, long-term goals), organisation (membership of a group, 'connections'), and measurable success (avoidance of arrest, scale of rewards). Shover (1973), for example, highlights the diverse qualities of technical competence, reputation for integrity, specialisation and 'success' (value stolen and time served), scoring each interviewee in order to categorise his sample. He himself admits the arbitrariness of his scoring system.

Several alternative labels have also been suggested to replace the problematic term 'professional'. Thus Jackson (1969) prefers 'career thieves', Einstadter (1969) writes of 'career robbers', Shover (1973) of 'good burglars', Mack (1975) of 'able', 'substantial' or 'heavyweight' criminals, and Letkemann (1973) of 'experienced' thieves or 'rounders'. Each struggles with the definition of his or her term, and most admit that they are not fully satisfied. Perhaps Jackson (1969:24) best sums up the general frustration when he confesses: 'Most easily, I'd like to be able to say, a career thief is a thief like Sam'.

At a purely empirical level, we found these dual classifications unhelpful as a means of describing our interviewees. There were among them a small number who were clearly (and no doubt always would be) hopeless failures as thieves, being arrested repeatedly for petty, poorly executed, spur-of-the-moment burglaries, often under the influence of alcohol, and in contrast at least three who qualified on most of the grounds mentioned as careful, well-organised and 'well-connected' thieves. However, the majority did not fit into either of these categories. Most seemed to oscillate between behaviour and attitudes associated with each end of the spectrum. They were committed to crime as a 'trade' (which a number claimed to have come close to mastering) and had on occasion been involved in lucrative offences carried out with considerable skill. On the other hand, in comparison with the three who stood out in every way as the 'best' burglars, they were disorganised and unsuccessful criminals. A period of two years without arrest was a comparative rarity, and they too often broke the rules they set themselves—for example by 'grassing' to the police under questioning, letting too many unreliable people know what they were doing and engaging in risky enterprises in between those chosen more sensibly. The overall impression we received was of people who had before them an image of how they should behave in order to give themselves the best chances of making burglary 'pay', but who were always in danger of being deflected from this path by other considerations and circumstances that arose.

The above observations convinced us that if a broad classificatory system is to be used to distinguish between persistent burglars it should include at least three basic patterns of behaviour. One such system had already been put forward by Black (1963), who divided offenders into 'crude', 'run-of-the-mill' and 'good' burglars. However, in our view this terminology attached too much importance to technical skills. We wished to explain why it was that so many thieves who were technically equipped to become 'good' burglars failed to use their talents to their best advantage. We came to the conclusion that the answer lies in some fundamental problems and contradictions which face anybody who becomes involved in property crime to a significant degree. These concern the central goals that people hope to achieve by engaging in a life of crime, and are at their most acute in the area of relationships between criminals. The classificatory system which we put forward is based upon the relative success or failure of individuals and groups in solving these problems, and concentrates more upon social and operational organisation than upon the act of burglary itself.

The behaviour of persistent burglars can be seen as falling into one of three patterns, which we have called simply 'low-level', 'middle-range' and 'high-level'. We considered employing analogies from the sporting world such as 'first division', 'lower division' and 'amateur league', and although the connotations are not quite right, there are some useful parallels. We would stress that although individuals tend to remain at one level for long periods, they can also move between them, and that it is more important to understand the systems of behaviour and the reasons behind them than to attempt to 'type' each burglar according to a set of personal characteristics. Finally, it should be noted that although in practice each level tends to be associated with a different scale of theft (stealing property of low, medium and high value), even offenders displaying 'low-level' behaviour patterns occasionally steal large amounts and vice versa. The next section discusses the problems inherent in relationships between thieves and the attempts at solutions which seem to distinguish different levels of criminal behaviour.

Relationships among thieves

Most persistent thieves know a great number of others. This is a result partly of shared custodial experiences, partly of the universal tendency for people with similar interests to congregate together, and partly of the need for co-operation and assistance in locating, stealing and selling property. Although 'one-off' offences may be committed by people acting entirely alone, anyone with ambitions to obtain a reasonable income from crime is almost bound to become involved with other thieves. Basic skills and techniques have to be learned, and others can provide invaluable help as extra 'eyes and ears', as drivers, as storers and receivers of stolen property, or merely as moral support. The higher a burglar sets his sights, the more important such co-operation becomes. Barnes (1971) goes as far as to say that: 'The professional burglar must be alert and inventive, but above all he must have connections, the right kind of connections. Without them he cannot live.'

Most of the burglars we interviewed had been involved in

delinquent behaviour as children or teenagers. At that stage they normally entered houses with companions. The extent to which juvenile burglary is a group activity is indicated by the fact that, in the Thames Valley area in 1975, 50 per cent of detected cases involving people under seventeen produced more than one offender. This proportion falls as burglars grow older (to 23 per cent in detected cases involving adults), but our interviewees indicated that they worked in pairs much more often than the figures for arrests imply (about half said that they 'usually' burgled with a partner). More important, the actual commission of the offence is only one aspect of burglary. Unless he is exceptionally lucky, any young male who makes a habit of stealing from homes will before very long find himself in borstal, detention centre or prison, where he will be brought into contact with a strong culture with its own rules, values, language and traditions.

The process of arrest and conviction will already have pinned the label of 'thief' firmly upon him and this identity will be postively reinforced by others who accept it willingly. He will quickly widen his circle of criminal acquaintances, learn new techniques and be encouraged to try his hand at more lucrative offences. Contacts made in prison are likely to be extended on his release through association in pubs, clubs and cafés frequented by local criminals. These provide focal points for people engaged in all kinds of criminal activity: they use them to meet, swap experiences, team up with others and arrange the disposal of stolen property. It is the nature of his relationships with this 'criminal world' and the life-styles it fosters that has the most significant consequences for the shape of an individual's career.

From the thief's point of view, association and co-operation with others have both advantages and disadvantages. While they increase the range of criminal activity open to him, they contain severe risks to his liberty. We isolated three basic problems that face thieves in their efforts to form mutually beneficial relationships. The first problem arises from the competing claims of actions undertaken for the good of the group and actions undertaken for the good of the individual. Although co-operation is usually of mutual benefit, there are also times when it appears wiser to revert to behaviour based solely upon selfish ends. This is particularly common when people are arrested or questioned by the police. There is then the temptation for a man to betray his associates in an effort to bargain for preferential treat-ment—for example, to be granted bail or to have certain charges dropped.

The maxim 'honour among thieves' and the widespread contempt for (and sometimes exaction of physical reprisals against) people who 'grass' in such circumstances reflect a general attempt to combat this temptation. However, as we shall see, the sanctions are by no means fully effective. Frequently-heard phrases like 'you've got to look after number one' and 'it's a jungle' represent the self-justifications of those who succumb. Quarrels, suspicion and bad feeling between thieves can also seriously weaken bonds of loyalty. Unlike most legitimate forms of co-operation, there are no formal remedies for the breaking of agreements or the cheating of associates, and many convictions are obtained by the police's exploitation of feuds between former partners.

A second major problem is caused by the contradictory desires for status and secrecy. As in any other 'profession', thieves want recognition as skilled or successful exponents of their work, and this can only be achieved if fellow-criminals have some knowledge of what they are doing. Allied to this is the need to advertise one's abilities to others who may be looking for a partner for a particular 'job'. Yet every person who has even second-hand knowledge of a thief's activities is a potential threat to his freedom. The police are always anxious to know who is 'active' at a given time, and can glean 'whispers' from paid informers who mix socially with thieves. People who boast about their exploits may gain a widespread reputation for daring, or for undertaking 'big jobs', but by drawing attention to themselves they are more vulnerable to arrest than those who manage to contain knowledge about their activities within a small group of trusted associates.

The third problem arises from the total lifestyle that involvement in crime tends to bring with it. The social life of persistent thieves often revolves around hedonistic pursuits such as drinking and gambling. Money is easily come by and quickly spent, and the ever-present threat of arrest and imprisonment further encourages emphasis upon short-term rewards at the expense of long-term plans. Hence when thieves meet socially they tend to value personal qualities such as 'smartness', daring and sociability. It is difficult to combine this kind of lifestyle with the opposite qualities—prudence, planning, consistency—which are necessary to the pursuit of a successful 'criminal career': despite their lip-service to the principle of keeping 'business' separate from pleasure, many thieves fall into the traps of burgling after an evening's drinking, taking risks for 'the thrill', or being talked into an ill-considered enterprise by a group of friends. Frequent association in public, particularly if accompanied by ostentatious spending, also gives the police clues to current groupings of thieves who are particularly active. The epitome of the successful criminal, the American 'Mafia boss', is often said to live a sober and respectable social life, indistinguishable from that of his executive neighbours (cf. Ianni 1972). Despite their admiration for such characters, most of the young men who become persistent burglars would find such an existence boring in the extreme. Unfortunately for them, the value they attach to pleasure, excitement, bravado, companionship and admiration from others can work directly against their chances of avoiding imprisonment.

The three broad categories of burglary identified earlier are distinguishable largely in terms of the abilities of groups and individuals to solve the problems just outlined. What we have called 'high-level' burglary is in essence a criminal behaviour system which results from the most successful solution: the formation of deliberately exclusive sub-groups within the criminal community. Sometimes called 'cliques' or 'firms', these consist at their most effective of small networks of careful and committed criminals who closely vet prospective recruits before entrusting them with knowledge about their activities, and who follow codes of conduct designed to protect members from acting against each other's interests. They may remain on friendly terms with other thieves, but will not normally become involved in schemes suggested by people they are 'not sure of'. They also tend to move in the world of saloon bars and clubs rather than in the public bars and cafés where lower status thieves, particularly young adults, are more often to be found. And by dressing well and meeting in small groups they are usually less conspicuous to the police or potential informers.

Such cliques do not operate as a unit in the sense of planning all their crimes together or sharing the profits. Members sometimes act alone, sometimes with one or two partners, and, between them, may be involved in several different forms of crime. Individuals can also move between groups, using 'references' from previous associates to gain acceptance in a clique elsewhere. What primarily distinguishes them from criminal groups or networks at lower levels is their strict exclusion of people whose weaknesses could threaten others' safety. By accepting only a small number of thieves who have proved their commitment to 'business before pleasure', the ability to keep secrets, and a technical competence in committing crimes, they have a much better chance of controlling the flow of information about their activities, and of maintaining sufficient internal loyalty and discipline to minimise the risks of betrayal. What they can offer to encourage loyalty is the availability of help and expertise when the individual requires it, and, above all, access to lucrative outlets for valuable property in the shape of major receivers who will deal only with thieves they can trust.

'Middle-range' burglary exhibits only temporary or partial solutions to the problems outlined. It is characterised by larger and less exclusive networks of thieves of varying individual ability, reliability and commitment, by less consistent adherence to articulated codes of conduct, and by consequent difficulties in establishing connections with important receivers. 'Low-level' burglary is characterised by a lack of discrimination in relationships between thieves, lack of direction or foresight in the commission of offences and the disposal of stolen property, and the prominence of factors other than profit in the decision to steal. Consideration of specific areas of burglars' activities will illustrate the themes that have now been introduced.

Selling stolen goods

Although disposing of stolen property is chronologically the last step in a criminal enterprise, it plays a crucial part in its conception. There is little point in a thief stealing items which he cannot sell or consume. If he keeps anything that can be identified as stolen, he runs the severe risk of its discovery in a search of his house. The capacity to sell stolen property safely and profitably usually increases with age and experience. However, more importantly, the range and quantity of goods that can be sold increases most dramatically when a thief is fully accepted into a high-status criminal group. People who deal in significant quantities of stolen antiques, for example, are normally very careful in choosing the burglars they will buy from. If possible, they will keep their identity secret from all but a few thieves they can trust to be discreet. Inexperienced offenders or low-status older offenders will rarely find important buyers willing to deal with them directly. If they steal anything of high value they are often reduced to hawking it around second-hand shops or local jewellers, or trying to sell it to friends. Not only is this highly dangerous, but they are likely to receive a very low price. They are thus limited primarily to thefts of cash or of easily saleable consumable goods such as cigarettes or alcohol. For anyone with ambitions to make a significant income from burglary, finding a 'good fence' is a major priority.

The burglars we interviewed varied widely in their access to outlets for stolen property. At the lowest level were a small number of offenders in the situation of 'Richard' and 'Alan' (Nos. 12 and 13), two very unsophisticated burglars in their late 'teens who committed most of their offences together in Reading. They did not hide the fact that they found difficulty in disposing of stolen goods. Their general policy was to 'stick to cash', but they often found the temptation of stealing other items irresistible and took things against their better judgement. Many of these they eventually threw away, gave away to friends or, most unwisely, kept for their own use. Richard told us:

> Alan usually looks for tapes or records and sits on the floor going through them looking for ones he wants to keep for himself. He's got quite a collection at home—which he loses each time the police bust him.

Most others without regular outlets were not so naive as to keep stolen property in their own houses for any length of time, but took the risk of attempting to sell it openly:

> No. 2:   You get a lot of buyers in pubs. You just ask around if anyone wants anything. They probably know it's stolen. Sometimes my mate asks around for me.
> No. 18:   One time I nicked 2,000 fags and everyone in the pub had a packet for 20p. They didn't care where they came from.

Their main alternative was to sell to second-hand dealers in shops or on market stalls, but again, unless the thief knew the dealer personally, he was running a great risk:

> No. 2:   They won't ask questions, but you never know if they'll be on the phone as soon as you're out of the shop.

Even dealers well known among the criminal population as 'fences' were not helpful to thieves they did not know well or respect. These were often wily old characters who struck very hard bargains and, it was widely suspected, kept the police 'sweet' by acting as informers.

However, generally speaking it was only the least experienced and most incompetent burglars who were forced to sell property in these ways. It did not seem particularly difficult even for young adults to find more reliable receivers if they showed a serious interest. The first step was sometimes to sell to 'agents' or 'middle-men', thieves who made extra money by exploiting their contacts with networks of receivers to take a 'cut' on transactions, protecting the buyers from direct contact with people they did not know. These agents were wary of new faces, but could be 'cultivated' quite easily if approached in the right way. Middle-range burglars might be introduced to them by other thieves or might learn 'on the grapevine' where they could be found. One London burglar described his method of selling property as follows:

> No. 38:   Each pub has its own little group. It pays you to buy them a drink when you've got some money, drop in and have a chat. Then one day you might casually mention you've got a TV someone might want. They won't answer you right away, but you come in another time and someone will buy you a drink. A bit later he'll get round to the point, and you'll do a bit of wheeling and

dealing. You can get rid of anything in the end, but it's a dodgy business. You never really know who you're talking to.

Another kind of outlet sometimes used by middle-range burglars is provided by formerly 'straight' shopkeepers or small businessmen who have recently been persuaded into buying stolen property. News about such people tends to spread quickly among thieves, with the result that they are inundated with offers and can quickly find their involvement growing out of control. In some towns there seemed to be 'too many thieves chasing too few receivers', a situation that could , eventually work against the interests of thieves and receivers alike. A good example is provided by the case of a small shopkeeper who had been in financial difficulties and was persuaded by a thief to buy a stolen television set. He later sold it to a regular customer. The thief told a partner about it, who told another friend, and so on, and within a few months the shopkeeper was being visited almost daily by people asking (and in some cases virtually forcing) him to buy stolen property. Inevitably, the activity eventually become known to the police, and surveillance and questioning resulted in the conviction of more than ten people, some of whom shared the dock with men they hardly knew.

A comparable case involved three young men who shared a house and began a part-time business dealing in hi-fi equipment, some of which they bought from friends involved in burglary. They allowed these friends to visit regularly and often to stay the night. The guests gradually expanded into 'friends of friends'. and people began to bring stolen property to the house to leave for safe-keeping. Too much late-night noise and activity led to complaints from neighbours and attention from the police. A raid eventually produced enough evidence to convict some of those involved, who in turn gave information which netted several others. In both the cases cited, the thieves involved were comparatively skilful burglars, stealing property worth hundreds of pounds. Their downfall came not from individual incompetence, but from their inability as a group to control the spread of information about their activites. As one of the original trio remarked, in bewildered fashion:

> I can't believe it ever got this far. It started off as a quiet fiddle and just grew and grew. It was all a game really. I'm not a criminal. We were living in a dream world.

Selling to 'agents' or to buyers known to many other thieves widens the scope of burglars, but it is by no means safe and the prices paid are generally very low.[3] The next step up the ladder is the acquisition of direct access to a regular buyer of stolen property who

is discerning in his dealings. This is usually a matter of cultivating
associations with thieves who already have such contacts and
persuading them to make an introduction—a process that can take a
long time. For example, No. 30, a 24-year-old Reading man, said
that it had taken him nearly five years to find the kind of 'fence' he
had been seeking, and that in the few months he had dealt with him
he had made more money than during the previous five years:

> He keeps plenty of cash in his house and will always take a good
> quality colour TV or good quality stereo. I never let my mates
> know where I take the stuff. As far as I know, there's only one
> other bloke who uses him. I get about £100 to £150 for a good TV.

Another (No. 22) said:

> I can get rid of gear half an hour after I've stolen it. I never keep it
> in the house—there's too many people caught like that. I just ring
> this guy up and he meets me in his car and puts it in the boot. He
> gives me £20 down straight away and the rest later.

Such relationships can also lead to 'stealing to order', whereby the
receiver gives a list of his specific requirements and the thief sets out
to find them.

Those who claimed to have their own 'fence' were reluctant to say
very much about such people, but they were generally described
either as 'businessmen' who did not have criminal records, or as ex-
thieves who had used their experience and contacts to become
dealers. One phrase used to describe them was 'working-class villains
made good'. The impression some had was that much of what they
sold passed along a regular chain of receivers before eventually being
put on sale to the public on market stalls or in shops in other towns. In
other words, they implied that the 'fence' could himself be regarded
as an agent for larger dealers, in the manner of companies with a
network of subsidiaries. However, one of the most experienced
burglars, who had dealt with many receivers, saw the system simply
as a market of independent dealers who each sold to a variety of
sources in the manner of ordinary small businessmen: 'It's not all run
from above by some Mr. Big. It's just a normal market with people
buying and selling and taking their cut.' (This description supports
the account of 'stolen property systems' given by Walsh, 1977).

Once a thief has 'broken through' to direct contact with a regular
buyer, he is likely to expand his horizons considerably. If the buyer in
question cannot take everything he offers, he may put him on to
another, and so on. Eventually he may develop a wide choice of
possible outlets. A London burglar (No. 25) who had been convicted
for offences in Gerrards Cross told us:

We go for colour televisions, stereos, a bit of 'tom' (jewellery) if it's around. I can always get rid of this stuff. I've got one fella who will just about take anything off me: colour televisions, stereos, silver, jewellery. A few others ask me to get things for them such as special kinds of antiques. These are usually bona fide antique dealers taking a bit on the side. They ask me for a little bit of this or a little bit of that; they know they can get it a lot cheaper than anywhere else. They're not really fences, they just like the chance of getting something cheap. Quite often I will have to go out and get a clock or a certain kind of antique. They might even tell me which area or which road I might be able to get it in—sometimes which house.

This man did not present himself as a particularly sophisticated offender, despite the value and quantity of goods he stole. He also admitted quite cheerfully that he was often given a very poor price for what he stole, but rather than argue or go elsewhere he would usually settle for cash in hand. His case illustrated the important point that it was much easier for thieves at all levels to dispose of stolen property in London than in smaller urban areas.

The three men we interviewed who could be put without any doubt into the 'high-level' category had not only acquired reliable outlets for the most valuable kinds of property, but were able to negotiate more favourable returns. One claimed that he sold direct to important and respected dealers who, although they had no criminal records themselves, had established long-term relationships with a small number of thieves they could trust:

I have a number of buyers, all from London. They're generally big legitimate dealers in their particular markets. One of them was a gold dealer in London who would buy absolutely any quantity of gold that you could give him. It's the same with silver or antiques; I always go to the biggest buyers. But it's very difficult to get in on it—they won't buy from just anyone. It took me years before I could get to sell anything. I had to go through a friend of a friend, gradually getting nearer to the man himself. In the end the man became like a god. All I ever heard was his name; I had never seen him, I had only ever heard people talking about him. Eventually, when you become trusted you see the bloke and you go out for a meal with him and you discuss things. After that he will take any quantity off you. I could give him a pound of gold or a pound of silver and he would take it.

Another was in no doubt about the major factor that had boosted his 'career':

That's what it's really all about. Ten years ago if I'd stolen a £10,000 brooch I'd have quickly flogged it for £40 and been happy. Now I'd want at least a grand and I'd know where to get it.

Chapter IV will demonstrate how the criminal career of a man who, despite exceptional skill and resourcefulness, had for several years been averaging no more than £100 per offence, was transformed by the establishment of a regular outlet for antiques and jewellery into an astonishingly lucrative 'business'.

'Grassing'

As has been mentioned, the majority of thieves we interviewed were not averse to working with a partner and did so on many occasions. The reasons given ranged from the purely psychological ('It makes me feel safer'; 'It gives me some company') to practical considerations such as the help provided in transporting goods, acting as lookout, or driving the car to a pick-up point. However, although few had any difficulty in persuading people to work with them, finding a partner they could trust, and then keeping him, presented all but a small minority with serious problems. Disagreements about where, when and how the burglaries should be committed, or simple clashes of personality were sometimes reasons for this, but more important was the stress put on any partnership when the police began investigating the people concerned.

Although most of those interviewed paid some lip-service to the maxim 'honour among thieves', and considered 'grassing' (informing) upon others contemptible, they also appreciated the temptation to respond to inducements from the police, and some even admitted having made statements themselves which incriminated companions. A man in his early twenties took a philosophical view of the situation:

> I've got nicked a few times, but I've never been caught in a house. It's always because my mates grassed me up. Usually it's because they want bail. I don't hold it against them, I'd probably do the same thing myself. That's how the 'Old Bill' work isn't it? I don't go screwing with them again if they grass.

He clearly understood that most partnerships are based on self-interest and not on any deep belief in loyalty. While it suits the members to act in the group interest they will do so, but, as another put it, 'as soon as the shit hits the fan it's everyone for himself'.

A much more experienced and thoughtful thief in his mid-thirties accepted the argument that ultimately crime is a selfish activity, but declared nevertheless that it was in every thief's own interest in the long term to adhere to the code of no co-operation with the police. He also pointed out that even in the short term there could be advantages in refusing to betray a partner:

> The idiots today try to do deals with the police, but it doesn't help them. My partner would probably gain more by keeping me on the

outside. I'd be able to run errands for him, look after his wife and kids, that sort of thing. It's well known that I wouldn't grass. When the police do their usual thing of telling the others that I've dropped them in it, they don't believe it. They know I keep my bargains.

This man, who called himself 'one of the old school', was convinced that the code had been seriously eroded over the 20 years of his career (cf. also Shover 1973). Although nostalgia for the good old days may exaggerate such changes in older offenders' minds, he and others said that among petty thieves one could now in some circumstances openly admit to having 'dropped others in it' without attracting much opprobrium. In the past, on the other hand, such a person would at the very least have been sent to Coventry and probably 'given a good hiding'. One memorable illustration of this came when a burglar broke off a conversation to wave at another prisoner and say: 'That's my mate Ginger. He grassed me up.'

Burglars face dangers of possible betrayal not only from fellow-thieves who aid them in the execution of offences, but also from people to whom they sell stolen goods and, if they regularly mix with the local 'criminal community', from loose talk in public houses or clubs. The 'high-level' burglars we talked to said that they had learned to avoid conspicuous groups of known offenders—which, they claimed, consisted mainly of petty thieves and 'mugs'—and although they still knew them 'to say hello to', were careful not to reveal what they were doing to any but a few trusted friends. Indeed, even among less successful burglars there was a clear awareness of these kinds of dangers. Some said that they had made efforts to keep away from such groups, only to lose their resolve when bumping into old acquaintances while out drinking. The threat, it was stressed, was not that of direct evidence that a statement from a former partner can provide. It was that of gossip which allowed the police to obtain a clearer idea of who was active in a particular area, who was working with whom, and so on—all information which could be useful in questioning suspects or as a preliminary method of linking offenders with specific crimes and opening the way to finding harder evidence. (cf. Steer 1980: Chapter 3).

Some claimed that they used association in public to deliberately confuse the police, for example, drinking with thieves they did not work with. However, most were sure that apart from betrayal by partners, the main risk to their liberty came from the 'grasses' who were thought to abound in places where thieves congregate.

'Grassing' is as destructive to criminal groups when it is imagined as when it is real. We were surprised at the prominence the subject seemed to take in discussions among thieves, and came to suspect that in many cases people were seeing 'grasses' where in fact it was their own mistakes that had put them behind bars. If the police suddenly raid a culprit's house, his first thought is 'How did they know?' and he will immediately start thinking of people who might have betrayed him. This fuels a general opinion held among thieves and expressed in the following sentences which are typical of sentiments articulated in our field notes on numerous occasions:

> Reading's full of grasses.
> You can't trust anyone in this game.
> They'd turn their own grandmother in.
> There's grasses everywhere.
> The thieves in this town they're an evil-minded bloody lot.
> They'd steal your last halfpenny and shop you into the bargain.

At the sentencing stage, too, suspicions creep in: 'When you get two years and the bloke you did it with gets probation, you begin to wonder why.'

In such an atmosphere, people are already half-way to believing the police when they tell them that their companion has made a full statement. If the police combine this information with vague promises of lenient treatment, it then becomes particularly tempting, even for those who believe in the code against giving information, to change their minds. Moreover, even if no betrayal actually takes place, there is often a lingering suspicion which acts against future trust between partners.

Among low-level and middle-range thieves, the taking of reprisals against suspected informers is rarely performed in the organised manner portrayed in television films. Individuals who have suffered will sometimes physically attack the person who has betrayed them, or more often seek revenge by damaging or stealing their property. However, if incarcerated they are unable to effect revenge (if the 'grass' is also in prison, he will normally be kept apart from his potential attacker), and, as time passes, the resolve is likely to fade. As groupings among ordinary thieves are generally temporary and in flux, once a series of offences has been cleared up there is no 'organisation' remaining to administer discipline. On the other hand, if the 'wronged' thief has the character to become an influential member of the prison community, he may succeed in labelling a man as a grass and mobilise the general hostility towards informers to ensure that his enemy has an unpleasant time in prison. However, the extent to which a prisoner who is a suspected informer is punished also depends upon his own character and influence. Those who have to seek protection under Rule 43 are often weak figures without the ability to counteract the vague rumours upon which most accusations of 'grassing' are based. Generally speaking, unless a man has actually made a statement to a court, it is not known for certain that he has informed and principles of scapegoating rather than of proper evidence usually decide which of the many candidates for group hostility actually receive it.

Among the much smaller number of 'high-level' burglars, more deliberately planned and more severe reprisals may be taken. The 'supergrasses' frequently in the news are in real danger, and people who risk several years in prison for lucrative offences have much stronger motives for punishing informers. The tighter groups with which they work also tend to survive for longer periods, and friends remaining outside may take revenge on behalf of those imprisoned. (It is interesting that receivers who made statements to the police were said to be forgiven more easily than thieves, perhaps because they are not seen as full members of criminal groups.)

Overall, the safety from betrayal of a criminal group depends upon its ability to make members believe that heavy reprisals will be taken against informers, and this is another mark of the higher levels of criminal activity. At lower levels, the same ideology is present, but most know that a man can often 'look after number one' without great risk to life or limb.

Choice of offence and specialisation

Most of our interviewees were fairly narrowly limited in the range of property offences in which they could become involved. One of the primary limitations, as we have already seen, is access to receivers: there is obviously no sense in hijacking lorries or in holding up jewellers if one is unable to sell the proceeds. Equally important, many crimes a:e excluded by a lack of technical knowledge or of special equipment, or by a lack of access to exploitable systems such as computer files or company accounts. Thus, for example, few people have the capacity to defeat bank security systems, to forge bank-notes or to engage in embezzlement. The majority of working-class thieves who become involved in crime as juvenile delinquents remain restricted for the rest of their criminal career to a group of relatively simple offences. These may involve ingenuity or dexterity, but are in essence attacks 'from outside' on the weakest points at the fringes of systems protecting wealth. Their choice lies mainly between crimes such as housebreaking, shopbreaking, petty theft, car theft, robbery, shoplifting and cheque frauds. Although some had ambitions of eventually widening their horizons by joining London gangs, most recognised and accepted their limitations. This section examines their methods of choosing between the possibilities open to them.

Nearly all had fairly strong ideas about the relative merits and disadvantages of each type of offence, and over the years had developed preferences for a 'line' which, other things being equal, they considered the best. Although most in practice had committed more house burglaries than other offences, this was by no means always their first choice in theory. It is interesting to look at both the reasoning used to establish preferences and the circumstances which sometimes deflected them from their supposed optimum strategy. As one would expect, the scale of rewards and risk of detection played a large part in their deliberations, but were not always the deciding factor. For example, a 20-year-old (No. 8) with five previous convictions for burglary and four for other offences argued somewhat obscurely:

> I burgle when I get bored with shoplifting. Shoplifting's harder work, but you can make more money . . . Burglary's easy but you know you're risking two years. It's worse in the long run because you're bound to get caught sooner or later and then you're going to go inside . . . Shoplifting you just get a fine usually.

This provides a good illustration of the confusion of ideas about the relative risks and rewards of criminal behaviour that can be caused by conflicting goals and values. This man recognised the logic of the purely 'economic' equation of financial profit versus risk of imprisonment, but considered the avoidance of hard work and boredom sufficiently strong attractions to overrule its conclusion.

Probably the most common reason given for choosing burglary was the opinion that it is 'easy to get away with'. We heard many times the argument that the chances of being caught for any one burglary were as slim as 'one in a hundred'. On the other hand, relatively few took the further step of noting that in order to make a substantial amount of money the offence had to be repeated many times, thus greatly increasing the statistical risk. There was a common tendency to take a short-term view of the situation, reminiscent of the type of gambler who remembers his wins more clearly than his losses. Moreover, the fact that burglars are rarely caught in the act obscured, in several minds, the fact that many are caught later (through information given to the police by partners, receivers or others), and offences are not 'finished' once the burglar has successfully escaped from the scene of the crime. All these elements were present in the reasoning of a 26-year-old man (No. 35) with over 20 convictions for burglary and theft:

> Burglars get the shit end of the scale. There's a lot of bird in it. But you don't get caught many times. I must have done hundreds of

houses and I've only ever been grabbed once. I only get caught when other people drop me in it . . . But I don't keep balance sheets. I take the jobs one by one. If I've got away with it I put it behind me and look for the next one.

Those who took a more far-sighted view of their situations, and particularly those who had more single-minded ideas of what they wished to achieve from burglary, putting financial gain above factors like companionship or excitement, were divided in their opinion of the relative profitability of burglary as against other offences. A 21-year-old Londoner (No. 17) starting a comparatively long sentence for some high-value commercial burglaries as well as two house burglaries, said:

I did a lot of houses between 15 and 17, but I've hardly done any since then. Housebreaking's for stupid criminals. You can do 20 on the trot, it takes you hours and you get nothing for it. These days I go for shops. At least you know there's something in there worth stealing . . . Yeah, it's a trade, isn't it? You start off with burglary, then you try smash-and-grabs or shopbreaks. Every time you get caught you learn a bit and you change your style.

A 40-year-old man (No. 24) with only three convictions, but clearly a sophisticated and experienced criminal, took a quite different view:

I suppose I cottoned on to burglary late. I used to do wage snatches with London firms but I came very near to getting a 15 stretch when one went wrong. Burglary isn't so·sensational, but if you go into it properly you can make a lot of money. I go for antiques and paintings and I pick them very carefully.

It has already been pointed·out that only five of our interviewees lacked convictions for offences other than burglary in a dwelling. Moreover, only three of these claimed to have 'specialised' entirely in burglary over the years, the most interesting example being Denis, the Gerrards Cross offender described in chapter II. A much more common pattern of offending was what might be called 'short-term specialisation'. Many recalled limited periods in which they had become involved in a specific type of crime to the virtual exclusion of others. However, these periods did not appear to follow any common sequence, but arose from a combination of reasoning about previous experience, assessments of the current 'market', what the 'fashion' was, and chance factors such as partnerships with others who had particular preferences. At the same time, habit, familiarity with techniques and personal preferences were always likely to draw them back towards their 'main line', the type of crime they felt most at home with.

Finally, it was interesting to ask to what extent our interviewees considered that either choice of offence or degree of specialisation affected the status and respect that individuals achieved among other criminals. House-burglary is often regarded by criminologists as principally the province of young or inexperienced thieves of low status. (Walsh, for example, 1980:148-51, sees it as a kind of training-ground for people who may later move into more complex and more lucrative areas of crime such as wage-snatching or armed robbery). However, several asserted that this is not necessarily the case. Status and success, they claimed, come not so much from the type of crime that a thief selects but from the way he goes about it. In spite of No. 17's statement above, burglary is not only for stupid criminals. To be known as a burglar does not in itself bring either admiration or contempt from fellow criminals: status is conferred or withheld according to factors such as the scale, skill and rewards of the crimes committed as well as the character of the offender and his dealings with others. Individuals may be dismissed with phrases such as 'he only does kick-ins' or 'he's only a baby burglar', but, equally, a good country-house burglar can earn respect even from wage-snatch gangs or other important criminals. As Jackson (1969:144) put it, to become a 'character' (a respected thief) it is not enough to engage in a particular type of crime. A good thief 'has to have a few other qualifications. In other words you have to be a sharp thief.'

Our interviewees also questioned the frequently-made statement (greatly influenced by Sutherland's 1937 study of a professional thief) that professionalism is associated with specialisation. It was argued that many 'top London villains' engage in a variety of offences, and, moreover, that one sign of a good thief is his ability to respond to new opportunities and to changes in markets (cf. also Letkemann 1973:32-6). Others pointed out that the man who blindly follows a single *modus operandi* in one area is a relatively easy target for the police. The message was clear: it's not what you do, but the way that you do it.

Choice of target

The question of how burglars select the individual houses from which they steal is now considered. The first point we would emphasise is that the vast majority of burglaries described to us were 'planned', at least in the sense of the offender having set out from home or from a café or public house with the intention of burgling a house. In other words, the initial impetus came from a general intention formed elsewhere; it was not a spontaneous reaction to a specific opportunity that presented itself while the burglar was out for another purpose. As one interviewee pointed out, burglars usually get in through back windows, which are out of sight of the street: therefore, it can hardly be the sight of the insecure entry point which sparks off the idea to break in. Some admitted that they had occasionally committed spur-of-the-moment burglaries when under the influence of alcohol, but such behaviour was regarded as characteristic mainly of 'children and drunks'.[4]

For adult and young adult persistent burglars, the selection of targets was a much more complex affair. Most of those we interviewed had preferences for particular kinds of area. To some extent this was a matter of habit and experience. They felt more comfortable in relatively familiar situations, knowing either the layout of streets and alleys or the general habits of people living in the area. Thus a 23-year-old burglar of Asian descent worked mainly in a town-centre area with dense housing where he could use back alleys rather than roads. He worked particularly in one part of town with a high proportion of Indian residents because 'I know they keep money in their houses' and 'they don't like calling the police'.

Even when travelling by car to other towns, many were reluctant to venture into totally unknown territory. A Reading man expressed a common attitude:

> I stay within my own area. I never go more than about 20 miles from home. It makes me feel secure because I know all the little roads to get back home if I'm in trouble. It sounds strange but I've never been stopped by the police at night.

Over the years such a preference can develop into regular patterns. A Reading policeman used an interesting metaphor when he described local thieves as foxes with a hunting-ground of about a 20-mile radius around the town, using well-worn paths to carry their booty back to their dens.

Of course, the choice of area is also determined by the type of property thieves are looking for, itself largely dependent upon their contacts for selling stolen goods. Those without reliable receivers often chose to concentrate mainly upon cash, and despite some token claims of reluctance to steal from the poor, here it was generally recognised that working-class areas offered good opportunities:

> No. 2: Working-class houses are OK because there's more money in them. People keep money in all sorts of little tins and pots about the house, one for rent, one for the meter, one for this and that.

Council housing was particularly attractive to those seeking cash because of the standard layout of the property and the presence of pre-payment meters in practically every house. Nearly all our interviewees lived in or close to areas containing this kind of housing, and although they did not often burgle houses in their own immediate neighbourhood ('you don't shit on your own doorstep', as one put it), it was not usually necessary to walk more than a mile or so to find what they considered a suitable area.

Those looking for items such as televisions or electrical goods sometimes headed for what they described as 'better class' areas, although the point was also made that nowadays houses of all kinds may contain valuable colour television sets. It was only those who seriously claimed to avoid working-class housing 'on principle', and more importantly, those who had good outlets for valuables such as silver and jewellery, who consistently went to wealthier districts. On the whole, the latter were approached by car rather than on foot, as the housing is more often spread out and there is usually further to run to reach a place of safety if a quick escape is necessary. Moreover, cars allow the transportation of bulkier and heavier goods. Only one man who regularly visited middle-class housing said that he never used a vehicle, and explained:

> If you are on foot you can see a police car coming a mile off. You can pick your time when it's safe to go in; if necessary you can hide gear and come back for it later. If you're in a car and they stop you, you're dead.

Once within what they consider a suitable area, the primary concern for most burglars is to select *a house which is unoccupied*. There are two exceptions to this. The first is where the burglary is committed in the small hours of the morning, and the second, much rarer, where the burglar deliberately takes risks in order to provide excitement. We shall return to these exceptions in a moment.

Several methods of ascertaining whether a house is empty were mentioned to us. On dark evenings most burglars aimed for a house where there were no lights, preferably where neighbouring houses were also in darkness. Although they recognised that some houses with lights on were also unoccupied, interviewees said that unless there were other good reasons for choosing a particular house they would not normally bother to find out. Indeed, even if there were no lights, many wanted further evidence that the house was in fact unoccupied. A 25-year-old man whose preferred time of burgling was shortly after dusk stated:

> We would usually drive along a good-looking road, about eight or nine o'clock in the evening. If we see a place with the curtains open, no lights on and no car in the drive we stop and go straight round the back.

During the day other signs of occupancy would be looked for. Some mentioned the well-known signals of milk bottles and newspapers left on the doorstep. Ironically, two of the Gerrards Cross burglars said that, particularly in the summer, a house could look 'too well-locked-up' to be occupied, and they might take more interest in such a property than in one with several windows open. Overall, however, burglars said they simply 'knew from experience' or 'had a feel for' whether a house was occupied or not. As a final check, some knocked on the front door and if there was an answer asked for directions or a fictitious person. A few even claimed that they took the trouble to find out the telephone number and telephoned the house, although this was not believable in every case.

Occupancy was not a factor to consider in the case of night-time burglary. This was practised more often by the younger thieves we interviewed, but, although it was considered more exciting than day-time offending, the consensus of opinion was that the risks of capture were no greater:

> No. 29:   I don't care if there is someone asleep upstairs. Most people are in such a deep sleep at two o'clock in the morning that they don't wake up.
> No. 30:   You can make a lot of noise but they hardly ever wake up. You put a chair at the bottom of the stairs so anyone who comes down will fall over it and you leave the back door open so you can get out quickly.
> No. 26:   You have the advantage that you're awake and they're still half asleep, so you can be long gone before they cotton on to what's happening:

No. 26 had formerly made a practice of stealing jewellery from bedrooms in which people were asleep. He, like other 'creepers', had stories of people half waking up but going back to sleep when he said something in a reassuring tone:

> I was looking through the bedroom cupboards and she called out, 'Is that you, Tom?' So I said, 'Yes, I'm just going to get a drink of water' and she accepted it for a second or two. Then she twigged and started to get up, but by the time she got to the top of the stairs I was out through the front door.

A small number of thieves admitted that at times they took extra risks in occupied houses purely for fun or excitement. Two men in their mid-thirties, who both said they had since become more careful, still took pleasure in recalling earlier days when they had been 'tearaways':

> No. 14:   I used to purposely go at night and walk around the bedroom—doing a bit of cat-burglary like climbing up the drain-

pipe into the bedroom window and walking around the bed while they were asleep. It used to give me a thrill. I used to like doing semi-detached houses because I knew the neighbours were right there next door and the slightest sound and I would get caught. I also used to get a kick out of doing places early in the morning before they went to work. Once I walked past the bathroom of a place to get to the living-room with a bloke shaving in the bathroom mirror. That gave me a hell of a thrill.

No. 25: When I was younger I used to purposely go into houses where they were in. I used to hide behind doors while they passed me and go upstairs when they came down and things like that. It was sort of pitting your wits against them.

Such escapades are the exception rather than the rule, but illustrate the excitement that most burglars experience at some time during their careers. Even one of the most clearly 'professional' of our interviewees admitted:

It can be very exciting being on premises where you know it is breaking the law. In fact I think, crazy as it sounds, people do get almost addicted to the buzz you get from the adrenalin pumping through your veins. I'd grown out of this myself by the time I was 18 or 19 and had begun to realise I was in the game for profit.

Apart from occupancy, there were a number of less frequently mentioned factors involved in selecting a specific target in the area chosen. Thieves interested in jewellery or antiques tended to select the 'richest-looking' house possible, judged by factors of size, acreage of garden and style, but the choice was tempered by other considerations. Several stressed the importance of escape routes. For example, a house in a *cul-de-sac* was generally to be avoided whereas corner properties and those with alleys at the side or back offered at least three escape routes for the burglar. Where to leave a car, if used, also came into the reckoning. Denis (the 'specialist' described earlier) went so far as to say: 'We used to look at whether there was a driveway, where it was, how long it was, where we could park the car, all these were important.'

A further consideration he and some others mentioned was the degree of cover offered by walls, trees, shrubbery or other buildings; there is clearly a greater risk in entering a house in full view of neighbours' windows. On the other hand, in town centres and particularly in housing estates such cover is not always sufficient. Other burglars took the view that in such circumstances a bold approach was preferable to trying to sneak in, since the latter approach would constitute suspicious behaviour in the eyes of a chance observer. Thus they would walk confidently into a garden and around the back of a house as if they were a resident or frequent visitor. Paradoxically, as one pointed out, the more pedestrians in the area, the less 'visible' such an act becomes. People do not expect burglaries to take place in broad daylight in full view of passers-by and therefore disregard what they see. It was said that one well-known local burglar regularly took this principle to extremes, walking up to weak front doors in poor housing areas and kicking them in.

Our earlier remarks (p. 42) about the apparent success of burglar alarms in deflecting offenders from a house were supported by most interviewees. Only five claimed with any conviction ever to have burgled properties with alarms fitted, and some of these were pre-planned burglaries of houses in which they knew there was something particularly valuable. Among the higher level burglars there was confidence that if they so wished they could deal with an alarm, but as there were so many unprotected houses containing valuables the extra risk was not worth taking. A similar attitude prevailed with regard to dogs. Most offenders said they would leave a house alone if they saw or heard a dog before they had entered. This was considered particularly important at night:

> No. 12:   We have a routine I make Alan follow. We always shine a torch around inside the house to see if there is a dog. If there is, we leave.

Even so, most claimed that, if necessary, quitening a dog presented no great problem to them (by a friendly gesture, a firm slap, or throwing food), and if they were already well embarked upon the burglary before seeing the animal they would be more likely to silence him and continue stealing.

In talking about target selection, almost the last factor burglars would mention (if they mentioned it at all) was the ease or difficulty of actually breaking in. Most assumed that they would rarely find a house they could not enter, an attitude summed up in the memorable statement: 'If it's made of bricks, wood and glass I can get in.' However, it was recognised that some types of security required more time and effort than others to breach and, as in the case of dogs in the house, sometimes 'tipped the balance' and sent the offender elsewhere. For example, aluminium-framed windows were considered a 'nuisance' compared with wood-framed windows. Where doors were concerned, mortice deadlocks (usually referred to as 'Chubb' locks, although other manufacturers also make them) were often said to present a major problem. One of the more competent burglars remarked:

> Security locks don't usually bother me unless there are Chubb locks. You can't open them. There's no point in breaking a

window to get in because everything has to be carted out through the window, which is a bit difficult if you've got a £400 colour television to get out.

All factors mentioned—occupancy, size and style of the house, possible exits and escape routes, cover and visibility, presence of alarms, dogs and security locks—play some part in influencing burglars' choices of which particular houses they enter and which they avoid. However, personal preferences and reasoning on such matters vary considerably among burglars, and an individual's mood on any one day may cause him to take more or less risk than usual. The general belief among thieves that burglary is 'easy' and their knowledge that few burglars are caught in the act mean that, although they are aware of risk factors and may think about them in detail, in practice they often feel safe enough to break their own safety rules and do not spend a great deal of time selecting the optimum target. As one of the most perspicacious pointed out, the greatest danger to a burglar's freedom can be his own over-confidence. One man said that after a number of successful burglaries he 'began to feel like Superman', and felt he would never be caught. This kind of attitude took an extreme form among some young adults:

> No. 10:   Sometimes I've gone out in the morning, the afternoon, the evening and then again overnight. Sometimes we would just start at one end of a street and work our way to the other. Working all day and all night means that you end up doing every type of place.
> No. 29:   Usually there were two or three of us. We'd have a drink in the evening, then hang about till about midnight, but we'd still drive maybe 40 miles so we'd be doing the burglaries between one and two in the morning when people are in a deep sleep. We never really bothered where we went, we did so many. We'd do whole estates sometimes. Other times we'd just stop here and there. We never worried because we never got caught.

Many of the replies burglars gave to our questions about target-selection were consistent with the impressions we had formed from visiting the scenes of crimes in Banbury, Reading and Gerrards Cross. As mentioned in chapter II, houses with back alleys, those situated on or near main roads, those near the ends of streets, and those surrounded by cover in the form of walls, trees or shrubbery all appeared particularly vulnerable to attack. The answers given also support the conclusions of Winchester and Jackson (in preparation), that the factors of 'access' and 'surveillance' appear to be more important in explaining patterns of victimisation than levels of household security. In other words, houses with good locks and bolts, but situated in a high-risk position from the point of view of easy and unnoticed access, may be more likely to be burgled than homes with little 'security' which are less conveniently sited from the burglar's point of view. (See also Chapter VI).

Retirement from crime

The depressingly high reconviction rates for burglars make it difficult to argue that the experience of imprisonment deters many offenders from burgling again. Indeed, the general belief we found among our interviewees that burglary 'pays' remains a serious obstacle to any effort to persuade, frighten or cajole a persistent offender to give up the activity. Even those who had spent many years in prison were inclined to remember only their more successful periods. For example, one man boasted that he had made £2,000 in three months, for which he had received only a six-month sentence, but in claiming that this represented a good return he failed to take into account the three-year sentence he had served earlier for stealing a smaller amount. Nor did he consider the possibility that he could have earned more money by legitimate means during the total time he had spent either burgling or 'inside'.

Equally problematic is the fact that the 'cost' of a prison sentence is a subjective cost. Not only do individuals vary in their assessment of its unpleasantness, but incarceration can mean much more or much less to a person at different times in his life. If it can eventually be said to have played a deterrent part in ending a lengthy criminal career, this is most likely because the offender's attitude towards prison has changed, or changes in his social circumstances (for example, marriage or fatherhood) have made it appear more painful than in the past.

The other major 'deterrent' against crime—increasing the chances of the offender being caught—likewise seems to have little hope of success in the case of burglary. Not only is it extremely difficult to improve detection rates (see chapter VI), but even dramatic improvements may not be interpreted by offenders as one might expect. As already pointed out, burglars tend to believe that the offence is successfully completed once they are clear of the house they have attacked. Subsequent arrest is usually blamed upon 'grasses', a problem that, it is believed, can be overcome by more careful behaviour in the future. As one put it: 'You've got to think positive.' Unfortunately, 'positive' thinking tends to distort realistic assessments of chances, and as long as people can escape with scores of burglaries without being captured in or shortly after the act, they will continue to believe that the offence is both easy and profitable.

However, despite the insistence that burglary could provide them with a good living, the very fact that most convicted burglars are young suggests that many thieves do eventually change their habits as they grow older. We did not interview people who had 'retired' completely, but we asked active burglars whether they foresaw an end to their 'careers' in crime and what would be the reasons for it. Some young adults had ideas of making enough money from crime to retire in luxury, or at least to 'buy my own business', but in the light of their achievements so far this seemed an unlikely outcome for the majority. Men in their thirties were more realistic. There was fairly general agreement that 'burgling is a young man's game' and that sooner or later they would have to look for alternative sources of income, whether legal or illegal.

The impetus to think seriously about retirement from crime altogether seemed to come in many cases from a gradual disenchantment with the criminal life in its totality: the inability to trust people; the frequent harassment by the police; the effects on wives and children when the offender is in prison; and the whole 'snakes and ladders' process described earlier. As people grow older such a process can become more painful and depressing and the optimistic outlook can give way to a feeling of being caught in a trap. The decision to steal, which many younger men insisted was a free one taken in full knowledge of the consequences, comes increasingly to be seen as forced upon the older man as the only way out of his situation. Unfortunately, for those with a genuine desire to leave it, crime is not a profession with a pension scheme, and the legitimate jobs open to a man with a long record of imprisonment and unemployment are few and badly paid. A 34-year-old man bitterly pointed out the ironical fact that, when younger, he had been given probation or other 'rehabilitative' sentences, but having no wish to end his criminal career, he treated them as a joke. Now, when he was thinking more seriously of retiring from crime, he was 'written off' by the penal system as a habitual criminal and 'automatically' given prison sentences for relatively minor offences, receiving no help or encouragement from anybody.

Others had notions of giving up direct crime like burglary and making a living from what they called 'dealing'. This might mean acting as a receiver, a go-between or a seller of information about likely targets, all of which could be seen as entering the 'service industry' surrounding crime. Of course, this solution, like that of starting a small business, is a viable one only for those with the character and ability to make a success of it. By the time a man with insufficient foresight reaches the point of wanting to change his lifestyle, he is unlikely to have any of the necessary qualities left in him.

IV. Peter Hudson: From Sweets to Antiques

This chapter contains an account of the criminal career of a 33-year-old man, mainly in his own words, charting his progression from petty thefts as a juvenile, through a 'wild' period as a young man, to his emergence as a careful country-house burglar in his early thirties. Peter Hudson, as we shall call him, was interviewed in prison many times over a two-year period, and the material presented is built up from detailed notes taken during these interviews as well as from pieces written by himself. Names and places have been changed, but as far as possible the intention was to let him tell the story in his own way with only minor editing and comment to link together different parts of the account. He had an excellent memory for detail and a talent for bringing incidents vividly to life. Although he may have added a certain amount of 'colour' to the story, we are satisfied that it is true in all essentials.

At the time of our first meeting, Peter was beginning a long sentence for over 150 charges of burglary in dwellings. In many cases the value of goods stolen ran into thousands of pounds, and the total value recorded was in excess of £200,000. He estimates that during the two-year period that these offences covered he had in fact stolen property worth more than half a million pounds. The offences on the indictment represented only the most serious and those he could best remember when admitting his activities to the police. Sentenced with him were a number of receivers and a man who had been his driver. The victims were mostly very wealthy people living in country properties, some of them well-known public figures. The burglaries covered a wide area of southern England and a certain amount of property was recovered in London and on the Continent. The police operation which finally trapped the burglar was the culmination of several months work by a special squad.

Despite his undoubtedly professional approach to crime, Peter did not present himself as a 'hard' character. The first impression he gave was of a friendly, intelligent person with a great deal of wit and charm. He was a fairly well-built man of average height, looking neither younger nor older than his age, with a pleasant but not particularly memorable face. He had a natural manner of speaking that made one feel at ease and quickly encouraged a relationship of trust. He seemed extremely observant and appreciative of others and at the same time capable of introspection without self pity. In answering questions about his criminal behaviour he was not aggressive or boastful, nor, on the other hand, was he deferential or over-anxious to please. Where prison life was concerned, he had no time for the 'screws', but did not try to provoke them either. He was well-liked and respected by other prisoners and had quickly got one of the best jobs in the prison. Yet despite being 'one of the boys', he was very much 'his own man' too. He gave the impression of knowing what he wanted and was usually clever enough to get it without causing any great fuss. The long sentence he was serving had hit him hard, but he was already working out how to make the best of it, how to keep his mind active, how to help solve his wife's problems and how to give himself the greatest chance of parole.

Despite the charm and resourcefulness he displayed, as our relationship developed he revealed a much more vulnerable side to his nature. He had to some extent buried his feelings over the past few years. In prison he was beginning to think about the sort of person he had become, in particular in his relationship with his family. At times it would have been easy to turn conversations with him into amateur therapy sessions, but efforts were made to avoid this.

*   *   *   *   *

Peter was born in a village near the south coast, the second youngest of five children. His father ran a small business. While he was alive this provided quite well for the family, but unfortunately he died when Peter was 12. It then emerged that debts had been mounting up to such an extent that his widow had to sell the house and business, and the family moved to a terraced house in a poor area of a coastal town.

It was here that, within six weeks of his father's death, Peter began to get into trouble. First he became friendly with a boy four years older than himself who was already stealing regularly. This boy, who had been brought up by a circus family, seems to have been the first of a series of charismatic characters, usually older than himself, that Peter admired, followed, and in some cases modelled himself on, during the next ten years. He was attracted by entertaining, energetic people, free of any ties, and in their company acquired a taste for travelling, drinking, gambling and stealing. From the 'soft emotional person' he described himself as at the time of his father's death, he gradually changed into a more extraverted, dare-devil character, and eventually became a persistent thief. He says of this first friend:

> He encouraged me to play hooky, and he taught me the ropes
> where thieving was concerned. We were always shoplifting, or
> getting round the backyards of shops. The first place we broke into
> properly was a market-holder's warehouse. We kitted ourselves out
> with new jeans and windcheaters, and I felt really smart for days
> walking around in them.
>   Then we started stealing sweets and cigarettes and selling them
> to other kids. We'd go shoplifting in the afternoons then break into
> the lock-up shops on the sea-front in the early evening. Mostly we
> only took things like sweets or apples.

His first appearance in court was for vandalism—smashing all the
windows in an empty house—for which he was fined £15. Peter
cannot remember anything else about the occasion, and is sure it
made no impression on him at the time, neither frightening him nor
making him feel important. The police and courts seemed irrelevant
to his everday life. At 13 he was put on probation for stealing 2,000
cigarettes, but dismisses the supervision as a 'waste of time': 'I used
to hang around all the time with older kids, mostly villains. A probation officer couldn't compete with them.'

He gradually began stealing more valuable items and found people
who would buy them. Eventually, at 14 he was arrested for the classic
petty criminal's offence of stripping lead off a church roof. He was
sent to an approved school, one of the toughest in the country. He
was caned frequently by, he says, 'a genuine sadist', and he reacted
by becoming 'the biggest troublemaker in the place'. He stayed for
more than twice the average length of time and left at 16 . . .

> much harder physically and mentally than I would ever have been
> without going there. I had learned the law of the jungle. I was only
> a kid, you know, and underneath I was soft but I learned you either
> had everything taken or you took it.

He began work, somewhat ironically, as a roofer, but within two
months was 'hanging about every night with the left-overs of the
teddy-boys', and began being late for work or missing days. Another
month and he was out of work.

At this stage he started breaking into houses. This was simply, it
seems, because his needs had changed. Instead of sweets or cigarettes
to consume or to sell cheaply to friends, he wanted cash. In fact, he
wanted enough money to live on and to enjoy himself. Gas and
electricity meters were the prime target, and the more he burgled
houses the more he realised how easy it was and how unlikely he was
to get caught. He estimates he broke and entered at least 100 houses
in a year without being caught.

He was still also burgling shops and pubs, and stealing lead and scrap metal, which were 'good sellers' at the time. At 17 he was caught in the act of stripping the lead guttering off the roof on an abandoned building. This time he was sent to a detention centre.

Peter's family, meanwhile, had not deserted him. None of his brothers or sisters ever became involved with the law, but Peter remained his mother's 'favourite' and she never threatened to reject him. She did not approve of his lifestyle, but as time went on simply accepted him as he was. Whether or not this stable background would have eventually influenced him enough to 'go straight' if he had stayed at home is impossible to know. Peter thinks it might have. As it was, after leaving detention centre his life entered a new phase. He left home to take a job on a large construction site. One consequence of this was that he had less contact with the small-town-centre petty thief culture; but another was that he began to spend his time with older men who, in his own words:

> were hard men, hard-drinking, hard-gambling. They were people who had done a lot of things in their lives. They'd travelled all over. They had a lot of money and they spent a lot of money.

Still under 18, he was greatly impressed by these companions:

> One sort of adopted me. He was what you'd call a real character. He was six-foot-four, with a great handlebar moustache. He'd been all round the world. The only things he really cared about were his boots and his banjo. We used to go into pubs and he played all night for as much as we could drink. I used to drink whisky by the gallon. We'd stagger out and sleep in old railway carriages or under hedges. When we weren't drunk we stayed up all night playing brag. He was the site bookmaker and I ran the bets for him. One day he comes up to me at work and says, 'Come on Peter, it's time to leave.' He'd been fiddling all the bets, so we had to do a bunk.
>
> I stayed with him for a while. We got tied up with all sorts of characters, like gypsies and knife-grinders. They used to know tricks to con money and drinks out of people. There was one tinker who used to bet people he could tie a knot in a piece of string with one hand in five seconds. He just flicked it somehow and it worked. Or he'd say, 'I bet I can drink all the beer in that glass and leave enough in it to fill another one.' So what he'd do was drop a shilling in the glass and drink the beer. I used to like people like that. The trouble was, they got me stealing. We'd go up to a pub after closing and they'd force a window to steal some drink. But it was always me they gave a bunk-up to go in. None of them were stupid. They'd run off if anything went wrong.

After a short time moving around the coast enjoying the company of these characters, Peter went back to his mother's house. Out of

work and short of money he soon started stealing in a more deter-
minedly mercenary manner. He teamed up with two local thieves for a
while, and together they burgled a number of premises, mainly
garages, clubs and offices around the town. He learned that, if only
one had a reliable market for the stolen goods, there was more money
in stealing property and selling it than in just searching for loose cash.
Peter was lucky in this, unlike many thieves of 18 who are limited to
the dangerous outlet of the local second-hand dealers:

> I had by now established a pretty sound relationship with a great
> character, Joe, who was my first real fence. He was around 50 and
> was a well-known person to the police. We called him the Dinosaur
> because he was so ugly. He'd been a pretty successful bloke owning
> a house and a caravan and a boat. He also had a landrover which
> we would often run stolen gear out in. Joe obviously had many
> contacts. There was one who used to send absconding Borstal girls
> to him and he'd harbour them, moving them from his boat to his
> house and the caravan before they moved on. I saw six or seven
> that I recall.
>
> I suppose you might call him a 'Fagin' type. He used to go
> round the cafés picking up kids of about 17, sometimes as many as
> 15 of them. He'd pile them all in the landrover and drive off to a
> holiday beach somewhere. First of all he'd charge them all two bob
> for petrol, so he was making a profit before he started, then he'd
> get them to nick anything that wasn't nailed down, deck-chairs,
> beer-glasses, towels, anything. He bought and sold everything. He
> even used to chug across to France in his motorboat buying and
> selling.
>
> Joe was very fly (smart). He'd never be in the same place twice.
> He kept moving his boat and his caravan so the police never knew
> where he was. He got caught a few times, but he never got a big
> sentence.
>
> He was a cunning bastard, but he'd never let you down. One
> time I had a suitcase full of cigarettes I'd stolen. I went to stash
> them in the station left luggage so I could go and look for Joe. I
> didn't know then, but the woman there was suspicious and she
> looked inside after I'd gone and phoned the police. Lucky for me I
> saw Joe almost as soon as I'd got out of the station and he told me
> to go and get them straight away. Anyway, I went and asked for
> my case back, but I noticed the woman was stalling me, she kept
> questioning the ticket and everything, so I guessed there was
> something wrong. I grabbed the case and jumped into Joe's van. I
> was going to throw it out of the window, but he just said, 'Tip them
> out in the back.' Then he filled the case up with old socks and odds
> and ends he had in there and told me to walk back past the station.
> Of course, the Old Bill saw me and grabbed me, but all they could
> find was the old socks, so they couldn't prove a thing. Things like
> that helped me learn never to panic if it comes on top.

He described his partners in theft as follows:

The others I mentioned were really rough lads and between the three of us we got into a lot of scrapes. Although I was only 18 I already spent the majority of my time in the pubs or billiard hall, and drink and playing cards were always priority providing I had cash. If not it was scheming where to get it. Our speciality became garages, and any batteries, tyres, etc. were bought by Joe. Neville, by the way, was a couple of years older than me and already had a drinking problem. Brian was well known in town and probably regarded as mad. He was from quite well-off people, his father had been a doctor on the liners before he died. His mother owned two large houses on the front. She boarded old folk and nursed them, usually till they died. She was loaded and Brian and I used to go to see her once in a while on the sponge. We'd buy prawns or peanuts and throw the heads at passers-by or sit on someone's wall and pull the heads off people's flowers, then stand and laugh at them in defiance. Brian had a thing about calling everyone a senile cretin. We were both pretty popular with the girls. At this time we were both wearing drape jackets and skin-tight pants, waistcoats and beetle-crushers, a fashion that was already dead.

One night Neville, Brian and I done a garage where we found two safes. We took a sledge-hammer, a crowbar and two tyre-levers from the workshop and broke open the first one to find £150, an awful lot of money in those days. Brian and I wanted to do the other but Neville said 'No, why take the risk? We may have been heard and we've already earnt well.' Anyway he persuaded us to leave. I was sick when I found out later there was over a thousand in the other safe.

But of course Neville was over the moon as he didn't gamble and he knew he'd be on the beer for a fortnight. Anyway a couple of days later we hit another garage and had to chop the doors off. We had about £30 and the following morning Brian and I went to London. Neville wouldn't come with us to 'waste' money up there. Brian and I stayed in London a week during which time we both rigged ourselves out in Petticoat Lane. Both went skint and done another garage in New Malden to get money to come home with. When we got home we learnt Neville had been caught in a garage; we were duly arrested on sight and questioned. Of course we knew nothing and Neville being one of the old school didn't shop us (a rare thing these days). Our clothes were taken for forensic but came up negative as they were new. One of the detective constables tried a stroke on me. He picked up a cash box we had taken from a safe and saying 'Have you seen this before?' threw it at me. Catching on, I let it fall to the floor—he was trying to get my fingerprints on it. Anyhow I had my own back on him later. I stole his son's brand new bike from outside his house.

Neville was eventually done for three jobs and got three years corrective training, which was a heavy sentence then.

Another friend disappeared to Borstal in a somewhat comic fashion:

He was a jock we called Mac. He and I done a few jobs together, usually shops. He went out one night on his own to do a hairdressers. As it was near to occupied houses he took a sheet of brown paper and a pot of jam [an old-fashioned method of putting in a window quietly]. He had done the job, had £25 and a load of women's tights and went back to his brother's for the night. He was amazed to be woken in the morning by the Old Bill. He was arrested and charged still puzzled. Then they showed him the brown paper. On it was his brother's name and address.

Brian and Peter carried on regardless until ultimately their luck changed:

Brian got a bit sweet on a local girl (whom a friend and I used to take money from for finding her clients). Brian moved in with her in this dingy terraced council house. I had my room of course. Another room was used for the ferrets we kept. Anyway we were at it non-stop. One of our favourites was hoisting people's wallets, cameras etc. off the beaches. Brian got done for demanding money with menaces but was only fined. Then one night we had no grub we went to get a bit of vegetable and a chicken off the allotments. Well it probably sounds wicked but at the time seemed funny to me. I'd never realised you can walk in a hen-house at night, lift a chicken off its roost and stretch its neck without it making a sound. Well we ended up with 13 chickens and a sack of vegetables and went back to the house. We got Sheila up and she made a stew. We sold the remainder of the chickens to Joe the next morning and a day or two later broke into a pub. We spent all night carting the cigarettes and booze across fields to the house and had a few pounds cash. Well someone caught on the next day. We suspected a neighbour (Brian wanted to burn her out). The police came and we were arrested and remanded in prison. Eventually we all got our Borstals.

Peter was allocated to a Borstal 300 miles from his home, and stayed there about 14 months. His friend Brian, he says, had a much better deal. He married his girl-friend Sheila in order to be allocated to the Borstal nearest to home, and he only served a few months:

He got out by using his head. He got Sheila to kick up awful scenes on visits, refusing to leave. She'd sit outside the gate all night until the governor had to take her home.

Meanwhile Peter was receiving his Borstal training:

I spent my time doing nothing constructive. I was always one of the lads and had a hand in anything going on, baroning tobacco and other goodies. I played rugby, but not for the sport, only for the treats that went with it.

Every other week we would play away and always went to the team's clubhouse. The officer who ran it was a bit of a fairy and I still think he only done it to see the lads in the shower. Anyhow we always had a good meal and the opposing team always saw we had a crafty pint or two by taking 'fairy' for a walk round the club or field.

I can't say Borstal taught me anything except to attempt to be a little more shrewd and become a bit more professional. I didn't enjoy being there for 14 months and I came out determined to be a lot craftier so I wouldn't go back.

On his return he immediately resumed his old way of life:

When they let me out, I caught the train, went to . . . walked from the station to the Bells, my old pub. Walked in. One man at the bar, 'I've been here every morning for eight months. What kept you, you cunt?' 'Nice to see you, Brian.'

He had actually been every morning to the Bells knowing that the day I got home I'd head there first. Well we teamed up again and were now very canny about what we done and how we done it. We worked on and off, here and there; we had a short period at the same site but were sacked on suspicion. We'd been stealing the copper. Then we worked together on a new sea wall. We were working nights under floodlight but had the sack when we rebelled and threw all the shovels in the sea.

Our drinking, gambling and general pattern of life changed little but we'd got pretty shrewd about burglaries and travelled some distance and put in a bit of waiting and watching before we done things. We both bought shotguns and loved a day's shooting. We had ferrets and a guy going abroad gave us two greyhounds. We had many a ruction over them, usually on buses. On one occasion a conductor had to be knocked out.

Another of Brian's favourite cracks was if we'd had a good day and shot a few pigeon and a couple of pheasant or rabbit. He'd splash himself with blood to get on the bus and, when we got into town, insisted on going in the milk bar in the High Street. He loved shocking people. He'd pick scraps off a plate someone had left and eat them with his hands covered in dried blood. He laughed like a drain if someone was visibly revolted. I suppose he was the original punk.

Despite such exhibitionism, Peter survived for six years without another conviction. In that time he estimates he must have stolen over £20,000 worth of goods. To commit crime on this kind of scale without detection is unusual in so young a thief, and shows that while enjoying himself and fooling around with wild characters, Peter always retained a calculating mind, taking no silly risks, not advertising his serious criminal activities, and above all constantly learning. Every 'job' taught him a little more, and he was ready to listen to older experienced criminals. One example of the latter was Henry, a London man with a good knowledge of jewellery, who, in their brief acquaintanceship, taught Peter to recognise different precious stones and to tell good pieces from cheap. He also acted as his 'fence' for a few months, encouraging Peter to look for jewellery and silver as well as cash. Peter described him as 'a proper London villain—nightclub bouncer, smash-and-grab artist and part-time fence.' He had connections in the entertainment business as well as with professional East End criminals and, to ambitious young thieves, was 'in a different class' from most of the local criminals.

Peter first met him when he began going to a cellar coffee bar owned by Henry and a man called Phillips, in a neighbouring town. Philips was known as 'Phil the Pill' because of his interest in drugs (this was the time when 'purple hearts' were very popular). Peter had no interest in drugs and had little to do with Phillips, but was immediately attracted by Henry, who like Joe, or Brian, or his gypsy friends, or the banjo-player, was different and exciting, 'a right character'.

> Henry was the size of a brick shit-house. He was as wide as he was high but what one would term a gentle giant. Mind you by that I don't mean he was no pushover. He could and often had to eject anybody from the place. He could lift a man clean off his feet with one hand, but this kind of presence he had about him calmed blokes before he had to use force. He had a mate called Bernard. He was a similar shape and size to Henry and had a reputation of being an animal in a scrap. Together they looked like Tweedledum and Tweedledee in gorilla outfits but were really nice guys to those who knew them. They were a pair of shrewdies. They also had shares in a dance hall and drinking place.

A few months after leaving Borstal Peter and Brian began travelling the country with a specialised construction firm. Most jobs took only a few weeks, which gave them enough time to plan and execute fairly substantial crimes and to be gone before the police became wise to their activities. They mainly burgled garages, pubs and offices, in several cases stealing or breaking safes. Generally they found digs in small towns, but sometimes found themselves at Government or Services establishments out in the country, where they developed interests in poaching game and burgling villages. Yet despite the more serious nature of their crimes, the dominant image of this next year or so is still one of a carefree life, with pleasure and 'laughs' as important as the financial rewards of stealing. Neither could be described at that time as a professional criminal. They were working hard full-time and earning good wages. Crime was still a sideline, although a profitable one.

> Brian and I always tried to avoid living with the others to allow us to continue our hobby: robbing people. One time we were on a long job near Huddersfield. We had digs with an old lady. She welcomed us but kept saying her regular boys would be back soon. Well, we didn't worry—'We'll soon get rid of them.' Apparently she had a couple of regulars who were on holiday. We met a bloke who was a barman at the Crown and he seemed OK. We gently

asked if he was able to move stuff, which he agreed he could. Two nights later we had a shop over. We took the gear, cigarettes and tobacco, back to the digs in two cases. We had no worry of the old lady as she always went to bed early. Next morning the old girl said her boys were coming back today. Roger (a workmate) picked us up, we threw the cases in the boot and delivered them on the way to work, having arranged for payment in the pub that evening. When we came in from work covered in shit with a couple of rabbits we'd shot with the sawn down 12 bore I carried in my case, the old lady's 'boys' were there. We went to wash up for our evening meal. 'What a pair of pricks they look.' 'Yeah, right pair of clowns' we were joking. We went down for our meal. The other two were eating. We sat down and they asked what we did. We told them and asked their jobs. 'Police cadets,' they replied.

That night we met our barman. He paid us OK and said everything was sweet. We asked if he knew where we could get digs and he invited us to lodge at his house at £4 a week full board. We moved out the following morning and dropped our cases at his place on our way to work. On returning in the evening we met his wife, a huge girl called Jean—very pleasant though. Our food was always first-class and she'd pile massive servings of everything on to us. They had a three-bedroom flat above a shop where Tom (the barman) had worked but was dismissed for something or other. He had a bulldog he thought more of than his wife. We had a good time there as they often had parties, the booze coming from the Crown.

This seems to have been a fairly typical scene. Brian and Peter were very quick to sound out locals who could help them dispose of anything they stole, as well as to size up possible 'jobs'.

Brian and I watched points at all times, never letting an opportunity to make a pound pass us. We always noted 'habits': if shopkeepers appeared lazy or publicans liked to be one of the boys and drank too much. One day we discovered where the riggers on the site we were working housed their scrap, mainly copper wire and copper plate. Two nights later, borrowing Tom's motor, Brian, Roger and I drove up to as near as we could to where it was. We had to walk a long way across fields to the sheds. We had the lock off and to our amazement and joy found all the scrap bagged up. What is more there was literally tons of it. Well, a bag each over them fields was killing but we struggled on. Two trips was a car full. So we done a shuttle. Roger took the car to his place, Brian and I carried more bags. We worked till we were exhausted and it began to get light, then knocked it on the head and went to Tom's.

His yard was stacked with bags. We had a few hours kip then Tom went to see a totter [scrap dealer] he knew. Everything was laid on but we had to deliver. We set out with the first load and went through the city, but halfway up a hill the car stalled and we had to roll backwards to the kerb. It started but couldn't pull the weight. We daren't try to roll all the way back down because of heavy traffic, so were virtually knackered. We daren't abandon the car in case a copper saw it. Anyway we had to unload the six bags and carry them to the top of the hill. What a pantomime. If we'd been seen by the law we'd have been nicked for sure. Well, the diddycoy agreed to come for the rest in his lorry but of course knocked the price down. We eventually got rid of it and drew our money.

We used to use another pub in the same road sometimes. One night the landlord was getting well slushed so we left a toilet window open. We returned later and cleared out the bars. We could hear him snoring. Unfortunately his safe was bricked in so we got no money. The spirits and cigarettes were sold via the Crown.

Although such crimes gave them money for short periods, it was soon spent, and the pair were often broke.

We were always squandering the money we stole. I was already well into the Gordon's gin and I loved to eat well. Whenever I had money I had good steaks for supper.

We were paid Fridays but usually boracic lint [broke] by Monday what with drink and gambling.

One Sunday after a heavy weekend, Brian and I returned from the pub for lunch. We had the crack [chatted] with Tom who was also skint so began to get our heads together. 'Take the dog for a long walk Jean, a very long walk,' he said. That left us to scheme. I went upstairs for a pony [to the toilet] and spent a few minutes hanging out of the bathroom window. Looking over the roof, I saw a lead valley on a building 50 yards up the road. I called the others up. 'What's that place Tom?' 'The GPO sorting office!' Brian and I were out of the window across the roofs and surveying the prospects. 'There's a nice few bob here all right.' We soon worked out a way across the roofs and were shortly hard at it stripping out the box gutters, 'valleys and ridges, carrying it and dropping it in Tom's yard. We had it all off in a couple of hours, went and borrowed the motor and took it to the Diddy. He paid us out and we were well pleased and soon getting togged up to go on the beer.

Not long after that we had to call at a builder's supply yard to get rope and noticed the safe. Taking note of the layout we went back and had it a day or two later, scoring good bread.

Despite getting involved in all kinds of trouble, neither was a particularly good fighter, and Peter, who has generally avoided violence since, learned this lesson, he says, in Huddersfield.

One night we gave a couple of the local lads a good hiding over some silly argument. A few nights later they caught us with a few of their pals and we both took a right lacing. Fortunately I was well pissed and it didn't hurt too much till the next day. I think that's when I realised the foolishness in fighting. 'Fuck this Brian, there's no profit in this game.'

When the job was finished, the team moved south to a small town in Kent. It is interesting that the vigilance of the police in this town kept their criminal activity to a minimum: 'We had a touch or two but played it a bit cool, as we found the law were pretty lively'. They soon moved back north, and things continued in much the same vein until one day Brian suddenly decided to give up the job and go back to live with Sheila. Peter has seen him only occasionally since then, and it appears that he has 'gone straight' and become an ordinary family man. Meanwhile, it was the less wild one of the partnership, Peter, who was to go on to a serious career in crime.

> We went all over the place from there. I done very nicely down in Hampshire working on my own. But I soon teamed up with another guy in the firm. We went to Dundee and didn't even have a tickle then, but done quite well in some other places in Scotland.

However, at one stage he almost gave up stealing, mainly because of the style of life in a particular town.

> It was one of the few places I would have stopped in. Certainly the only place in Scotland. The people there are so friendly it's really peculiar. Everyone: milkman, postman, people in the street, coppers, old ladies, kids, everyone speaks to you. It's even funnier as you get to know people; they all seem to have two jobs. The postman worked as a barman, the croupier in the casino was a teller in the GPO, another guy worked as a doorman in a hotel (the only place you could get a drink on Sunday) in the evenings and worked in a shop all day. Then when the bars turned out everyone was up the casino. Brag was the game everyone played. I didn't do any thieving for two reasons: one was that we were very popular there. Everyone liked us and knew us. We had an old ambulance which was an attraction to all the kids (and a few of the girls as it had two beds in the back). I felt I would be too easy to recognise if anything went wrong. Apart from this I was never short of money. Every time I went up the casino, which was every night it was open, I won money.

After returning to England, Peter carried on as before. But without Brian a lot of the fun had gone. Brian had a 'golden touch' he said. 'People were attracted to him like a magnet.' 'He made everything seem exciting.' Within a year Peter too met a girl, married, and gave up the travelling life, settling in a small town in the Thames Valley. However, unlike Brian, he did not give up his 'hobby'.

> My gambling got worse and I became very much the friendly neighbourhood burglar. I was at it in a pretty big way from the word go, but in those days used to work as well. My main targets were the local shopkeepers. I reckon I had 80 per cent of the local business people over five or six years. Either their premises or their

houses, sometimes both—it was like a one-man vengeance against
the town. How I used to work was quite simple. I'd take note of
how I thought they were doing. Then watch as they left at night,
noting bags or similar being carried when they drove off. Then I'd
be waiting in town the next night hoping to spot them in the night
safes. Or I'd follow on foot. I'd find their address from the telephone or *Who's Who* book. Quite often I'd fancy them to leave the
bread in the shop. This being so I'd go in buying something to get
the lie of the land. Trying to spot safes or alarms etc. I had a knack,
a way of smelling money out. Maybe it was something I'd learnt
over the years, something like instinct. Well the scope was endless
and they were going over every week. Not huge sums of money but
£150-£200 a time wasn't bad dough. I think the fact that I was not
known to the local filth [police] was the greatest thing in my favour.
I was never stopped at night—I wasn't normally out later than the
pubs turning out. I liked working early, the earlier the better, so it
was just after dark as a rule. That way you aren't on the street late
getting yourself noticed.

Peter said that he would literally walk down the streets of the town
centre mentally ticking off which businesses he had not yet burgled
and working out the best way of remedying the deficiency. It is
astonishing that, despite being probably the most prolific thief in a
small town and getting away with thousands of pounds in regular
thefts over a period of years, Peter was virtually unknown to the local
police. He puts this down to the facts that: (a) although having plenty
of criminal contacts, he did not mix with the 'obvious villains' in the
town-centre pubs and cafés, so was not seen much by policemen or
informers; (b) he was married, working, and had started to buy his
own house, and (c) he had not been arrested for several years. He
seemed on the surface to be a reformed juvenile delinquent who,
having sown his wild oats, had settled down to become a responsible
family man.

A good example of his technique at this time—his ordinary appearance and apparently innocent questions to gain him information;
then his logical approach to stealing the money—was demonstrated in
this incident:

One day Jane and I were buying a piece of furniture in a shop in
town. The salesman was a fool. I started chatting about how
annoying it is the banks closing early and he straight away tells me
about all the problems shops have with banking money: 'See that
supermarket across the road? The manager goes to the night safe
the same time every night. If I was a crook I'd have a motorbike in
that alley and have it off him on a Friday.' Well, I thought, here's a
right plum, so I start agreeing with him. 'Yes, you can see how
these things are done easy enough. You only have to look round
and see how careless people are. I suppose you're pretty secure

here aren't you?' 'Well,' he says, 'We cash up every night and put it in the bank bag, but as none of us go near Barclays we hide it in the shop until the morning, then one of us will walk it up the bank.' 'Hide it in the shop? That's a good idea,' I says. Two Fridays later I watched, saw nothing leave. Saturday was the same, so that night, thinking I had all night tonight, all day tomorrow and all tomorrow night to find it, I went to do the place. This shop is three storeys and all various departments: bedroom, dining-room, carpets, lounge, curtains, and so on. I got in at the back by forcing a window, walking through the place to the office. I rang the till up. Nothing. Right, I thought, where would I hide a money pouch? I walked through the carpet department and into the bedroom suite. The second drawer I opened I found the bag. I couldn't believe my eyes. Well it was locked and I couldn't open it so I took it with me. I went home, opened it by cutting it with a lino knife and copped for £300. Needless to say I was well pleased, especially as I could have been there a weekend.

Where houses were concerned, he rarely went in merely on the off-chance of finding something worth stealing, and normally took care to find out where the occupants were so that he would not be disturbed. Yet he could not always bargain for the unexpected, as a particular event, related by Peter with relish, shows:

I'd been watching a bloke who owned a good electrical shop —radio, tele, stereo, records, in fact most things. He was a real Flash Harry and although I did not know him personally I disliked him immensely. He lived in a large terraced town house. One night I saw him drive through town. I was round his place in a few minutes. Well the front is a pretty busy street so I just looked to see if there were any lights on. None. I went round to the back which is in another street, down an alley into his garden. No lights, so I think it's OK. I climbed through the kitchen window into the sink and went through to the living-room. Spots his wife's bag and scores £30. (I should have thought then, but it never entered my head. A woman rarely leaves her handbag behind if she is out and almost always takes her purse.) Well I searched the ground floor and found nothing so went upstairs. At the top of the stairs were two doors, one on the left, one on the right. I went into the left one but soon found it was only a spare bedroom. As I came out crossed the passage and was about to turn the door knob of the next room, a voice said 'Shall we have the radio on?' With that music began playing. I nearly crapped myself on the spot. I froze for a second then spilled off down the stairs and away. I still smile to myself wondering who the other person was in the bedroom. I take it one was his wife. They had no children and he was out for the evening. No doubt she had a bit of explaining to do.

Security measures rarely presented any problems to him. Indeed, he took a perverse pride in beating them.

Another was a delicatessen in the main High Street. All I done was reached up and pushed aside the two arms holding the light above the door open. Then I scrambled up and over the door. I had a quick look round and found little so I tried the till. It was unlike any I'd seen and was very modern. I pressed the different knobs and keys, expecting it to roll open but nothing happened. All this time I'm on my knees behind the counter. Well, it's either locked or had to be switched on electrically, I think. So I look for a switch and find one a foot or so from the back of the till. Flicking it all the lights in the shop come on. 'Christ' I think, and immediately flick it off. At this very second someone walks by the window and looks, in. Fortunately the fool doesn't look up and I'm OK. I gave it a minute and went back to the till. I eventually hit out the right tune and it opened. I snared £50 odd and left by the yale lock. Next day I saw the guy had a bloke fitting bars to the light. Of course with the smell of the cheeses and various food they needed a circulation of air. Exactly one week later I done the same place again by squeezing through the bars. I was well pleased as he still left the cash in the till. You know I'd love to be a fly on the wall the next morning to see some of these people's faces or hear what they have to say. Really it must be quite funny sometimes.

Dogs, too, were also dealt with easily although they were one of the factors several other burglars mentioned as an effective discouragement to burglary.

Another night I went after a particular person. They owned a classy ladies' hairdressers. Previously the shop had been done by someone else and I knew no money was found. By watching I was pretty sure it went home. Home was a large detached house in a pretty good neighbourhood. Well I've gone round with a mate and watched them go out. We were hiding in the back garden. We went up to the house but as soon as we approached a dog began to bark. Normally that's enough to put me off. It certainly is nowadays. Nevertheless I keep going round the house till the dog comes into the kitchen. It's one of those basset hounds and, although he's barking like mad, I get the impression that he's all front and really a softie. I open the window with a steel comb but try to get my mate to go in first. He wouldn't have any of it so I had to go in. Well, the dog's really a big pudding and after a few minutes I've got him behaving well. I found a box of chocolates and he seemed quite contented eating those. Well we turned the place upside down and found the takings, £118 and a bit of tom [jewellery]. The pooch is following us all over the house and I was well pleased with the situation when I tucked him up in the king-size double bed before leaving.

His attitude to the victims, many of whom he knew personally or by sight, was essentially that they were 'fair game', either because of their character (many of his descriptions of offences began with references to the victim as 'a right plum', 'a fool', 'a bad tempered old bag'), or simply because they were comparatively wealthy. He enjoyed the thought of 'the look on their faces' when they discovered that they had been outwitted, and was particularly pleased in one case actually to witness the results of his 'cheeky' theft.

One evening my pal and I were having a pint, we're skint and wondering where we could score. 'How about the King's Head?' he says. Well its summer and still broad daylight. We both knew this woman was loaded and deserved to be had. She was abusive and ignorant, never ought to have had a boozer, but being as it was on an estate a mile's walk from the town centre, she had a monopoly. The off-licence was like a shop. Well, we walked round just to look but I've spotted the kitchen window open on the side. Convinced that she had plenty of dough in there I get my mate to check she was in the bar. Yes and there's quite a few in there, so she's busy. We slipped round the back and trying to avoid being overlooked by keeping below the ledge took a quick look. Well I opens the window, gets in to the sink and into the kitchen, as I open the living-room door I hear a low growling and there is a poodle sat in a chair opposite. Well I knew if it barked the old boot would come through to see why, and as the living-room led straight in the bar I'd have been snookered. Well, I've started talking to this pooch, 'There's a good boy' and all daft things and gradually steps in the room, talking to the mutt all the time. He settles down and just watches as I begin going through all the drawers and cupboards. All over I'm finding bits of cash—four fivers in a beer mug, five fivers under the clock, a few quid in this drawer and a couple of tenners on the sideboard. I spotted her handbag, opened the living-room window and passed it out. But being as she knew me and so did most of the people in the bar I got a bit windy and left. On counting up I had over £200 and there was £120 in the handbag. But what really made me wonder was a couple of days later when we went in for a drink. She was talking with a couple of her regulars. 'I can't find my handbag anywhere. I wonder if I left it in the Off Sales and one of those kids took it.' She honestly didn't know I'd been. She'd not even noticed all the drawers had been turned upside-down or the money missing.

Only occasionally did he experience qualms of conscience about what he had done, but even in the following example these were subordinate to his annoyance at the low value of what had been stolen. Having heard that an old man possessed a 'fantastic coin collection', he and a partner broke into his house:

We removed all the boxes, bags and albums until I'd got the lot out in the passage, then closed the door and bagged up. We left, walked down the road over a recreation field and then decided to have a look. We went through the lot. Well to be honest I felt bad. It was just a lot of old halfpennies and threepenny bits, a few tanners, a few half-crowns etc. There wasn't a piece of gold among it. What annoyed me was that we'd probably broke the old boy's heart for nothing. We took them out to the road, put them under a lamp-post and left them, hoping someone would find them and hand them to the police.

This incident also illustrated a recurrent theme in Peter's conversation. He is of the opinion that information from other criminals about the location of valuable goods is often false and can lead to trouble.

I rarely work on information nowadays—usually it's very unreliable. My first question is always, 'If it's so good why doesn't the bloke do it himself?' I find these people always without exception exaggerate. Maybe in their own mind they think they are getting in with you by talking that way, maybe not believing you will, or hoping you won't, work on their word. It's very odd but even basically honest people like to mouth off about what they know. As a matter of fact one person who used to give me information is now known by all that matter as a police informer and is in for a very nasty time when a certain man is released from prison. Another odd thing is that bum information is often related to coins or stamps!

Indeed, Peter's first conviction for six years stemmed from a burglary that was suggested by a 'tipster'.

I'd met a bloke from town who was a bit of a villain and he would tell me of the occasional job. He was known as Mickey, but that wasn't his real name. He'd pop over and see me when anything was coming up. He got a lot of his information from a geezer who had his own building firm. What his game was, when he was working in houses, just keep his eyes open and ears flapping.

Anyway, I had a 'phone call: 'Come over now and come pre-pared, have transport and bring a mate.' One 'phone call later a pal picked me up and we bombed in to see Mickey. The briefing was quick. His mate had dealings with a bloke who owned a pros-perous shop and also bought and sold good class cars. 'He knows this guy has two grand in the safe at all times. The safe is in a cup-board in the kitchen and the family has all gone out, taking the dog. They will not be back until after 11.00. We want 40 per cent of the cash. Anything else is down to you.' We'd heard enough. A few minutes later we're in the house, but as you've guessed, there's no safe in the kitchen.

Well, we began searching the ground floor and eventually after finding a few quid here and there found about £200. Then we shot upstairs and began turning over the lounge. The geezer had a Parker Knoll recliner and next to it had a cabinet stacked with every drink imaginable, the biggest colour set I've ever seen and an all together nice gaff [home]. Still we don't score much in there and proceed to the bedroom. I'm over the moon when I score for what must be the old gal's tom box, a quick look reveals some good pieces. Next we've had a butcher's in the daughter's room and had it off again for her tom. Another quick spin round and we were ready to leave. We put the gear by the front door and my mate went for the van. While he was gone I took as a bit of bonus a bottle of Gordon's, a bottle of Courvoisier and a few hundred Benson's. As he drove in to the block I just walked down the path with a large box, he hopped out, opened the back door, I slid it in and off we went.

We went back to the flat where Mickey and his pal were waiting. Well I've explained that the info was correct up to the point of cash and produced the £200 saying '40 per cent of the cash is £80. Paid.' Of course a little argument developed concerning what else did we get. 'Hang on cock, anything else is down to me, remember your words?' But I say, 'When I've had a look at what's what, maybe you'll be good for a bit of bonus.' Mickey was fairly knowledgeable as far as tom was concerned, and I brought in the boxes to allow him a gander. This proved to be a mistake. The boxes revealed a quantity of pretty classy tom, this in turn brought in the greed and another little argument. 'If it wasn't for us, you wouldn't have got the stuff: we must be good for a split.' 'That wasn't the agreement and anyway if it wasn't for me and Dave you'd have nothing. Neither of you had the arsehole to do the burglary yourself. If you had then you'd have had the lot and there would have been no need to 'phone me.' Then it was the old crack of 'Well, can I have this and that?' A couple of pieces changed hands and we left after a promise of a drink according to what it fetched. Next morning the geezer screamed £8,000. This brought another 'phone call from Mickey but the stuff had gone to earth and that was where it was staying. I also put with it the tom from a previous job. It was five weeks later that I removed it from earth, planning to take it to Henry, if I could find him, in London. Mistake number two, I told Mickey, who told his mate. Me and Dave took the stuff and drove out of town. (Here I'd like to add that a reward of 10 per cent had been on offer.) Dave and I went first to a guy he knew in north London. He proved to be a flyboy and tried pulling the oldest trick in the book. Offering first money for individual pieces of mediocre jewellery, pushing aside the cream. Glass in eye, he'd pick up first a string of glass beads: 'Crap, son' he'd comment. Next a brooch of reasonable quality: 'This is nice, yeah, nice little ruby in this one, son; few bob there.' Maybe another fair piece next and similar chatter. Then he'd pick up a piece of class, maybe a solitaire diamond or a cluster, always precious stones: 'Crap, son, coloured glass', and push it in with what was crap. This he'd continue until every piece was examined, then it would be 'Well, how much do you want for this?' Now I argue that the pieces in the crap pile were really the cream. 'Rubbish, son, I know my business, look it's worth nothing.' He then takes a handful and goes to throw it on the fire. 'Hang about pal, I'm sorry but I know that one, bag it up Dave, we're off.' His game was to throw it on the fire thinking we were dumb enough to think it would burn. After we'd gone he'd have raked out the ashes and sifted out the stones, which would have been re-set in any case. We pulled out rapid and shot off hoping to look up Henry.

I knew he'd been out of nick for some time. However a tour round the local haunts proved fruitless. In the end we were told he was in . . . , where he'd opened a café. We drove down for a look. He wasn't there, but I left a message for him saying I'd be back and we shot back to London where I outed a few pieces to cover expenses. Then we drove back home. Well we hit town about five. I'd previously 'phoned the wife saying when I'd be home and to put on my dinner. I got in the house and reckon about 10 minutes later Jane put my meal out. The tom I'd tossed in a cupboard thinking it would be alright for an hour until I put it back to earth. Well I'd just put me ass in the chair and the door knocks. Like a prick I go straight to the door thinking it's Dave forgotten something. Course I opens it and in storm the filth, warrant and four-handed. 'What's your game then?' 'From information received we believe you have stolen jewellery on these premises.' Well I didn't see much point having those pigs raking all over the house, so I said, 'Not stolen jewellery, the only stuff I have is this.' And I takes them to the cupboard. Didn't even get to eat my meal. They whisked me off like I was Ronald Biggs. Well they held me all night. I said nought and acted a bit stupid. Next morning I'd made up a simple story which I told them. I said I'd gone up the dog track a few days earlier and had it off. I said I won about £200 and came down into town for a few drinks. I was stood minding my own business when a guy comes over and asked if I'd like to buy something nice for the wife. So I said yes and he showed me a watch but I wasn't very impressed. Well, come outside and I'll show you more. This I done and ended up giving £200 for the bagful. 'What's he look like?' 'Well,' I says, 'He's five-foot-eight, slim, dark hair and was wearing a light mac.' 'Oh, yeah, the man in the mac again.' 'That's him—you know him then?' Well, they charged me with burglary and handling for the £8,000 worth and burglary and handling for the other job and whipped me before the beak who bailed me out. A few weeks later I went up before the magistrates. It was peculiar as my solicitor was convinced I was going to Quarter Sessions with it. But then they dropped all the charges and brought in one of dishonest handling. The magistrates listened to the copper, then my geezer and retired. 'They'll send you up the steps, I'm afraid it's too serious for them.' Next thing the door opens, in they come, and give me six months' imprisonment, suspended for three years! 'Course I was well pleased!

I thought about it all and although I knew I was shopped never narrowed it down to which one actually done the business on me. So all I could really do was drop the pair of them although I wanted to revenge.

Whether or not it was Mickey who informed on him, Peter had learned a lesson about such tips from fellow thieves. They can be grossly inaccurate and can lead to dangerous arguments. The best ways of finding lucrative targets, he maintains, are through his own observation and by piecing together information which can be wormed out of 'straight' people. He had, for example, patiently coaxed a man who had idly speculated about how easy it would be to steal the wages from a local firm, but would never have considered actually becoming involved in such an enterprise.

One time I did get a really worthwhile piece of information. I can't say too much about him but a very genuine man (never been in trouble, upright member of society and as honest as the day is long) gave me a cracker. He knew I was basically a waster, drinking and gambling, but he saw no real harm in the drink as he loved a few scotches himself, and he always wanted me to get on. Well, one day he and I were both pissed up and he was on to me a bit about my ways. He said something about if I had to be the way I was then to do it once only and make it a good one. He said some cackle about one day he'd tell me something. Well at the time it didn't mean anything to me. However a few days later at work it all came back to me so I done a bit of thinking about what was said and he just laughed it off. 'Oh, I was drunk, you mustn't take any notice of me when I'm like that.' Well I suppose I'm a devious bastard so that weekend I made a point of going to his local and getting him on the scotch real early in the evening. Then I said was he coming down town? Off we went and had a good drink but me ensuring I never had too many to get paralytic. Well when they chucked us out I suggested a meal and a couple of bottles of wine and he was game as ever. Over the meal I slowly got into him. Well what was it he was going to tell me, and 'I was only curious', this and that until I got him talking. But still he was talking round it all the time. Anyway it appeared he had a pal who was a cashier for a very large concern and in idle chatter had let a few things drop that began to add up to a very big job.

Over several evenings, with reassurances and 'gentle persuasion', Peter gradually extracted enough information to discover where and when large amounts of money were kept on the premises overnight, and eventually acquired the reluctant co-operation of his informant in providing full details.

I suppose it was a fortnight before I knew all there was to know. But he made me promise that I would take a long study and he must not know when I was going to do it. I also had to promise him, would you believe, that I would not get caught!

Following the theft, which was successful although it did not net as much as he had been led to believe, Peter offered the man £200 for the information, but 'he wouldn't take a carrot, just didn't want it. Believe me, it took weeks for him to get over it.'

After his conviction for the jewel burglary, Peter once more took stock of his situation.

Regarding the whole matter as a near miss I stayed low for a while and knew I couldn't afford to make similar mistakes. I became a bit craftier again and continued my activities but took more care all the time.

He decided that house burglary was the 'safest bet', because he could 'size up most of the jobs for myself'. For another three years he worked mainly alone, concentrating on the homes of local business-men and on large houses in the surrounding countryside. However, as time went on he began to get over-confident again and to 'team up' with other local thieves in ill-considered crimes. The involvement of others seemed to encourage him to take bigger risks, and he was also let down on occasions by unreliable partners. He escaped from several risky situations through ingenuity, but, as a further incident shows, he was once again beginning to tempt fate too often to hope to remain free for very long. Having burgled a local factory at four in the morning, he and another man went to meet their driver at a pre-arranged point:

We waited for 45 minutes for matey to show. No joy. We wonder what's what. We get impatient and I send me mate off on foot to see if he can find him. About 30 minutes later he comes back. No sign. Well it's another wait and a discussion of what we do. If we go back as we both want we only have an hour or so before it's light. We're both covered head to toe in shit. 'Go get a car, any car, get us out of here mate.' Off he goes. Ten minutes later I could have died (I'm laid in a field). A taxi stops on the road, 20 feet from me. And out gets my mate, he comes over the fence and whispers, 'I've told him you're with a bird.' I nearly had a heart attack. 'You're joking.' 'No, it's the only thing I could think of.' What this taxi-driver must have thought I'll never know. I came out of this field, head to toe in mud, a donkey jacket, screw-driver in the pocket, woolly hat and turtles [gloves] on saying, 'Well goodnight Doreen, thanks for everything.' I got in the back and never said a word. Every time my mate spoke I just grunted. Anyway we re-routed him to a couple of miles from home and my mate made an excuse to get dropped at his auntie's 'where we'd spend the night'. Fuck did we run when he drove away. We knew our way and went by field to his place. Well we were boiling over about this other geezer and couldn't come up with any excuse for him. No way was he getting a penny piece. He told us that 'the clutch went' but we knew the only thing that went was his bottle [nerve].

Eventually the inevitable happened. For the first time in 12 years Peter was 'caught on the job'. The story has elements of farce in it. It provides a good example of how technically-skilled and resourceful criminals can become so over-confident in their own ability that they behave in a quite irrational fashion. As Peter put it: 'The trouble is, you come to think you'll never be caught. You're so clever and everybody else is stupid.' He described the occasion:

One evening a pal of mine came round and we were discussing what to have a pop at. We more or less went through the whole of town and came to think of the local post office. Now this geezer who ran the place can only be described as an ignorant pig. He can't keep staff because he's rude to them and makes his wife slave all day serving on the shop side while he puts his fat arse at rest in the post office side. Well, the plan was hatched at 12.30 a.m. Bruce and I were to brace and bit through the back door, once we'd made a hole big enough one man in and open up, then we'd go from there. So that's what we tried. But after one hole through the door taking about 10 minutes we realised we wouldn't get through in reasonable time. We also knew if we didn't get in now we'd blow it for the future. We were both pretty stupid and kept geeing one another up. My pal got on the roof and tried going through the slates but found it boarded underneath. I went up the drainpipe to try the upstairs window. Anyway we ended up taking two jemmies and taking the front door off. If you could see the place the shop was positioned I doubt you'd believe it could be possible without waking someone up. Still we did it, got in, hopped the counter and bandit screen and almost passed out at the size of the peter [safe]. It was huge. No way could we lift it, so we dismantled the bandit screen and demolished the counter. This enabled us to slide the peter over the tiled floor to the door. We now realised we couldn't get it in the car even if we were to take out the seats. So we left, propping up the front door, and went in search of some kind of transport. We found a two-wheeled barrow-type hand-truck and removed it from a do-it-yourself shop yard by lifting it over the fence. We pushed it to the shop and after almost breaking our backs got the safe on the truck. Why we wouldn't pass and admit defeat I don't know but we wouldn't. It was now getting light and the weight on the truck was so great it made loud squeaking noises as we went up the road. It was so bad people must have heard so I took two milk bottles off a step and chinked them together, 'Two pints at number 28 George', and began to act as milkey. Well we managed to get it to the park and then broke open a couple of sheds to find a axe, chopping away at the back and making a terrible din. Now this was the silliest yet. We got a hole in it and removed all that was inside—bundles of cash, PO stamps, savings stamps, the date stamper, everything. As we were beginning to bag up my mate discovered another compartment. 'We've got to put another hole in her.' 'No way' I said, 'We got plenty, let's go while the going's good.' But I let him talk me into it. I guess it took 10 minutes and that was our downfall. Someone had heard a noise and phoned the Old Bill thinking there were vandals in the park. They came 10-handed and actually captured us in the park. We both gave them a good run and me dipping for a bundle of fivers before legging it. I went one way, my pal the other. In fact my pal was given a good sticking for fuck-all other than refusing to name me. The three who caught me weren't interested about anyone else and were just chuffed to have made a capture. Well I think the most stupid thing I've ever heard was said that night, convincing me anyone with big enough feet and a pointed head to fit a helmet can become a copper. There is a three foot by two foot six safe weighing about six hundredweight, around it are books of stamps, Postal Orders, Premium Bonds, all scattered on the ground, along with bundles and bundles of cash, and this copper says to me, 'So you've just done the tennis club, have you?' They took me in and left me in the charge room, handcuffed in the charge of one bobby. In my hand I was still clutching what turned out to be £900. In fact I tried bribing this cop saying make sure my Mrs. gets half and keep the rest. But he would not bite. He said, 'Come off it, where would I put it?' 'On top of your head,' I said, 'with your helmet over it.' When the other came back and brought my mate in they crashed us away. Now the real annoying thing was when we learnt there was over £5,000 in cash and negotiable bonds in the compartment we opened first. And, in the one we stayed to open, only a watch and ring worth £300. Sick, I should cocoa!!

An unexpected bonus of the manner in which they were caught was that the court was persuaded not to regard them as serious criminals and they escaped with comparatively light sentences.

We were held a couple of days and given bail at magistrates. Of course we kept a pretty low profile for a few weeks. Both knowing it was a certainty for a jail sentence, we had a couple while we were waiting to go up, then got a job to go to court with. Our luck was in when we eventually came up, as we ended up in front of a Recorder. Both of our barristers made a big play on how amateurish it was and would a criminal really go about such a serious raid in such a slapdash way. Anyway, we didn't do badly. My mate copped for 18 months and I got a deuce [two years]. Seeing as we both thought about four or five years we weren't too upset. I went to an open prison and he a semi-open as he had violence on his record.

Now approaching the age of 30, Peter found even an open prison an unpleasant experience, and in one sense it proved a 'deterrent'. It convinced him that the risky and adventurous offences into which he had been periodically drawn would finally have to be put behind him. The alternatives as he saw them were either to give up burglary altogether or to find more lucrative targets that would enable him to burgle less often and thus reduce the risks of being caught.

Well I guess now I'd done plenty of thinking and assure you I hated every day of being in prison. I never wanted any more. No more dragging round the country for my Mrs. and kids. No more heart-aches for them, they didn't deserve it. But after a couple of months I realised I was going to be at it again. So I thought change your style and get smarter, why take chances? There's no profit sat in jail. If something looks bad or hard, then pass and find something less risky. The shopkeeper and businessman game was alright but I'd played most of them out, plus it was hit-and-miss. I could never

be sure of scoring. So often I'd have been out hours following and
waiting, just to draw a blank.

The 'breakthrough' finally came through a chance conversation:

I got talking with an acquaintance who was getting interested in
antiques. He thought it was definitely the game to be in. There's
plenty of scope and an awful lot of money to be earned, he told me.
I thought it over for a time, because I didn't want to break my jam
roll [parole], but in the end we made an agreement that he'd take
from me any antiques I could get hold of.

The first haul of antiques he stole was selected in haphazard fashion
from a house he and a friend came across when returning from a
roofing job in a village. Out of habitual curiosity they stopped to look
at an unusual, isolated building and, finding that it was unoccupied,
looked in through the windows.

'Here, look at all this old gear he's got in here.' My pal knew no
more than me, but we could see that what was in there was
valuable. It took us about 10 seconds to decide to break in. He
pulled the car round the side of the house. I put my socks on my
hands and with a steel comb slipped the window catch. 'You load it
up as I pass it,' I said and hopped in and began taking what I
thought looked nice; I didn't have a clue what was what really. I
passed him a clock, a couple of paintings, a card table and chair,
then I ran upstairs and had a search for jewellery, bringing down a
couple of boxes, one a writing box and a tom box. He began to
panic a bit now as he's loading up in full view of the road and a
couple of cars have passed. 'Come on, I can't get anything else in;
that'll do us.' 'Yeah. OK.'
Now at this stage we didn't even know where we were taking the
gear but headed towards home. On the way we spoke of where to
take it first and he came up with a pal's garage, so agreeing, we
took it there. Drove in, unloaded and left. I went and found the
guy who I'd spoke to earlier and he came to see it. Well, to my
amazement, he was quite happy with it and was making what
seemed good offers for it; however, my mate argued like mad,
saying he was taking the piss offering so low. Eventually we hit on
around £400 and all left happy. My mate later admits he knew
nothing and was just spoofing over the prices. We all met that night
to discuss further details and over a few jars of ale said we'd supply
more as long as he paid fair bread and that was the beginning of the
end.

Peter was quick to realise the difference that specialised knowledge
would make.

At first it was more or less bits and pieces. I'd dive into a place, cop
a few items and we'd do business, but all along I knew I was most
likely leaving the best stuff and, like a jackdaw, just taking what

shone. So I paid the library a visit and began a bit of homework. I invested in a few books of my own and a silver guide, a guide to pricing antiques in general and an eye-piece. Shortly I began to know what kind of bread I could expect for certain items and how much they were really worth.

Over the next few months, Peter and a partner who became his regular driver gradually developed a system of stealing antiques which reduced risks to the minimum and brought them high rewards from relatively few offences. The description he gave shows how much attention was paid to detail and also provides a good illustration of how experienced burglars are able to 'read signs' that houses are unoccupied, develop a sense of where and when it is safe to break in, and deflect suspicion on meeting people when 'casing' a house.

Now I was beginning to get pretty canny at sussing houses out, I could look at a place and say to myself, yes there'll be antiques in there. Day or night it made no difference. But all the time looking for houses to do. I had a few cars on hand available to borrow at short notice so was not using the same vehicle every day. If I spotted one that didn't go off, I returned in a different motor. It's only a matter of deduction but I got very keen at spotting houses where the occupants were out. There are many signs to look for, but the routine was something like this. My mate would pick me up and we'd head off a different direction every morning. Now we'd top up the tank and drive a few miles just watching the mirror to make sure we weren't being followed. Maybe we'd hit a by-pass or motorway where we'd put our feet down for a few miles, take a turn off round the roundabout and back where we came from. Or we'd go out to the downs and drive over them giving us a choice of routes and a clear view behind to ensure we weren't tailed. Once we were happy we were on our own (say an hour or so) we'd find a boozer and have a few pints and a roll and get off. Now we never hit a place within five miles of a stop, so we'd be off searching out villages. 'Lose me,' I'd say. 'I want you to find a village we've never heard of.' So we passed continually through the countryside, every time we hit a main road we'd take the next turn off and back into countryside.

Now the driver's job was just to drive and remember. If we needed he had to get us out of places quick, credit where it's due, my driver can drive too. The remembering is when I'd say to him, 'I want to come back here tonight,' or 'I want to be here next Friday at 10.00 in the morning.' I can't recall him letting me down on one occasion when I asked to go back. Maybe I'd noticed a woman coming home to a good-looking house and I'd deduced she'd been shopping. I spot her arriving home at 11.30 and guess it's probably a regular Friday morning shopping trip, therefore 'I want to be here at 10.00 next Friday morning'. On occasions I've been back and watched the occupant leave. And on various occasions seen the whole family going out for a day, dog and all, heaped into say a big Merc or an XJ6, that's nice. Maybe as we pass through a village I see a very likely prosperous target that I know I can't get at now, so I fancy a look at night, then it's, 'we got to be here just after dark'. On occasions like this we'd stay in the locality within 20 miles.

Remember, we would put 200 miles on the clock on an average day, sometimes even 300 miles. We was usually well stocked with gum, sweets and cigarettes so we had no call to stop, and if the need arose I'd prefer to drive to the next town rather than put my face up in a village shop. It's uncanny how they take interest in strangers, always nosing to see what type of car you're in.

Sometimes we'd head out early, say to Sunningdale–Windsor way when an event like Royal Ascot was on, spotting for people off to the races. So we're out, we know we're alright, had a pint and we're getting down to a serious bit of work. As we drive along I'm looking at the signposts, all the time leaving out places saying 'So-and-so village only' as it's nearly always a dead-end and also 'single-track road' as we don't want to get screwed up behind a bloody great tractor after hitting someone's Mickey Mouse [house], do we? So I may see a sign saying 'do-dah 1 mile, watsit 2 miles and thingy $3\frac{1}{2}$ miles.' Now that tells me for about four miles I'm going to see isolated houses so off we go. As I see a decent size place come into view (normally over £35,000), I say 'Slow' and he gets down to about 20 m.p.h. Sometimes it's instinct I suppose but other times the signs are there to see. Now the object of the exercise is to ascertain whether there is anyone in without knocking the door and, as you will appreciate, it's not easy. If you knock and someone answers it means driving on for several miles before you can strike. I'm now looking for anything to either say they are in, i.e. a car in the drive (usually in the day a woman's car, maybe a Fiat or Mini), a window open and washing on the line or I want to see signs that they are out. Milk, papers are the obvious but there are many others, open garage doors, no car and open gate, empty dustbins by the road, the position of the curtains on hot days, no open windows indicates no one in, the same as tools, i.e. a wheel-barrow or spade in the drive indicates a gardener is about. Also as I say, often you just know it's either OK or no go.

Assuming I believe it's empty my next move is stop directly in view of the house (the logic here being if anyone is in it's best to let them see a car rather than think who is it and how the hell did he get here), get out leaving my mate at the wheel where he's studying a map and walk up the drive. Maybe as I'm approaching the house I see a geezer in the garden; if he's not noticed me I'd wheel round and go, if he had seen me I'd carry on, put on a smile and approach him. Various excuses as the mood took me, nearest garage, looking for High Crest Farm, or directions to another village. One of my favourites was only suitable for very large mansion-type houses, 'Good-day, is this the Military Academy of Music?' The funny thing about that one is whenever I've used it I've always ended up with directions! 'Oh, you must mean the so-and-so school; now if you take the next left . . . ' Also funny is the larger the house and the more class the people have the less likely you are to get odd looks or questions.

Well, assuming I've got to the door and no answer, I holler 'hello' through the letter-box, give it a second and round the back, check the garden and look in the kitchen for dogs—if you do get a dog he's usually in one room, shut in. From the back I now look in to see what they have on offer, usually one glance will tell if I'm going to earn or not, the furniture will tell you plenty. Right, so I see a carriage or mantel clock, look down and see a Persian rug, I know that's between £200 upwards to maybe a monkey [£500], according to how good they actually are. Seeing that is enough to go to work. I go back to the car making a mental note of the size of the house and how long I'm likely to be. 'OK, gloves. Better give me 15, come in the same way.' Then I'm away to do the business.

My mate now takes the car at say 30 miles an hour and drives for seven and a half minutes, turns and drives back, giving me 15 minutes. He knows when he comes back to the house that I will either show myself and get picked up, or if I'm not to be seen either I need longer, which means five minutes only and he's to be back again. Or thirdly something has gone wrong: that's why I've told him which way to come for me as that's the direction I'll be travelling like a long dog. Fortunately, the latter only happened once.

He's away, then I walk straight back to the rear of the house, pop a window and in. Just looking, I go straight from room to room and into the kitchen where I open the fridge. A glance tells me plenty: whether there are several people living there or just one or two, but I'm really hoping to find it's empty which would mean they are away or, on odd occasions, everything covered in mould when they've gone away forgetting the fridge. Next I go to the front door hoping to find letters or papers; if there are some there I check the dates. This is to see how long since anyone's been and whether, if there's plenty there, I can come back after dark. Then its upstairs as fast as I can move, find the master bedroom, check the time and head for the dressing-table where its almost certain the jewellery will be. If I find a tom box I have a quick look, it's nice to know what class of money I'm dealing with. Sometimes I find they just toss their tom in a drawer. Either way, with or without finding anything, I take a pillow case from the bed, a very quick look in cupboards and drawers and leave the room; the only time I bother with other bedrooms is when I know I have more time or I've found good tom in what I assume is the wife and mother's room and I look to see if an elder daughter, who may also have a good tom, lives there.

I now head down, quick look out down the drive,—OK—and begin bagging all and sundry that appeals to me. Occasionally getting greedy, humping one bagful and then popping back for barometers, swords or other bigger but manageable pieces. I leave by the easiest route and get myself down the drive where I can see my pal returning, finding a blind spot to put the stuff I have. I let him pull in beside me, open the door, he watches the road, I load up, hop in and 'Goodnight nurse, thank you very much.' Now obviously most breaks are pretty similar as it's in and out, swagging what I can in the time I allow myself, but sometimes things are different.

For example if I see before I enter that the place is loaded with good pieces I'll pass and re-visit until I catch them away for a day or two, or if it's a large enough house and I see no trace of a dog, i.e. water bowl, chewed up ball on the lawn, scratches on the door, I may decide to come back and do it at night with them in bed when I can take my time and clean up. A good sign once inside a house is to find interior doors locked, usually this means they are away but I would empty the room I entered, in case I was wrong and missed out, coming back later to find people in.

Once we've got gear in the motor we always follow the same procedure. Leave the scene as quietly as possible, no dramatic wheelies or mad rushing. Just a natural 30-mile-an-hour cruise out of the villages. It's not always possible but I now like to cross a major road as soon as I can. This may mean driving from the scene three or four miles back to the last major road, a mile or so up this till we find another B road on the opposite side from where we came; from now on I'm looking for a spot to clean up. As he's driving I have a quick look at what I've copped for and usually estimate how much it will fetch. The tom especially fascinates me, I do like a nice diamond or a decent lump of gold. I wrap the tom separate and put it with the other gear bagged ready to put out. As soon as I spot a copse, a field of corn or any half decent spot we wait for a clear road and out I dive and stash it. If a car comes along as I'm stashing or returning to the motor I fiddle with my zip like I've just been for a gypsy's kiss. We drive off now in the direction we're heading and note the next signpost. Another mile or so we stop and check nothing got dropped in the car. Gloves in the glove compartment and we begin looking for another. We've had three in a day and another at night but a safe bet would be to say we'd average one every two days.

Now the reasons for placing the swag rather than taking it straight away. Well I think the main one stems from one night when I got stopped eight years ago on a routine check with a van full of stolen gear. On that occasion I was dead lucky, the copper let us go only to realise five minutes later what he'd done; when he came behind us I jumped out and shot off. I was later arrested, in the meantime my two mates had admitted the burglary. I denied it and three months later in Crown Court was found not guilty. Ever since I dread travelling with stolen gear but of course it is necessary in my line of work or should I say chosen profession. But to my way of thinking should that burglary I've just done be discovered soon, I could well be stopped by some dozy copper getting ambitious and he's got a nice capture for nothing. On the other hand if I hide it and clean up and I'm stopped, there's no evidence to suggest anything. Plus I know where it is, they haven't a clue, so I can pick it up at leisure. However it was usually picked up about mid-day the next day (after pre-arranging a meet with the buyer). The reason mid-day was to allow the filth plenty of time to go in and play at detectives and splash their powder about looking for fingerprints. Also when picking up we now come in from the opposite direction, pick up, turn round and even if it means a few miles extra never have to go within 10 miles of the break. And apart from all this I had a terrific person who would often pick up for me and was less likely to get stopped than a vicar.

While developing this 'system', the burglars were still in a very subordinate position in relation to the receiver, Sam. Peter became increasingly aware that while they were taking most of the risks, he was paying them only a fraction of the value of the antiques. The next stage of his development was a deliberate manoeuvre to 'cut out the middleman' and deal directly with a bigger buyer. The cunning way in which he did so shows not only his skill in manipulating people but also the value of old 'contacts' he had made many years before in London. He first ceased trading with Sam and then used a new local 'fence' as a means of locating the type of receiver he wanted.

Well, as I said at first I was quite happy with prices I was having to take, that is until I realised what some of it was worth. Plus the geezer made a few mistakes by bragging. 'You know that repeating carriage you had from Lambourn? I got £430 quid for that.' Well obviously he thought he had me by the balls as he was the only bloke I knew who would buy bent antiques, but his mistake came when he tried to tuck me up over some coins. One night I done a gaff and had a load of coins, so when he sees them and has a look he says 'How much?' After a bit of haggling we stick at £700. 'Take this for now,' giving me £300. 'I'll pick you up on Monday and we'll go to the bank and I'll give you the rest.' Monday comes, up turns matey with his excuse. 'Look' he says, 'I made a bloomer, it's not difficult in this game; I overpriced them but I can't afford to pay the other £400 as I'd be chucking my money away. However to show no ill will, will you forget the £300 I've given you and you have the coins back.' All I can do is agree but of course when I go through them I see that they have been very cleverly sorted out and the cream ones are gone and I've got all the less valuable. Then, as if to rub it in, a day or two later a mate is chatting away to me and comes out with, 'Oh, I went down to London with Sam yesterday. He took me to Spinks' to value all his coin collection. Do you know he has some there worth hundreds?' Exit one buyer.

A week or so later I was talking to a vague acquaintance in a boozer who had a crummy shop which he had the nerve to call an antique shop. In fact it contained mostly junk, bits of bric-à-brac and a few cheap pieces of Victorian and Edwardian jewellery. The whole contents of the shop would easily go in the back of a mini-van. This guy also worked, he had to as the shop made peanuts and he left his wife to attend it. Anyway this night we were just chatting about things in general but as always matey keeps whining on about his mortgage and the price of things; his car had just failed its

MOT. You know the sort, a real pain in the arse. Well I thought I'd put him to the test and began a few subtle questions regarding his buying habits. He twigged what I was going on about and said we should go back to his place to chat later. So a few pints later we walked down to his place where I asked was he interested in some coins. After the obvious chatter regarding how bent they were, he agreed he was very interested as he knew a guy who was really into the things. So I laid them on him a bit cautiously, a few at a time and he moved them. This proved OK and all were happy. As it happened it was he who asked if I was able to get more stuff, mainly decent silver, clocks and jewellery. I agreed I was able to but queried his ability to pay for such items. 'Look', he says, I know a bloke who is a big dealer but he also likes a bit on the cheap; he's as good as gold and I trust him implicitly. I'll have to do all the business as I know him well and know he wouldn't meet anyone else, but you know you can trust me and I'll work on a commission.' I agreed to give it a bash but knew full well this weasel intended to have me over when and wherever possible. So I began doing business by doing a drum, informing him so he could tune his geezer, then I'd deliver the goods the following day and get paid a couple of hours later.

Now as I said I knew he was out to rip me off and it was hard to avoid. It should have been a matter of trust and he having his agreed 15 per cent but what the creep was doing was selling my goods for say £550, he'd then pay me £475 and I'd have to pay his commission of say £65–£70. In my mind I knew exactly what was what and he was getting fat off me but my hands were more or less tied; I either went through him or had to find another fence. The other obvious thing to do was find out who his buyer was and stab the creep in the back by approaching whoever it was with a proposition. Either he bought from me or got nothing. To make things even worse and very annoying, creep was now beginning to get even greedier. I do a drop at 11.00 at his place, maybe leaving a suitcase of silver and an amount of tom. Creep, while awaiting his guy, at say 11.30, went through it all. The smaller pieces of jewellery which were pretty common or nondescript he filtered. Yes, what a liberty, he was actually stealing from me, the hand that fed him. Well, it's no joke I assure you. As I've said previously I've a fair eye for a piece of jewellery and remember most pieces again. As time went on and the business increased I noticed his show case becoming more and more healthy-looking with bent pieces that I'd supplied. So he was in fact now ripping me off, getting his commission plus he would collar, for example, a silver propelling pencil, an eternity ring, a couple of gold charms off a bracelet and say a pair of earrings which he'd eventually knock out at top money earning say another £100. And every deal would be similar.

Now I've pulled him ain't I? 'What's your game here then?' I gives it, looking into his cabinet, 'That, that and that came from Henley, that, that and that from Cheltenham and that from Aylesbury.' He only denied it, looking me bang in the face and tells me it was a few pieces he bought at a fair. 'There's no point in lying to me I recognise those pieces, but what's more so could the owners. If ever anything goes wrong and the filth bounce you they'll plant three breaks on you in this display alone. What else have you got here?' Still he denied it so I just says, 'Right, get rid of it all.' The next drop I gave him was sorted out, all big lumps, swords, tea sets, tray, Victorian writing box, nothing he could score from. I dropped it, drove away, went round town, came back and hid up the road. Waited a bit and watched a car pull up and a bloke enter the house. I then copped the make and number of the jam jar but was unable to hang about to see the guy as I didn't want creep to see me.

A few days later I'm going by and see the same motor in the car park just down the road. Right, I thought, front it out and just happen to pay a social call. I knocked on creep's door and as he opened it I just stepped past him into the shop and walked through to the kitchen, up the stairs, out in the garden, all over the house. He comes in behind me, 'Oh, we were having a little party' he said. 'That's nice' I replied, 'I'll have a noggin of gin.' He was knacked, he just had to pour me a drink and say 'This is a friend of mine, Peter.' Now I more or less knew the guy I wanted was here somewhere but didn't know which one of about 20 or more but there was one chap I did recognise. I'd known him roughly nine or 10 years previously when I used to frequent a casino which he helped run. When he saw me he asked how I was and this and that and I returned similar chatter. 'What are you doing now Jim?' I asked. 'Antiques.' Bingo, I'd nailed him at last. Well I said nothing and creep didn't realise I'd caught on; I had a few drinks on the house and left.

Next morning I was ferreting through the 'phone book, got the number and rang this guy Jim. The conversation was easy, 'Hi, this is Peter, remember I met you at creep's yesterday.' 'Oh yeah, what can I do for you?' 'Well, I'd like to meet you for a drink and a chat.' 'OK, are you in town today? Do you know the Red Lion?' 'Yes, see you there 11.30.' 'Fine.' I arrived first: when he appeared I bought his drink and we sat in the corner. He had already put two and two together so it was easy to guess he was going to agree to cut creep out and deal direct. It didn't necessarily mean he was going to have to pay more for stuff, it was just to ensure I was getting a better deal. Plus, and most important, a safer one as we would now make various different arrangements and the stuff was never going near my own town. The other thing we did agree on which we felt was significant was for me to let creep have the odd piece, say a clock or a small quantity of silver. So as he doesn't get a notion he's played out; its best not to have too many enemies in this game.

This cutting out of the 'middleman' represented the final stage in Peter's development as a professional criminal. The combination of the skills he had previously acquired with the reliability and large-scale operation of the dealer, Jim, meant that there was virtually no limit to the amount of antiques and other valuables that he could 'turn over'. Very few other people knew about the arrangement and although the high stakes that Peter gambled with attracted police attention, it was many months before he was positively associated with country-house burglaries. Meanwhile the general increase in such offences during this period led to more urgent investigations by the Regional Crime Squad and other specialised police teams. Even after he was marked as a 'target' criminal, it took a squad almost another six months to trap him with intensive surveillance. When he was arrested they had gathered ample evidence to convict him and his associates, including Jim. Seeing that he had no chance of escape, he admitted as many offences as he could remember and helped the police to recover several thousand pounds worth of property. Even so, he received a very long prison sentence.

What happened at this point illustrates the essential precariousness of the position of even the most 'professional' burglar. He had gambled away most of the proceeds of his crime and after he was imprisoned his wife was faced with considerable financial hardship. He also realised that he would be a prime target of the police when he was eventually released from prison and would not be able to achieve the same level of comparatively safe stealing again. For this reason he felt that his career as a house burglar was to all intents and purposes over, and was therefore prepared to talk about his past without any fear of jeopardising his future. What he will do when he is released is a matter for speculation, but he hopes that if he can give up gambling he can make a reasonable living from working normally. This may be over-optimistic, but he has the advantages of intelligence, a skilled trade and the support of a wife and family. As he says himself, he was a successful burglar and if given the opportunity could be successful in other fields.

V. The Victims

This chapter concentrates on the effects of burglary upon victims. The findings are based on the 322 interviews carried out over one-year periods in Banbury, Gerrards Cross and Reading. Although the interviewees can be taken as representative of victims reporting burglaries in each of these areas,[1] they are not necessarily representative of burglary victims as a whole. For example, the exceptionally high proportion of middle-class residents in Gerrards Cross means that working-class victims are under-represented among the full 322 cases. When discussing victims as a group it is therefore often necessary to control for factors such as class, age and sex.

Considerable attention has been paid in recent years to the problems of victims of violent crime (cf. McDonald 1976, Bryant and Cirel 1977, Halpern 1978, Miers 1978) but little systematic research has been carried out into the effects of burglary. Waller and Okihiro (1978:36-9) included some questions on the subject in their questionnaire to 116 victims of burglary in Toronto. Although providing only a brief outline, the answers showed that the majority of victims were angry, afraid or emotionally upset upon discovering the crime and that over 40 per cent of female victims were afraid to be alone in the house for some weeks or months afterwards. Reppetto (1974:62) found that people who had already been victimised were more worried about the possibility of being burgled than those who had not. He claims that as many as 73 per cent of the former expressed 'considerable fear' of the offence being repeated. Unfortunately, the wording used in the question ('How worried are you about your home being broken into?') was somewhat ambiguous, and it is not clear whether they were expressing genuine fear or simply concern that it might happen again.

In England there appear to be no data specifically on burglary victims, but there are a few indications of the effects of crime in general. Durant, Thomas and Willcock (1972) reported that about two-thirds of respondents who had come into contact with crime had been upset by the incident, and more specifically that 28 per cent named 'shock' as the worst element. In 1975, the Bristol Victims Support Scheme (the voluntary group which pioneered the practice of visiting victims of crime in order to offer help and support) presented a short analysis of the 315 cases they had dealt with during the first six months of operation. Ninety-seven per cent of these involved theft or burglary. They reported that seven per cent of victims had suffered a 'severe and long-lasting impact, affecting their lifestyle', and that 'approximately a third of all victims were upset to a degree which called for some help in restoring normal coping ability' (BVSS 1975:2). The most vulnerable groups were found to be females, the aged, and people living alone. Other victim support schemes later carried out their own small studies with similar results (for example, Raynor 1977). Most recently, Haward (1981) found that as many as 70 per cent of victims of a variety of offences had been 'very distressed' by the experience.

In order to provide a more detailed account of people's reactions to burglary we asked our interviewees, most of whom were seen between four and ten weeks after the event, to recall their initial feelings and the effect upon their lives during the intervening period.

Initial impact
In the majority of cases, the burglar had disappeared long before the victim either returned home or came downstairs the next morning to discover what had happened. Seventy-eight per cent had been out when the burglary took place, 16 per cent had been asleep in bed, and the remainder had been present and awake. About 80 per cent realised fairly quickly that a burglary had occurred, usually by noticing a broken or open window or an open door, but the rest did not at first notice anything amiss or thought they had mislaid the stolen articles such as purses or radios. In the latter case it often took a combination of events for the burglary to come to light. Two or more people may have compared apparently unrelated experiences, or a series of small incidents may have suddenly 'fallen into place' in the victim's mind. For example, in one case (No. 151) a woman noticed a window open on a Wednesday afternoon, but thought no more about it. On Friday she could not find £10 she had put aside to pay a bill, and that evening her husband 'was ferreting around asking, ''Where's my lighter?'' '. At that moment she suddenly realised that they had been burgled and became extremely upset. She was unable to sleep properly for the next week and kept worrying about what else might have been missing without her having noticed.

Even among the majority who noticed immediately that something was wrong, a considerable number took 10 seconds or more to associate the signs they saw with the word 'burglary'. It seems that their first instinct was to find a more 'normal' explanation for the evidence before them. For example:

No. 37:   I saw everything on the floor and I thought my boys had been having a party. I was halfway up the stairs to tell them off before I did a sort of double-take.

No.100:   I looked over where the television should be and it wasn't there. It's funny, it didn't click at all, even then. It was only when I noticed the gloves that the truth began to dawn. It was a horrible sinking feeling in my stomach.

One victim likened the feeling to being involved in a road accident, with an initial refusal to believe what had happened, and a 'sense of unreality', followed about a minute later by 'sheer panic' when the truth became clear.

All victims were asked to describe in their own words their first reaction once they realised what had happened. The answers were fairly easily classifiable into six categories (see Table 8).

Table 8   *What was your first reaction on discovering the burglary?*

Reaction	Male %	Female %	All %
Anger/annoyance	41	19	30
Shock	9	29	19
Upset/tears/confusion	13	20	17
Surprise/disbelief	11	6	9
Fear	4	13	9
No strong reaction	21	13	17
Total	100 (N = 163)	100 (N = 159)	100 (N = 322)

While almost 50 per cent of female victims reported shock or some form of emotional distress, the most common initial reaction by men was one of anger. There was also a class difference: working-class respondents reported shock and distress more frequently than did middle-class interviewees (see Appendix 1, Table A13). Surprisingly, the age of the respondent did not emerge as a significant factor, although people over 60 reacted with shock slightly more often than did younger victims. The results in Table 8 can be compared with those of Waller and Okihiro (1978:37), who asked Canadian victims a similar question. They found 'surprise' (33 per cent) to be the chief first reaction, followed by 'upset' (25 per cent), anger (20 per cent) and fear (20 per cent). Unfortunately, the Canadian authors did not isolate cases of shock, which we found to be one of the most serious (as well as relatively common) immediate effects. However, assuming that these are categorised under 'surprise' or 'upset', the results are broadly similar: the only clear differences are that 'very few' of the Canadian victims 'remained calm' (compared with 17 per cent of our sample) and that a much higher proportion of the Canadians reported feeling frightened.

Of course, all the above categories can include anything from mild to severe reactions. In our study, those who experienced shock ranged from a women who 'felt the need for a glass of brandy' to one who 'shook and shook for several days'. 'Anger' ranged from indignation to blind fury, and 'upset' from mild depression to hysteria. Measurement of the intensity of reactions was difficult, as some victims were inclined to use exaggerated language (for example 'petrified', 'flabbergasted', 'fuming') to describe their feelings, while others played them down in retrospect. Nevertheless, the researchers' subjective assessment was that at least 20 (six per cent) of the 322 victims interviewed had suffered acute distress shortly after discovering the crime. Their reactions included severe shock, trembling, panic and uncontrolled weeping. The following are examples of such cases reported in the victims' own words:

> No. 536:   I went to pieces. I just couldn't believe it. I cried so much I couldn't 'phone the police. I was so frightened. I cried every time someone talked to me.
> No. 825:   It was the worst shock of my life. The doctor had to give me an injection. I couldn't speak a word.
> No. 1010:   I was hysterical. I ran screaming to my neighbour and hammered on her door. Then I went icy cold and shivered for hours.

One woman said she had been found by neighbours 'standing dumbstruck in the middle of the street', and two others reported being physically sick.

The extent of the emotional impact appeared to vary considerably between different social groups. Of the above 20 victims 18 were female, 11 were working-class and eight were pensioners: all three groups were significantly over-represented. It was also notable that 12 were widowed, separated or divorced, although only 18 per cent of the total sample fell into this category—a point that will be discussed later.

In addition to the 20 suffering acute distress, for a further 63 victims (19 per cent of the total) the initial impact appeared to have been considerable. Female victims were again over-represented among them (although not to such a significant degree), but there was little difference by age or class. A brief selection of cases from this second category is given to illustrate the kinds of feeling experienced.

No. 142:   I was shaken to the core. The idea of someone in my house—somehow I felt violated.

No. 144:   Everything was unreal. I was in a dream. There was just this feeling that someone had been walking about in my house.

No. 650:   I was really frightened—I was trembling. I thought they could have come upstairs. It never hits you till it happens to you.

No. 762:   It was the most terrible feeling to think that someone's been in your house. I nearly made myself sick with shaking.

No. 861:   I was very shocked at first. It's a feeling that you don't own your own house.

No. 920:   When I saw the window I practically heaved up. I didn't know what to do.

No.1597:   I turned to jelly for half an hour. I was very shocked and tearful and had to have a few drinks.

No.1717:   I got the spooks. I went round looking in all the cupboards and under the beds to convince myself they weren't still in the house.

No.1779:   I am used to crime [a barrister] but it was still a bad shock, much worse than I thought it would be. I felt so unsafe.

Lasting effects

We have seen that at least one-quarter of victims experienced some very unpleasant moments after discovering that they had been burgled. It is perhaps a matter for more concern that, four to ten weeks after the event, 65 per cent of victims interviewed said it was still having some effect upon their lives. The most common persisting effects were a general feeling of unease or insecurity and a tendency to keep thinking about the burglary.

Once the initial shock had worn off, most victims began to speculate about who had committed the offence. As only about 30 per cent of burglaries are cleared up by the police, the majority never find the answer to the riddle and the imagination can run riot. While some continued to envisage a frightening stranger (typically employing terms such as 'rough', 'scruffy' or 'unemployed' when asked to describe their mental picture of him), on reflection more than half came to suspect that the burglar was 'somebody local' who knew them, or was familiar with their habits.[2] On the whole, the latter conclusion was more likely to prolong the worry caused by the incident. Victims tended to re-interpret small events in the past—arguments with neighbours, visits to the house, prying questions, etc.—as connected with the burglary. For example, one woman stated that she now 'suspected everybody' of being the culprit. She was convinced that 'he knew his way around', as he had chosen one of the few times she was not in the house to commit the offence, and had easily found some cash she had thought well-hidden. She said she was 'racking her brains' as to who could have done it. 'You have this awful suspicion about everybody who comes near your house: the milkman, the kids, even people you have known for years.'

In at least three cases such feelings had developed into a state approaching paranoia, where the victims were convinced that somebody—they did not know who—held a grudge against them and was 'watching' them. Even in less serious cases people were inclined to search for reasons why *their* house had been chosen among all the possible targets in the area. This tendency (which might be dubbed the 'Why me?' syndrome) seems to have been responsible for a great deal of the anxiety produced by burglaries.

Another common consequence linked with the suspicion of acquaintances—one which was named by seven per cent of victims as the worst effect of the burglary—was a general sense of disillusionment with humanity. An example is provided by the case of a 40-year-old man, (No. 29) living alone, who lost a week's wages from his jacket. He said that prior to the burglary he regularly invited workmates back for meals and social evenings, and had people to stay overnight. He had always trusted people and welcomed them into his house. When he returned one evening to find his back window broken and the money taken he described his initial reaction as intense anger followed by a 'complete loss of faith in people'. As he guessed, the offender was a previous visitor to the house, but even after the arrest, the victim's attitude to other people remained radically altered. As he put it, he had changed from an 'open' to a 'closed' person, and was now reluctant to have anybody in his house.

Fifteen per cent of victims stated that they were still frightened at times as a result of the burglary. This normally took the form of fear when entering the house, or certain rooms in the house, or of being alone in their homes during the hours of darkness. Many of these thought that now that the burglar knew the 'layout' of the property he might return to steal what he had not taken originally. (In fact, only 11 of the 322 interviewed were burgled more than once during the period of study and most of these cases involved child offenders). The main physical consequences of such fear were difficulty in sleeping (eight per cent mentioned this), and the use of tranquillisers or other drugs not previously taken (three per cent). In all, six per cent said that their physical health had suffered as a result of the incident.

One of the most disturbing long-term psychological effects was experienced almost exclusively by women. About 12 per cent of all females interviewed used words such as 'pollution', 'violation' or 'a presence in the house'. Many made an explicit analogy with a sexual assault, expressing revulsion at the idea of a 'dirty' stranger touching their private possessions, and had felt impelled to 'clean the house from top to bottom'. Such feelings tended to persist for several weeks, and were so troubling in two cases that the victims had decided to move house to escape them. Five others had burnt furniture or clothing touched by the burglar. The following examples show the intensity of feeling that could be aroused:

> No. 539:   I shall never forget it because my privacy has been invaded. I have worked hard all my life and had my nose to the grindstone ever since and this happens. Now we can't live in peace. I have a feeling of 'mental rape'. I feel a dislocation and disruption of private concerns. I have destroyed everything they touched. I feel so extreme about it.
>
> No. 629:   I'll never get over the thought that a stranger has been in here while we were in bed . . . the idea that a stranger, who could be one of those horrible revolting creatures, has been mauling my things about.
>
> No. 976:   They had gone through all my clothes. I felt a real repulsion—everything felt dirty. I wanted to move—I had night-mares, and it still comes back even now.
>
> No. 1010:   It's the next worst thing to being bereaved; it's like being raped.

A final common effect upon victims was to change what can be called their 'security behaviour'. Forty-three per cent of those who had not been insured had taken steps to take out a policy, and 42 per cent of those who had been under-insured had increased their cover. Fifty per cent had improved the physical security of their homes by fitting new locks or bolts or an alarm. Eighty per cent of those who admitted they had been careless about locking doors or shutting windows prior to the burglary said that they had become more 'security-conscious' as a result (although some were already begin-ning to lapse). A small minority went to desperate extremes, nailing up windows, putting furniture against doors, or sleeping with make-shift weapons beside the bed. With the exception of insurance, the above activities were recognised by many victims as having as much a psychological as a practical purpose. The view was often expressed that it is impossible to create a 'thief-proof' house, but that, neverthe-less, to know there are solid locks on the doors greatly increases one's peace of mind. The very act of making it more difficult to get in also seems to have helped some victims to regain a lost sense of control over events. As one man put it, 'I felt I was fighting back.' Others simply said they 'felt better afterwards'.

In addition to describing their reactions, victims were asked what, in retrospect, had been the worst thing about the whole event. The question was put twice during the interview. On the second occasion they were asked to choose one or more possibilities from a prepared list. Table 9 shows the results of this second exercise.

Table 9   *What was the worst thing about the burglary?*

	Selected as worst %	Selected as second worst %	Total % (i.e. mentioned as either first or second choice)
Intrusion on privacy	41	22	63
Emotional upset	19	25	44
Loss of property	25	20	45
Disarrangement of property	4	4	8
Damage to property	3	2	5
None of these	7	27	—
Total	100 (N = 322)	100 (N = 322)	—

Sixty per cent selected either intrusion on their privacy or general emotional upset as the worst element. Of course, the small proportions who chose damage or disarrangement of property were to some extent produced by the comparatively few cases in which there was any serious damage or ransacking. However, even allowing for this, victims were much more likely to select an emotional element as the worst: only 16 per cent of those who had to pay over £15 to repair damage chose damage as the worst thing, and 14 per cent of those whose property was significantly disturbed selected disarrangement as the worst. Above all, a great many victims answered the question unprompted with almost identical words: 'The thought that someone has been in my house.' Almost 22 per cent used this phrase or a close equivalent. Even those who said that the loss had been the worst thing were often concerned about 'sentimental' rather than monetary value.

These findings underline the point that the emotional impact of burglary is more important to victims than financial loss. While there has been some discussion (Marcus *et al.* 1975, Miers 1978) of extending the use of compensation orders for property crime, our study suggests that, where burglary is concerned, the first priority in improving the lot of victims is to find ways of alleviating psychological damage.

Differential vulnerability

It has already been pointed out that certain categories of victim (female, pensioner, separated or divorced, etc.) appear to suffer disproportionately heavy initial effects. To test relative susceptibility to longer-term effects a panel of volunteers was asked to assess each case. Ten people from a variety of backgrounds were given a copy of each victim's account of the effects that the burglary had upon his or her life up to the time of interview. They were instructed to rate each one in terms of the overall impact the burglary had produced, using a scale from 1 (severe) to 5 (little or none). The answers were averaged, cases with an average of 1.5 or below being labelled 'serious effects', those with an average between 1.5 and 2.5, 'fairly serious', and so on.

The groups emerged as shown in Table 10.

Table 10   Rated seriousness of lasting effects

		Number	Percentage
Serious	(1 to 1.5)	43	13
Fairly serious	(1.5 to 2.5)	71	22
Moderate	(2.5 to 3.5)	100	31
Slight or nil	(3.5 to 5)	108	34
Total		322	100

This exercise confirmed that, as with the initial reaction on discovering a burglary, serious lasting effects are largely confined to female victims. Although almost equal numbers of males and females were interviewed, 34 of the 43 deemed to be worst affected were women. For this reason the remainder of the analysis is concentrated upon female respondents only, noting any significant differences between the characteristics of those women who were badly affected, and those who were not.

Table 11   Effects on female victims by marital status

		Married	Single	Separated or divorced	Widowed	Total
Number of cases with	serious effects	8	5	10	11	34
	less serious effects	67	30	15	13	125
Total		75	35	25	24	159

$(x^2 = 19.8$ with 3df p$\rangle .001)$

The most surprising finding was that no less than 21 (62 per cent) of the 34 worst affected were separated, widowed or divorced, although only 49 (31 per cent) of the total female population interviewed fell into this category (see Table 11).

Other variables of victim characteristics had very little independent effect. For example, female pensioners were more seriously affected than women under 60, but much of this difference could be explained by the presence of 18 widows among the 35 pensioners. (Only four of the remaining 17 suffered badly, compared with eight of the 18 widows. Male pensioners, too, were almost as resilient as younger male victims.) Working-class women were marginally worse affected than middle-class women, and women living alone worse affected than those living with others, but both these groups contained a higher proportion of widows and divorcees. When the figures were controlled for marital status, the differences all but disappeared. (Overall, the category of women emerging as most seriously affected was working-class widows over 60, but once classifications are subdivided, the numbers become too small to allow full confidence in the results: see Appendix 1, Table A12).[3]

Finally, it might be expected that, independent of the characteristics of the victim, the nature of the offence would make a considerable difference to its psychological impact: for example, that night-time burglaries would create more fear than daylight offences; offences where the victim was present more than those where the house was unoccupied; 'break-ins' more than 'walk-ins', and so on. However, none of these factors appeared to have any significant effect. Nor, indeed, did the type or value of the property stolen: people who lost nothing at all were as likely to be badly affected as those losing hundreds of pounds. The one exception was in the case of ransacking: eight of the total of 18 women interviewed whose property had been seriously damaged or disarranged were among those most seriously affected (Appendix 1, Table A14).

Explanations and implications

There is little doubt on the evidence presented here that a burglary is a significant event in the lives of a considerable proportion of victims. Almost all those interviewed had a clear memory of their reactions on discovering that their house had been entered. As many as 25 per cent (and 40 per cent of all female victims) were fairly seriously shocked or distressed at the time, and more than a month after the event only one-third of all victims said that they had fully recovered from the experience. Fifteen per cent were still in some fear, about one in eight women felt 'contaminated' or 'violated', and others reported worry, difficulty in sleeping, reluctance to leave the house unoccupied, and a distrustful and suspicious attitude towards strangers. Above all, the impression was of people struggling to recapture a lost sense of security.

The irony is that the event triggering off such responses was often objectively a fairly minor incident. Most of the victims quoted had lost relatively little and their houses had not been ransacked; more often than not it was daylight when they discovered the offence and there was no sign of the offender. Many even suspected local teenagers of whom they would not be physically afraid in a confrontation. Before any remedies for the problem can be suggested, it is important to attempt to understand its causes. There seem to be at least three possible explanations, which although not fully satisfactory, at least provide some illumination in a proportion of cases.

The first is that those who react badly are often people who are already experiencing a high degree of insecurity in their lives, and that *any* unexpected unpleasant experience might cause a similar reaction. This idea cannot be properly tested on our evidence, but might be supported by the preponderance of widows and separated and divorced women among those who suffered the worst initial impact. On the other hand, there were also a considerable number of victims to whom the above description clearly did not apply, and yet who described strong symptoms of shock: Haward (1981) has made the point that those he treated for psychiatric complaints following victimisation 'were no more vulnerable to psychiatric breakdown than any other random sample of the population'. Finally, the Bristol Victims Support Scheme data (see p. 175 n.3) shows that victims of burglary are much more likely to require support than those of other types of property crime: 13 per cent of the burglary victims were categorised as suffering severe effects, compared with the overall figure of seven per cent.

A second possibility is that the intensity of feeling aroused is related to the importance people instinctively attach to private territory—a concept explored some time ago by psychologists such as Lorenz (1966). This is supported by the frequent mention of 'violation', and disgust at 'the idea of someone in my house', and by the fact that the intrusion itself is often considered more disturbing than the actual loss or damage. However, there is no evidence to suggest that the greater the degree of emotional investment in a home, the greater the distress when it is burgled; nor that those who spend a great deal of their time in a house are worse affected than those who are often away from it (for example, housewives compared with women in employment). Although we found two specific categories of people with short-term homes—students in 'digs' and servicemen renting houses while stationed at a base—who were almost all unaffected by their burglaries, the numbers were too small for general conclusions and anyway special cultural factors may explain these specific reactions. Moreover, it transpired in some cases that owner-occupiers, who might be thought to have more emotional attachment to their property than those who rent, were less seriously affected than both tenants of private landlords and council tenants. Waller and Okihiro (1978:37) found no relationship between length of residence and severity of reaction; nor did reaction appear to depend on whether or not people had put extra effort into major alterations or decoration in their home.

The third explanation is concerned with the public image of burglary. For many people the word conjures up pictures of masked intruders, ransacked rooms and shadowy figures entering bedrooms while people sleep. These are all images perpetuated in fiction and in sensational media accounts of burglaries, but they are far from the reality of the vast majority of actual offences committed. Even without such influences, one has only to think back to childhood fears of 'noises in the night' to understand why burglary comes high on the list of crimes which cause most apprehension. It thus seems plausible to interpret the initial symptoms of shock so frequently mentioned (such as shivering, pallor, nausea) as a result of the combination of the unexpectedness of the event and of the imagination of the victim. As previously described, many victims are temporarily unable to understand what has happened. If this state of disorientation is followed by a moment of comprehension in which a word such as 'burglars' with its frightening connotations suddenly leaps to mind, all sense of perspective may be lost. The victim may react to his or her preconceived image of what 'burglary' means, rather than to the (usually less serious) reality of the situation. Many of those interviewed described their recovery from the initial impact of the burglary in terms of relief that the event had not been 'as bad as it could have been': perhaps such a statement manifests the replacement of flights of imagination by a more objective viewing of the actual incident.

The three explanations—which are not mutually exclusive —suggest a variety of possible strategies for reducing the adverse effects of burglary. The first points towards awareness of and action to help types of people particularly susceptible to distress. Victim support schemes have already indicated that the aged and people living alone are likely to require more support than most. Our finding that separated, divorced and widowed women are the most vulnerable groups provides a further insight and may help to direct attention where it is most needed.

The second implies the importance of restoring a victim's sense of safety within the 'territory' of the home. Many found it comforting to change locks or to install new security devices, and the visit of a crime prevention officer, or even simple advice from investigating officers, were also helpful in this respect. A possible conclusion is that victims should be actively advised and encouraged by the police to make some changes, if only minor, in the way their homes are protected.

The third explanation merits special attention, as it is relevant to arguments about a controversial approach to the problem of burglary which has gained some currency in the United States and Canada. Waller and Okihiro (1978), for example, have used the argument that fear of crime may often be as socially harmful as actual victimisation (cf. also Sparks *et al.* 1977: 208) to advocate a programme of 'de-dramaticisation' of burglary. This would involve fewer prosecutions for minor offences, elimination of fear-producing crime prevention campaigns, and efforts to educate the public 'by more frequent publicity of the peaceful nature of residential burglary'. They have also suggested that minor burglaries should merely be recorded over the telephone by civilian employees (with an explanation to the public of the scarcity of police resources), so that trained policemen can concentrate upon 'more serious offenders' (*ibid.* p. 105). Before commenting upon these ideas, the nature of the contact between the victims we interviewed and the police will be considered more closely.

The victim and the police

Once they had discovered the burglary, over 80 per cent of the victims we interviewed informed the police without delay. The normal procedure was to telephone the local police station, although about 20 per cent walked or drove there, and 15 per cent dialled '999'. Most of the 20 per cent who delayed reporting were people who discovered the burglary late in the evening and decided to wait until the following morning. A small number had resolved not to report the incident but did so when, for example, they had learned that neighbours had also been burgled, and thought that their information might help police inquiries.

The speed and degree of police response to reports of burglary varied enormously. In some cases several officers arrived within minutes, in others one constable appeared two or three hours later. To some extent this was a matter of chance. If there happened to be a patrol car close to the scene, or if the burglary was discovered at a quiet time, the victim might receive 'first-class service'. Indeed, one woman complained that her house was suddenly invaded by five policemen from three cars, as well as a dog and a handler, when all she had done was to report what seemed to her a minor burglary! At the other extreme, a pensioner complained that he was told over the telephone not to touch anything until an officer arrived, and consequently spent a winter's night and the whole of the following day with his living-room disarranged and a broken window letting in cold air. Of course, if it appeared likely that the burglar was still in the area and particularly if he had been disturbed, the police response was normally an urgent one. Conversely, victims who had delayed reporting the offence usually experienced a slow response. In all, in 49 per cent of cases police arrived at the scene of the burglary within 15 minutes, and in 79 per cent within one hour. The rapid arrivals were generally by uniformed police; CID officers appeared at a later stage.

It is interesting to consider exactly what a victim expects of the police when he reports a burglary. Victimisation surveys have invest-igated the reasons for victims *not* reporting offences to the police, but there is little published information on the opposite question. We asked our interviewees: 'Why did you report the burglary?' About 75 per cent replied that it was a normal or automatic response, and 10 per cent that it was their duty as citizens. Only a few pointed out that reporting was necessary in order to claim on their insurance, and nearly all of these said they would have reported the matter anyway for other reasons. Under 10 per cent mentioned the hope that the offender might be caught.

The puzzlement with which this question was usually greeted suggested that people did not have any clear ideas on what they wanted from the police. Although most *hoped* that an arrest would be made, expectations were very low. The majority had been pessimistic from the beginning; and where no offender had been caught by the time we interviewed them only four per cent said that they expected an arrest and 12 per cent that they were still hopeful.

Some of the pessimism may have been encouraged by the initial attitude of the investigating officers. In nearly 60 per cent of cases, it seems, the police indicated during their first contact with the victim that they thought there was little or no chance of an arrest (see Table 12).

Nevertheless, in spite of the general expectations of failure, 62 per cent of victims were satisfied that the police had done everything that could reasonably be expected to catch the offender. Thirteen per cent said that they could have spent more time on the case, and another 19 per cent that they could have followed up specific leads more

Table 12   Did the police seem optimistic about the possibility of catching the person responsible?

	Number	Percentage
Very optimistic	22	7
Fairly optimistic	41	13
Not very hopeful	36	11
Not at all hopeful	150	47
Did not indicate	65	20
Offender already caught	8	2
Total	322	100

thoroughly. The complaints were strongest in cases where there was a clear suspect but the police had not obtained enough evidence to make an arrest. Comments like 'They just don't seem interested', and 'I could make him confess myself' were typical in such cases. Victims also tended to be more critical when the police failed to take fingerprints, a procedure which 30 per cent said had not been carried out.

However, much greater importance was attached to what one might call the 'public relations' rather than the investigative role of the police. Although very few uniformed officers were faulted, CID officers came in for some criticism from over 30 per cent of working-class victims and 10 per cent of middle-class victims. Such criticism was expressed in comments such as, 'They treated us as unimportant', or 'They made us feel as if we were wasting their time.'[4] A related complaint was that after the first few days they had heard nothing further about the case. Only 24 per cent received any notification of police progress, and although one area had a policy of sending out 'progress letters', this was carried out in a minority of cases. Those who praised the police usually did so also in terms of 'the trouble they took' over the case. Significantly, their satisfaction was not affected by whether or not the burglar was eventually detected.

Table 13 shows the replies received to the general question: 'How satisfied are you with the operation of the police in your case?' It is suggested that the figures are more a reflection of the degree of success achieved by police in handling victims sympathetically than of their investigative abilities.

The fact that criticisms were made predominantly by working-class victims reflects what appears at first glance to be a difference by class in the time and attention given to burglary cases. For example, fingerprints were said to have been taken in 77 per cent of cases with

Table 13   Victims' satisfaction with police handling of their cases   (N = 322)

	All %	Working class %	Middle class %
Very satisfied	43	32	49
Fairly satisfied	27	30	25
Neutral	14	16	13
Somewhat dissatisfied	10	14	8
Very dissatisfied	6	8	5
	100	100	100

middle-class victims and 56 per cent of those with working-class victims; middle-class victims received three or more visits in connection with the burglary in 23 per cent of cases as compared with 10 per cent of working-class cases; security advice was proferred in 22 per cent of middle-class cases as compared with 11 per cent of working-class cases. These differences may be due not so much to class bias as to a natural desire by the police to 'catch the bigger villains', as middle-class victims were more likely to lose valuable property and to be burgled by professional thieves. (Working-class victims who lost valuable property received considerably more attention in the above terms than those who lost small amounts, although still not to the same extent as middle-class victims.) Nevertheless, as female working-class victims are marginally more likely to suffer serious after-effects than their middle-class counterparts, and as working-class burglaries are more likely to involve offenders known to the victim, it seems unwise both in terms of helping victims and of detecting offenders for the police to 'save time' on apparently petty cases.

The clear conclusion to be drawn from the answers to questions about victims' expectations of and experiences with the police was that victims were much less concerned with seeing an offender arrested than with receiving what they regarded as *the appropriate response to the incident*. In a state of considerable emotional upset, they had telephoned the police almost as an instinctive response, with the expectation that the latter would come along and 'do something' about the situation. The very routine of investigation—for example, taking fingerprints, recording details, examining the point of entry, questioning neighbours—if coupled with a sympathetic attitude and a willingness to listen to the victim's fears, was mentioned as having a beneficial effect in helping people to come to terms with what had happened.

As both the victim and the police were often well aware that there was little chance of an arrest, these actions can to some extent be regarded as a kind of 'ritual', but this does not mean that they have no value. What they achieve is to 'mark' the offence as an experience that others have been through in the past. As Wright (1977) puts it:

> A crime is, at the least, a disturbance, at the worst, a disaster in people's lives. It is natural for people to want something to be done, just as they do when there has been an accident. This is partly out of a desire for practical action to put things back to normal, as far as possible, but partly it is because people want recognition of the offence, appropriate to its seriousness, from recording the details of a petty theft which is unlikely to be cleared up, to a full-scale murder-hunt (or, in the case of an accident or natural catastophe, a visit by a government minister to the disaster area) . . . What offends people's instinctive sense of rightness is that the response is insufficient, rather than that it is insufficiently hurtful to the offender.

It is this aspect of the situation that produced intense criticism of Waller's suggestions for 'de-dramatising' burglary (Waller and Okihiro 1978). For example, McKay (1978), wrote:

> I would like him to be aware that the burglary was neither common nor dull for us. It was in fact an intrusive and psychologically violent act with long-term and enduring consequences . . . If anything, our residual anxiety over the act was heightened by what we perceived as the *lack of reaction* by the local police. Frankly, in the aftermath of such an incident one resents being treated as mundane routine. Contact with the local force reflected less than five minutes of total conversation on the telephone with the investigating officer and with a desk officer at the station.

Such comments draw attention to the tendency of both Waller and critics of his ideas to confuse general anxiety that a burglary might occur with the feelings produced in the victim when it actually happens. In fact, there need not necessarily be a contradiction between encouraging a less dramatic image of burglary and, at the same time, taking seriously the psychological impact upon those who become victims. In other words, while it seems sensible to criticise sensational reports which increase public fear, this approach should not be taken to the extreme of making victims feel apologetic or embarrassed to report offences or to ask for attention.

Attitudes towards offenders

All victims interviewed were asked whether they knew or had suspicions about who had committed their burglary. The majority of Gerrards Cross victims believed the offenders to be adult professional burglars strange to the area, but in Reading and Banbury over 50 per cent were convinced that their burglar lived near them; teenagers were blamed almost as often as adults; and few thought that 'professionals' were involved. Table 14 shows victims' answers to the question, 'How would you like to see the offender in your case dealt with if caught?' It can be seen that, despite the differences in the type of offender thought to be responsible and in the social characteristics of victims (95 per cent in Gerrards Cross being middle-class), the answers were remarkably similar in each area.

Table 14   How would you like to see the offender in your case dealt with?

	Reading & Banbury %	Gerrards Cross %	All %
Custody	29	29	29
Corporal punishment	8	9	8
Personal revenge, torture etc.	2	1	2
Community service/work	10	10	10
Probation	6	10	7
Compensation to victim	16	7	14
Fine	4	6	4
Caution/no action	5	5	5
Other/don't know/depends	20	23	21
Total	100	100	100
	(N = 240)	(N = 82)	(N = 322)

As a whole, we were surprised by the lack of vindictiveness among victims. Despite general agreement that burglary was a serious offence (67 per cent answered 'yes' and 19 per cent 'middling' to the question 'Do you consider burglary to be a serious offence?' cf. Durant *et al.* 1972:117), fewer than 30 per cent thought that 'their' burglar should receive a custodial sentence. Remarks like 'Prison does no good to anyone' were common. Even among those who chose custody there was a strong feeling that prison was unlikely to bring about any reform, and in many cases they chose it because of the lack of an effective alternative. If a general 'message' came through, it was that (a) the offender should repay his 'debt' in a useful way, either by straightforward restitution or by working for the community, and (b) if he could be reformed, other households would be spared the same experience. Purely retributive feelings were comparatively rare, although there were six cases in which the offender would be well advised to avoid falling into the victim's hands! The birch and the stocks also had some supporters.

Community service was chosen by 10 per cent of victims, and mentioned by many more as a good scheme. However, in some cases they felt that such work was not hard or disciplined enough to effect a change in attitude, or that prison was preferable in order that the offender did not immediately go free. Others toyed with the idea of 'work-camps', which they considered would be more likely than prison either to reform or to deter.

Those who had been most seriously upset by the burglary were the most likely to display vindictive feelings towards the offender. Twenty-one per cent of those in our 'seriously affected' group wanted personal revenge or corporal punishment compared with eight per cent of the remainder. However, they were no more likely than anyone else to favour a custodial sentence. Pensioners were also more frequently in favour of flogging than younger interviewees, while among the victims most likely to choose prison were those whose houses had been ransacked.[5] However, in neither of these cases was the variation statistically significant. In general we were struck by the similarity of attitudes towards offenders. For example, there was virtually no difference between male and female, or between middle-class and working-class respondents. As one might expect, those who believed that the offender was a 'professional burglar' were more likely to say he should go to prison than those who described him as an 'amateur', but again the variation was not very great. Indeed it was interesting that a greater desire to see a custodial sentence was expressed by victims who thought the offender was *in between* these two categories—that is, variously described as, for example, a 'semi-professional' or 'ordinary thief'.[6]

Despite the surprisingly lenient attitude of victims towards offenders when discussing their own cases, they often expressed a very different viewpoint where *hypothetical* cases were concerned. Towards the end of the interview we put the following question:

Forgetting your particular case for the moment, how would you like to see each of the following burglary offenders dealt with?
(a) An 18-year-old offender with no previous record of burglary;
(b) An 18-year-old offender who had previously been involved in a number of burglaries;
(c) A 30-year-old offender who for one reason or another committed a house burglary, although he had never done anything particularly criminal before;
(d) A 30-year-old offender who had been classified by the police as an experienced burglar and the offence in question was one of a series of similar offences.

Table 15 shows how the 251 victims who answered (the question was unfortunately omitted through lack of time in 71 interviews) thought each of the burglars described should be dealt with. Probation and psychiatric treatment or investigation were thought appropriate for first offenders (no more than 16 per cent favoured custody for a first offence), and a solid minority favoured community service and supervised work for all kinds of offenders fairly equally. In stark contrast, however, 54 per cent considered that an 18-year-old with previous convictions should be given a custodial sentence, and 75 per cent thought that a persistent burglar aged 30 should go to prison—one-third of these recommending a period of more than five years.

Table 15   Victims' recommended sentences for different types of burglar

		(a) 18-yr-old: no previous convictions %	(b) 18-yr-old: previous convictions %	(c) 30-yr-old: no previous convictions %	(d) 30-yr-old: previous convictions %
Custody	Borstal/DC/ Prison up to 1 yr	15	48	12	31
	Prison over 1 yr and up to 5 years	16 { 0	54 { 4	14 { 1	75 { 20
	Prison over 5 yrs	1	2	1	24
Corporal punishment		6	9	3	2
Psychiatric treatment/ probation, etc.		23	8	39	4
Community service, work, etc.		21	20	17	15
Compensation to victim		9	4	4	1
Fine		13	2	11	1
Caution/nominal		12	3	12	2
Total		100 (N = 251)	100 (N = 251)	100 (N = 251)	100 (N = 251)

These results introduce a contradiction: whereas only 31 per cent of those who thought they had been burgled by an experienced professional had wanted to see him imprisoned, when later asked how virtually the same kind of offender should be dealt with in a hypothetical case, nearly 80 per cent of these same victims replied that he should go to prison. How can this be explained? It may be that some had a different image of the offender in mind in each case. Again, it may be that, having suggested rehabilitative sentences for less experienced burglars, they felt the need to recommend prison simply in order to emphasise their comparative disapproval of the persistent thief.

We believe, however, that these figures underline the general point that the words 'burglar' and 'burglary' are imbued with powerful myths and images and that as soon as one moves away from personal experience into general discussion these images are quickly conjured up, distorting people's judgement. The victim who said, 'I'd hardly call it a burglary; he just walked in and nicked a radio' was unconsciously making the same point: while he did not think that 'his' burglar (whom he knew to be an 18-year-old with at least five previous convictions) should be sent to prison, he was quite prepared to see the hypothetical 18-year-old offender sentenced to 'three to five years', presumably for something he would consider to be a 'real' burglary.

In arguing for a general reduction in prison sentences and a more 'tolerant' attitude towards offenders, Hood (1974:14) conceded that this would be most difficult in the case of the kind of burglar we have been describing: 'There can be no doubt that public opinion is not very favourably disposed towards recidivist burglars.' Our research confirms that this is so if one asks generalised questions, but that when people are considering a real event in which they have been involved, albeit badly upset as a victim, they are much more likely to advocate a constructive policy.

Finally, the 'penal philosophies' people expressed during the interviews were, like those of professional penologists and practitioners, varied and contradictory. However, we found almost no support for the theory, partly embodied in legislation in California, Maine and other states in the USA, that there should be a fixed mandatory penalty for each category of offence. Victims generally favoured individualised sentencing aimed at reform, with prison only as a 'last resort'. The view of imprisonment as an expensive and ineffective response to crime was fairly widespread. On the other hand, if an offender consistently failed to respond to alternative sentences, many people were then prepared to 'lock him up and throw away the key'. Even those with very liberal attitudes had a tendency suddenly to lose patience and swing from one extreme to the other, an attitude reminiscent of what Bottoms (1977) has referred to as a 'bifurcation process' in modern penal theory.

VI. Prevention, Detection and Sentencing

This final chapter considers current efforts made by the police, the courts and other bodies to combat the problem of burglary. The first section discusses the particular difficulties involved in detecting a type of crime in which there is usually no previous link between victim and offender, and where investigations often commence many hours after the incident has taken place. The second section outlines recent sentencing policy towards burglars in both magistrates' and Crown Courts, and the third turns to the problems and possibilities of preventing burglary, through 'target-hardening' or other measures designed to protect houses. Finally, the 'summary and concluding remarks' draws together threads from the previous chapters and asks to what extent the police, the penal system and the community in general might alter their current responses to burglary in order to reduce its incidence or alleviate its effects.

The problem of detection

For burglary in a dwelling few police forces regularly achieve a clear-up rate of over 30 per cent, and in the Metropolitan Police District the rate has fallen below 10 per cent. In 1978 the lack of success of the London police spurred the former Commissioner of Scotland Yard, Sir Robert Mark, to make a controversial speech in which he admitted that the city's police were becoming virtually powerless to protect houses from the actions of burglars:

> Anyone reading the reports of the Chief Inspector of Constabulary and the Metropolitan Police Commissioner may reasonably draw at least two general conclusions. The first is that so far as crimes against property are concerned—that is burglary, breaking offences, theft and dishonest handling—the police in England and Wales have probably reached their lowest point in effectiveness in living memory. The second is that this situation is more than twice as bad in London as in the provinces. Only 6,600 or 9.8 per cent of 67,500 aggravated burglaries or burglaries in a dwelling were cleared up in London last year, the corresponding figure for the provinces being 67,300 or 34 per cent of 195,000...
>
> The simple truth is that crimes against property are now so numerous that both police and courts are of little relevance from the point of view of the victim and the insurer... I am suggesting

quite bluntly that for the first time in this century the belief that the State can, or even wishes to, protect people effectively from burglary, breaking offences and theft should be abandoned, at least in the great cities, where inadequate numbers of police have other and much more demanding priorities.[1]

Although this speech caused shock and condemnation in British police circles, it would not have aroused much surprise in the United States, where for some years academics and others had been exposing the limitations of police efforts to detect burglary. Greenberg *et al.* (1973) and Greenwood *et al.* (1977) had convincingly demonstrated the insolubility of the majority of burglaries by traditional police methods and with the resources available. In Canada, too, Waller and Okihiro (1978) and Engstad and Evans (1980) were beginning to suggest that the investigation of burglary should be given lower priority than hithertofore, partly because efforts to solve cases were not proving cost-effective. In fact, the English research graduate Chappell had anticipated many of these arguments several years previously when he quoted 'a number of experienced officers' who estimated that 'between 30 and 40 per cent of all offences of breaking and entering were probably undetectable from the outset' (Chappell 1965:305).

The two main reasons for the low clear-up rates for burglary appear to be that by the time most offences are reported the offender is well clear of the area and that in most cases there is no previous link between victim and offender to provide an initial suspect. Table 16

Table 16   Method of report, burglary in a dwelling, Thames Valley, 1975

Method of report		Number	Percentage
By public	Ordinary telephone	3,666	56.5
	999 call	921	14.2
	In person to police station	990	15.3
	Police patrol	226	3.5
Sub-total		5,803	89.5
By Police	Patrol	83	1.3
	Observation	13	0.2
	Other inquiries	408	6.3
Sub-total		504	7.8
Alarm		23	0.4
Not recorded		154	2.4
Total		6,484	100.0

shows the methods by which the 6,484 cases of burglary in a dwelling recorded in the Thames Valley area in 1975 came to the notice of the police.

In over half of all cases they were notified by means of a telephone call to the local police station, while '999' calls were made in only 14 per cent. This is one reflection of the fact that by the time most offences are discovered the trail is cold and there is no need for an emergency police response. In 70 per cent of cases, the victim had been out of the house or asleep in bed for over six hours and had no precise idea of the time at which the burglary had taken place. This normally unavoidable time-lag between offence and report significantly reduces the chances of catching the offender. In the relatively small proportion of cases (14 per cent) in which the police were called within 30 minutes of the event, the clear-up rate was 40 per cent, compared with an overall clear-up rate of 29 per cent.

Even more important to detection than the speed of notification seems to be the provision of information to the police by the victim or by a witness which produces a suspect or at least the description of a suspect. Recent research into policing has stressed this above all else. A great deal of evidence has accumulated showing that the classic method of detection portrayed in fiction—deduction from 'clues' at the scene of the crime—is relatively unproductive in terms of arrest, and that the major source of both arrests and clearances is early identification of the offender by members of the public. One of the most influential studies was that carried out in the United States by Greenwood (1977), who noted that the vast majority of arrests for property crime were made either near the scene of the crime or 'as a result of information readily available at the time the offence was reported'. He calculated that without such evidence the chances of clearing up a burglary by arrest were remarkably slim: 'The thrust of our analysis is that all the time spent on difficult cases where the perpetrator is unknown results in only 2.7 per cent of all clearances' (p. 227).

It was similar findings that provoked Greenberg (1973) to conclude that if there was insufficient initial evidence available, it was just not worthwhile pursuing enquiries into a burglary. He recommended immediate suspension of investigation of all cases where the evidence at the scene does not reach a minimum level of usefulness, defined by a weighted checklist of factors (headed by descriptions or names of suspects).

English researchers have not moved to this extreme, but have confirmed the diagnosis of the problem. Chatterton (1976:108-9), for example, estimated that 'at the very least ... almost half of all arrests for crime were cases in which the public had provided the police with a prisoner'; Bottomley and Coleman (1981:140) that 24 per cent of all clearances were produced primarily by 'citizen information'; Steer (1980:97) that in one-third of detected 'serious' crimes the identity of the offender was known from the outset or was deduced from a description by the victim; and Mawby (1979) that about 60 per cent of offences were cleared up because of evidence 'given' to the police. Another striking illustration was provided by Zander (1979:216), who discovered that in 87 per cent of a sample of cases at the Old Bailey, 'the identity of the accused was reasonably clear from the outset of the inquiry'.

As we have seen in chapter II, burglary victims rarely see the offender, and even in the council-housing area in Banbury where burglary seems to be a very local affair, in more than half of the cases reported victims were unable to suggest who might have been responsible. Chappell (1965:298) also found that in 28 per cent of undetected cases in his sample the police had no idea even of the type of offender involved (for example, 'juvenile', 'vagrant', 'local offender'), and had 'strong suspects' in only 20 per cent.

Lacking early identification of offenders in so many cases, the police are thrown back upon a number of other strategies. Physical evidence such as fingerprints, shoeprints or items left behind by the offender have been shown to produce few arrests directly. Steer (1980), for example, attributes only one per cent of detections to fingerprint evidence. (However, Bottomley and Coleman (1981) point out that physical evidence is sometimes helpful in furnishing extra evidence to convict suspects identified in other ways, or in convincing detained suspects to make a confession.) Police patrols and checks made in the street on 'suspicious' drivers or pedestrians are likewise of only marginal importance in capturing burglars. Again, Steer attributes only four per cent of all detections to 'stop/ checks', and Mawby (1979) attributes three per cent to 'police vigilance' (mainly by patrolling officers).[2]

Apart from information given by victims or witnesses, the most important method of clearing up burglaries is through the routine questioning of known offenders. Matza (1969) has emphasised the extent to which police work depends upon what he calls the 'method of suspicion'. He asserts that local people known to be involved in crime are continually being 'harassed' by the police (stopped in the street or in cars, visited in their homes, or taken down to the station for questioning), often on a kind of 'fishing expedition' to see if they can be linked to any recently reported crimes. It is not easy to find out to what extent this is the case, since police records rarely reveal how offenders initially come to be interviewed formally about particular crimes. Detectives we spoke to said that circumstances vary widely—some are named by informers, some are stopped for one reason and then come under suspicion for other offences, some are seen spending a lot of money, some are approached because a series of offences conforms to their *modus operandi*, and so on. However, whatever the prior events, there is little doubt that the interview situation is an extremely rich source of detections. Bottomley and Coleman (1981) found that 28 per cent of all detections in their sample were produced primarily through astute interviewing and that for burglary the proportion was considerably higher. Mawby (1979:109) puts down almost 40 per cent of detections to 'routine questioning'. Steer (1980), too, stresses the importance of police knowledge about local offenders and makes particular mention of the tendency of those questioned to implicate accomplices. He writes (p.115) that:

> the police interview emerges not only as an important means by which some offences are first discovered and detected, but also as an important and by no means infrequent means by which the identity of accomplices is established. And it is at this point perhaps that one finds justification for the very real fear of criminals of those who inform against them . . . The greatest danger to the offenders comes not from those in the circle in which he moves who know (or suspect) something of what he has been up to, but from those with whom he has actually commited the offence.

One might add that 'those in the circle in which he moves' are indirectly important in that they point the police in the right direction. Many police reports on detected offences in our sample included the words 'acting on information received' as a prelude to a description of an interview. Although such information may not be sufficient to convict a burglar, we suspect that it is as valuable as hints from victims concerning the identity of an offender in providing a primary lever for the investigating officer to work with.

The outcome of questioning of persistent offenders is often not merely one but a considerable number of detections. If the police are able to convince a burglar that they can prove one offence against him—ideally by catching him in the act—he will frequently decide to 'wipe the slate clean' by admitting to other offences, thereby avoiding the possibility of further charges being brought against him at a later date. Altogether, offences cleared up by confessions in the course of 'other inquiries' acounted for at least 37 per cent of all clear-ups of burglaries recorded in the Thames Valley area in 1975, and where offenders under 17 were concerned, the figure reached 60 per cent. Most of these offences are eventually presented in court as 'TIC's.[3]

They also include a number of cases which have not previously been reported by the victim and which are thus recorded and detected at the same moment. Inclusion of such cases in the totals of detections helps to boost the clear-up rate somewhat. We calculated that, if offences coming to light in this latter way were excluded, for 1975 the clear-up rate would have stood at 24 per cent rather than 29 per cent.

We did not go into as much detail about methods of detection as the writers discussed earlier, but we can provide some comments about how the 40 persistent burglars we interviewed had been caught for their latest offences. About half said that they had been persuaded into confessing to burglaries (including 'TIC's) in their most recent court appearances and they thought the police would otherwise have found their involvement difficult to prove. For example, two offenders were seen in a car that was recognised as stolen and were arrested after a chase; they later confessed to a number of burglaries. Another drove into a road block that had been set up in connection with a quite separate police operation and was detained because he was thought to be behaving suspiciously. Yet another was stopped in the street when drunk and on being taken down to the police station and questioned talked injudiciously about his recent activities.

It seems strange to an outsider that people should confess to crimes when there is no evidence against them, but many offenders believed that the police had a considerable amount of knowledge about their movements, and some of the more perspicacious remarked that policemen are expert at appearing to know more than they actually do. Moreover, there was general agreement that the 'pressure' to confess was very strong. While there were few allegations of physical force, there were many of deprivation of contact with family or solicitor, of long periods of 'interrogation' without respite, and of offers to make 'bargains' if the interviewee would accept some offences or would implicate accomplices. Irving and Hilgendorf (1980) have discussed interview procedures in detail, and many of their findings are echoed in statements by our interviewees. A typical assertion was made by a 21-year-old:

> When they take you down to the station they pressurise you till you tell them something. They know very well that I go out nearly every day doing jobs so in the end I tell them a few. They're only a drop in the ocean though.

In cases with more than one suspect, police questioning was said to be even more effective, as it is carried out in separate rooms and each suspect is ignorant of what the other has said. About one-quarter of those we interviewed were convinced, with good reason, that they had been caught for their most recent case as a result of being 'grassed up'. In some cases they knew this from written statements made by partners or by receivers and in others inferred it from the behaviour of the police. For example:

> When I get the stuff home I hide it in the loft and I never tell any-one where I keep it. I've had buyers come round my house and I always tell them to come back in half an hour and I will have the stuff. All I do is to pop upstairs and I get it down. On one occasion I was lazy and I got caught. I had some heavy stuff upstairs and I needed a hand to get it down. The buyer was there and I had known him for about three years, so I got him to help me carry it downstairs. He saw where I stashed all the gear. A little while later the police were round and they knew exactly where to look. The buyer had told them everything.

Almost another quarter thought that 'someone had grassed' but had no idea who or why. In most of these cases we came to believe that they were merely looking for a scapegoat for what had happened. The truth was that they had made mistakes or talked too much over a period of time, eventually drawing police attention to themselves. Some were found with stolen property in their houses when the police arrived with a warrant; others were arrested on suspicion of having been responsible for a certain group of offences, and confessed when questioned.

Only four of our 40 interviewees said that they had been 'caught red-handed' for their most recent offence. One had been heard by a resident and disturbed: 'I ran off out the back door. I ran across a few gardens and then came out into the street and went slap into a police car. I ran off but they caught me.' Another was stopped by a police car early in the morning after a night's 'creeping' and asked to turn out his pockets. He was unable to explain either the large amounts of cash or the tools he was carrying.

As our interviewees were mainly adult persistent burglars, the manner in which they were caught was not representative of how all burglars are caught. In the Banbury area villages, by contrast, most of the children arrested were initially identified by victims, and in the council-housing area in Banbury several of the arrests stemmed from victims' or neighbours' suspicions. Personal feuds were sometimes involved, as in the case of a man who had been staying with his uncle and returned to steal some money.

Both the main methods of clearing up burglaries described —information from victims and questioning of known persistent burglars—tend to capture particular types of offender: in the first case, petty offenders local to a small area, particularly children and teenagers, and in the second, offenders local to a town, particularly 'middle-range' persistent burglars. However, neither method is generally effective against high-level burglars, especially those who are more mobile and burgle houses several miles from their usual haunts.

During the 1970s, many police forces expanded the use of special burglary squads and Regional Crime Squads, whose primary mode of operation is to watch 'target' criminals, gathering intelligence about them and keeping them under frequent surveillance even when they move across wide areas. Surrey CID, for example, have claimed considerable success by such methods, both in the number of arrests made and in the reduction of high-value burglaries (cf. Burden 1980:87-9). Targets are selected by a filtering process: in Surrey information about London thieves known to have visited affluent areas of the county in the past is gathered, and those thought to be still active come in for special attention. The method has the advantage that once under the spotlight a thief has to be exceptionally careful to avoid arrest, but it can be criticised on the grounds that it is an extremely time-consuming procedure and takes resources away from other pressing concerns. Peter Hudson, for example, took up nearly six months of the time of a number of experienced policemen before he was caught.

Moreover, there is an argument that if too much effort is concentrated upon this type of offender, who preys on a relatively limited section of society, the police will be protecting the rich at the expense of the poor. Wealthy people are anyway more likely to be insured against burglary, and as we have seen, working-class victims are marginally more likely to be seriously upset by the offence than middle-class victims. On the other hand, targeting seems to be the only effective method for dealing with mobile professional thieves: for example, spot-checks on roads into affluent areas like Gerrards Cross have had only minimal success, and anyway cause annoyance to innocent people who are stopped.

Finally, while the general principle of 'keeping tabs on' a group of known offenders, whether petty, middle-range or high-level, is doubtless one of the major weapons the police have in the fight against burglary, it has the drawback of hardening the attitudes of offenders and ex-offenders towards the police. Several of our interviewees claimed that they had intended 'going straight' on release from prison, but had soon become embittered by the police attitude which did not allow them to forget their past. There were many stories of employers or new girlfriends being warned by policemen about an ex-offender's past (for example, by visiting a man at his place of work or stopping him in the street when he was with a friend). Bottomley (1981:138) quotes the father of a boy suspected of burglary angrily complaining that 'they always blame my lads because our name stinks round here'. There were many equally bitter remarks made by our interviewees:

> The police see you all as a group. If one of you did it, you all did it.
> They've got it in for me. Last time they couldn't nick me they said they'll get me again. If they can't prove it, they fit you up.
> The police always keep you in mind in case they need a body.
> They don't give you a chance. As long as I stay in this town, I'm a marked man.

Such comments may well be gross exaggerations, and in many cases the individuals involved were probably actively engaging in crime and hence minor forms of what they saw as 'harassment' may have been justified. However, civil freedoms must never be overlooked, and it is important when considering overall policy towards burglary to balance the aim of detecting crime with the possible harm that is done to the rights of individuals. Recent controversies over the 'sus' laws (now abolished) and over relationships between the police and ethnic minorities in high-crime areas have highlighted extreme variations of this problem, and Irving's (1980) study of interviews in police stations raises comparable questions. Our information on such matters was drawn primarily from comments by offenders and therefore gave us too one-sided a picture to make a balanced judgement. Nevertheless, we feel it important at least to mention the intensity of feelings expressed by our interviewees.

The sentencing of burglars

Despite the freedom that has been given to magistrates to deal summarily with cases of burglary, the majority of adult and young adult offenders are still sentenced in Crown Courts. In 1978, 64 per cent of people over the age of 17 charged with burglary in a dwelling were committed for trial or sentence to a higher court. The equivalent figure for burglary in buildings other than dwellings was 38 per cent, and for all other indictable offences was 17 per cent. Burglars were also more likely than any other major category of property offender to be remanded in custody: 29 per cent of those sent for trial were so held, as opposed to 11 per cent of people committed on theft charges.

The sentences passed reveal how serious a view of the offence is taken by both magistrates and judges. Table 17 shows the disposal in 1978 of male house burglars over the age of 17 in both types of court, compared with that of offenders convicted of theft and handling, fraud and forgery, and all indictable offences. Forty-nine per cent of

Table 17 Court disposal of male offenders aged 17 and over, England and Wales, 1978

	Nominal %	Probation/ community service order %	Fine %	Suspended sentence %	Custodial sentence %	Other %	Committed for sentence %	Total %
MAGISTRATES COURTS								
Burglary in a dwelling	6.5	15.7	32.3	12.0	18.5	1.7	13.0	100.0 (N = 4,819)
Theft and handling	8.1	8.6	65.8	6.6	6.6	0.6	3.7	100.0 (N = 125,620)
Fraud and forgery	10.0	9.1	56.3	11.5	9.1	0.5	3.5	100.0 (N = 12,126)
All indictable offences	9.3	8.7	63.0	6.9	7.5	0.6	4.0	100.0 (N = 221,707)
CROWN COURTS								
Burglary in a dwelling	2.1	15.1	4.3	14.5	63.6	0.5	—	100.1 (N = 7,716)
Theft and handling	4.5	11.4	17.8	18.7	46.8	0.8	—	100.0 (N = 19,351)
Fraud and forgery	3.6	8.7	12.7	28.0	46.5	0.5	—	100.2 (N = 3,278)
All indictable offences	4.0	10.6	14.6	17.0	52.5	1.3	—	100.0 (N = 59,995)

the burglars received custodial sentences, compared with 12 per cent of the thieves and handlers, and 17 per cent of the fraudsmen and forgers. For young adult burglars, borstal training is a particularly common sentence: 20 per cent of all males who were sent to borstal were convicted of burglary in a dwelling.

Once they reach the Crown Court, burglars of *non-residential* buildings are as likely to be sent to prison as house burglars. However, a much smaller proportion of the former are committed for trial or sentence, and magistrates also pass custodial sentences in a lower percentage of such cases. Altogether, about 32 per cent of those over 17 years of age who were found guilty eventually received custodial sentences from either judges or magistrates.

An important factor in the sentencing of residential burglars is their previous record. Over three-quarters of those charged have at least one previous conviction, and 20 per cent have been convicted five or more times (*Criminal Statistics* 1978:183, Phillpotts and Lancucki 1979:7). No other offence group exceeds these rates of recidivism, which clearly account for some of the differences in disposal. However, fraud and forgery offenders are also notorious 'repeaters' (18 per cent have five or more previous convictions) but are dealt with considerably more leniently.

The relative severity towards burglars is further expressed in the length of sentence they receive: 31 per cent of males sentenced to prison in Crown Courts in 1978 were given terms in excess of 18 months. The equivalent figures for non-residential burglary, theft and handling, and fraud and forgery, were 22 per cent, 13 per cent and 28 per cent respectively. The normal 'tariff' for burglary appears to be in the range nine months to two years. However Thomas (1979:147-51) concludes from an examination of Court of Appeal decisions that sentences of up to three years are not considered excessive for a single offence of burglary by an offender with a bad record, and that sentences below this level reflect the presence of mitigating factors. Even where there is some mitigation, 'sentences between twelve months and two years are not considered excessive'. He quotes a case (Davey, June 5th 1975) in which the Court upheld a sentence of 12 months upon a man with no previous convictions who had knocked on the door of a house intending to break in, but had fled when the owner returned unexpectedly. The reason given, that the 'gravamen in burglary or attempted burglary . . . is the terror which is instilled into people', is reminiscent of the arguments of Blackstone and other jurists of over 200 years ago.

In the case of R. v. Stoakes (September 4th, 1980), *Criminal Law Review* (January 1981:56) reported:

The court had frequently stated that those who commit burglary of dwelling-houses must inevitably expect, in the interests of the public, to be sentenced to a term of immediate imprisonment. Even for a person of good character, something in the order of 18 months' imprisonment can be expected for burglary of a dwelling-house.

In a recent judgement (Bashir Begum Bibi, July 21st 1980), the Court of Appeal used the platform of discussing a drugs case to state some opinions about the possibility of reducing sentences in general. Here it was clearly implied that burglary in a dwelling, however minor the case, deserves longer sentences than most other offences against property.

Many offenders can be dealt with equally justly and effectively by a sentence of six or nine months' imprisonment as by one of 18 months or three years. We have in mind not only the obvious case of the first offender for whom any prison sentence however short may be an adequate punishment or deterrent, but other types of case as well.
  The less serious types of factory or shopbreaking; the minor cases of sexual indecency; the more petty frauds where small amounts of money are involved; the fringe participant in more serious crime: all these are examples of cases where the shorter sentence would be appropriate. *There are, on the other hand, some offences for which, generally speaking, only the medium or longer sentences will be appropriate.* For example, most robberies; most offences involving serious violence; use of a weapon to wound; *burglary of private dwellinghouses*; planned crime for wholesale profit; active large scale trafficking in dangerous drugs. These are only examples. It would be impossible to set out a catalogue of those offences which do and those which do not merit more severe treatment. So much will, obviously, depend upon the circumstances of each individual offender and each individual offence. (*Our italics.*) (see Thomas (ed) 1980:178-9)

Finally, the comments of the Lord Chief Justice on the case of Buckland and Ayling (January 30th, 1979) show that persistent burglary, even where there is no evidence of violence nor evidence that any residents have actually been put in fear, is considered serious enough for a long sentence to be passed in order to protect the public. Upholding a sentence of seven years on each, he remarked:

One does not want to pile on the agony in regard to two men of mature age, of 40 and 41, who have been before the courts so often, but the plain fact is that these two men have reputations and records as burglars which it has not previously been my experience to meet. They have in each case consistently pursued this trade. Although they have not used violence, and although it is said no-one has been put in fear as a result of their activities, we for our part are not prepared to accept that. It is a commonplace that if a burglary is committed in a dwelling-house people are put in fear, even if it is retrospective fear. The wife of the house is upset by it. Furthermore, people who consistently burgle residential houses will sooner or later be confronted with the occupiers, and whether or not they will then break their previous record of no violence is a matter which has to be waited to be seen. [*sic*]

Buckland is 40. He has 15 previous convictions. They are all for dishonesty. Those two figures alone will show he has been in and out of prison almost continuously for the last 20 years. In fact it is rather more than that for his first recorded offence was when he was 16.

Ayling has a similar record. He is 41. He is divorced. He has 21 previous convictions, almost all for offences of dishonesty and that has been the basis of his life for the last 20 to 25 years.

Mr. Jones, who has said everything possible on behalf of these two men, has stressed the considerable efforts they have made to rehabilitate themselves. He has given us an interesting account of their progress in the higher education which is open now to persons serving prison sentences, and there is no doubt at all a great deal to be said for that.

But we feel that this is a case in which the protection of the public is absolutely paramount, and that there is far too much risk of these men drifting back to crime if they are allowed premature release from their prison sentences.

I did not mention that each of them wished to have ten other offences taken into account, most of them being burglary offences. That is some indication of how their thoughts have been moving since they last came out of prison in the early part of 1977. We think in this case that the protection of the public requires the retention of the sentence imposed by the trial judge, and therefore these two appeals are dismissed. (see Thomas (ed) 1979:44-5)

These clear policy statements from the Court of Appeal show that, despite the remarks of Burden (1980:145-8), the British judiciary has hardly been persuaded by the voices of those concerned with prison overcrowding into 'going soft' on burglars. About 4,000 people are sentenced to imprisonment for residential burglary each year, and burglars (including those convicted for burgling commercial property) make up nearly 30 per cent of the total prison population.

It has often been assumed that there is widespread public support for heavy sentences for burglars. Hood (1974:14), for example, singles out recidivist burglars as particularly opprobrious in the eyes of the general public, and recognises that arguments for shorter sentences or for greater use of alternatives to imprisonment find most opposition in this area. Certainly, our general questions to victims about how burglars should be dealt with (see chapter V) revealed that the great majority (often reluctantly) saw prison as the only suitable sentence for older recidivist offenders. On the other hand, it was surprising how few wanted to see the offender in their own case sent to prison, even when he fell into the latter category.

This suggests that 'public opinion' leaves some leeway for a gradual easing of sentences. The arguments for such a change are essentially negative or, some would say, 'defeatist'—that prisons are overcrowded and that alternatives are less expensive. Admittedly, too, corrective measures such as probation or community service appear to produce no better results (cf. Brody 1976). Yet the constant round of offending and imprisonment which characterises the lives of most persistent burglars itself offers a bleak and depressing picture. It is difficult to claim much success for incarceration in preventing reconviction or in deterring young people about to embark upon a career in crime. If there is an 'answer' to burglary, it does not lie in increasing levels of sentencing. The long sentences already given may satisfy a desire for punishment and express symbolically the public's condemnation of the offence, but our interviews with burglars firmly convinced us that while burglary remains such an easy act to commit without immediate detection, the threat of punishment is too remote in offenders' minds to act as a significant deterrent.

Finally, while there has been an upsurge of interest in the idea of 'incapacitating' persistent offenders in the United States, British experience with preventive detention (cf. Hammond and Chayen 1963, West 1963) should have convinced us that this is a disastrous policy. Those 'caught' by the policy at its height (1950-65) included more burglars than any other type of offender, but at the same time burglary figures saw an unprecedented rise. Any attempt to lock up the 'hard core' of persistent adult burglars would almost inevitably result in the expensive incarceration of the most incompetent and inadequate older offenders, while the bulk of offences continue to be committed by young adults and teenagers, with no observable beneficial effect on crime rates. Pease (1979) exposes many of the weaknesses of the evidence upon which advocates of such a policy rest their case.

Crime prevention and burglary

Few policy-makers or practitioners in the penal field would disagree with the old aphorism that prevention is better than cure. 'Crime prevention' is often said to be a vital complementary strategy to those of detecting, punishing or treating offenders, although, as most would admit, it has never attracted comparable resources or attention. Strictly speaking, of course, the term covers *any* activity designed to reduce the future incidence of criminal behaviour, a point clearly recognised by the recent Home Office Working Group on Crime

Prevention. They divided the field into 'legislative prevention' (legal sanctions to deter offenders), 'social prevention' (attempts to improve social conditions thought to breed crime) and 'opportunity reduction' (making offences more difficult to commit). Similarly, the US National Crime Prevention Institute writes of 'punitive', 'corrective' and 'mechanical' means of preventing crime.

However, the most common perception of crime prevention is of a very limited field of action: that of protecting property by means of locks, bolts and alarm systems. This narrow interpretation has to some extent been encouraged by government-sponsored television and leafletting campaigns aimed at persuading people to lock up their property, and by the large security hardware companies, who have made considerable efforts to expand the market in home and vehicle security devices. Moreover, since 1965, all British police forces have employed specialist Crime Prevention Officers with expertise in physical methods of protecting property, who give free advice to any commercial company or householder requesting their services. Gladstone (1980) states that five per cent of the total police manpower is now engaged in specialised crime prevention. A large proportion of these officers' time is spent visiting premises and recommending the fitting of better locks at vulnerable points.

At first sight, this so-called 'target-hardening' approach to crime prevention seems eminently sensible. The conventional wisdom has been that a great deal of crime is 'invited' through lack of attention to security, and that if the number of easy opportunities to steal can be significantly reduced, so eventually will be the number of offences. Where residential burglary is concerned, it is often said that, while there may be a small number of 'professional' or 'determined' offenders who can defeat even the most sophisticated security systems, sound locks are sufficient to deter the majority. In the words of the author of '*Homewatch*' (Hampshire Constabulary, 1978:31):

> It must be accepted right from the start that the determined and ruthless criminal will probably defeat your efforts to keep him out of your home. Fortunately, these criminals are few and far between and their efforts are normally directed to much higher values than you or I are likely to possess . . .
>
> . . . Almost all housebreakers are young, inexperienced and very frightened whilst at their criminal work. If we make entry to these budding housebreakers just a little more difficult we will send them elsewhere.

Unfortunately, this deceptively simple argument conceals many practical difficulties and begs a number of questions, some of which we will explore over the next few pages.

cf — a selfish act!

First, there is little doubt that, despite all the efforts made to date, overall levels of household security in England remain very low. Sixty per cent of our victim sample said that prior to their burglary they had had no locks beyond ordinary spring locks, bolts or window-catches. Moreover, Winchester and Jackson (in preparation) found in Kent that under two per cent of a random sample of houses which had *not* been burgled were fitted with mortice deadlocks on all doors and window-locks on all downstairs windows. Only 11 per cent had mortice deadlocks or double-locks on the front door and only 15 per cent had any window-locks at all.[4]

Equally important, whatever quality of locks are fitted, many householders remain very careless about using them. The Kent survey above found that 22 per cent of the non-victims interviewed had failed to lock up on the last occasion they had left their house. Of the 322 victims we interviewed, 132 (41 per cent) admitted that they had frequently gone out without locking doors or shutting windows. Baldwin (1976) also writes of about one-third of burgled houses in his sample having been 'left insecure to a marked degree'.

Unfortunately, there appears to be little hope in the short term of significant improvements in either the overall quality of security hardware fitted to houses or the security consciousness of residents. Results of experiments using persuasion have been negative almost without exception. For example, in 1973 a Marplan evaluation of a television and leaflet campaign in south-west England based on the theme 'Protect your Home' found that, although the public were aware of the campaign, there had been no change in security behaviour (Riley and Mayhew 1980:5). A more recent evaluation of a security advertising campaign carried out in the Harlech and Westward TV region, conducted by Research Bureau Ltd. for the Central Office of Information (No. 11751, August 1980), found no improvement either in the rate of installation of security devices or in the degree of care taken in locking up. Similar negative results are described in White (1975) for a wide variety of publicity campaigns by the police and other bodies in the United States. Although Van Dijk and Steinmetz (1981) report slightly more encouraging results from a Dutch campaign, they draw attention to a further problem: any improvements following advertising tend to be short-lived. The same caveat applies to recent police reports of successful localised campaigns, for example in Southampton, Durham, Sunderland and Coventry, where recorded burglary figures have fallen following intensive prevention publicity, but where evaluations have not been sufficiently rigorous or made over long enough periods to draw any conclusions.

The results have been disappointing even in crime prevention campaigns where personal visits have been made to householders. For example, a Department of Justice study (1973b:68-71) reports on a programme ('Crime Specific') carried out in six Californian cities, in which officers called on a large number of houses offering advice. Return visits established that only five per cent of those visited had made any changes, and that the cost of each change effected was roughly 50 man-hours.

Legislation to *compel* people to improve the security of their homes is a theoretical possibility, but is hardly feasible politically. A few local authorities in the United States have experimented with such legislation in a limited way. For example, White *et al.* (1975:24) describe an ordinance in Arlington, Virginia, which made it compulsory to fit deadbolt locks and special latches on doors and windows in apartments below the second storey. However, many householders strongly resent the idea of being forced to spend money to protect their own property. The only area in which compulsory improvements are currently feasible is that of new housing. It has recently been agreed that British building codes will be tightened up to enforce minimum standards of security in new houses—a welcome development, but naturally one that will have little effect upon overall security levels.

One of the major factors which have to be considered by proponents of target-hardening is that of 'displacement'. By this is meant the problem that if a thief is foiled by security measures at one target, he may simply seek out another which is less well protected, hence defeating the major object of preventing crime. Members of the Home Office Research Unit, who published several studies concerned with opportunity-reduction (for example Mayhew *et al.* 1976, 1978; Riley and Mayhew 1980, Gladstone 1980) have stressed the point that success in crime prevention depends heavily upon how high a proportion of the total 'pool' of possible targets can be equally well protected. They argued, for example, that while only a minority of cars were fitted with steering-column locks, thieves could easily find others to take; but if and when, as the eventual result of compulsory installation in new cars, the vast majority on the road were so protected, only the most determined and skilful thieves would be in a position to steal cars at all. By contrast, the virtual impossibility, in the foreseeable future, of effectively protecting a significantly high proportion of houses appears to leave little defence against 'displacement'.

Even so, it can be argued that the problem of displacement is no excuse for doing nothing. On the contrary, White (1975:40) argues that evidence of displacement is evidence of successful crime prevention, and should provide encouragement to more people to follow the example of the wise:

> As a matter of fact, the very essence of security is that you will turn the criminal from the protected premises to the unprotected ... Critics of mechanical prevention must bear in mind that actual lowering of crime through the mechanical approach may take several years before significant results can be shown.

It is possible, too, that some results may be achieved by the less ambitious policy of concentrating intensively upon selected small areas with high burglary rates. An interesting experiment is under way, at the time of writing, in Newcastle-upon-Tyne. A council housing estate has been 'fortified' at public expense, each house being fitted with thief-resistant locks. The experiment is being monitored to ascertain the effect upon crime rates, both in the estate and in neighbouring areas.[5] The results should provide some test of assumptions which have been made about both specific and general displacement. For example, if, as is likely from evidence discussed earlier, most of the burglaries on the estate are committed by local people, and if the security devices are as effective as is hoped, potential burglars may be forced either into travelling to less familiar territory· or into turning to different forms of crime. Mayhew *et al.* (1976:6) suggest that both courses of action are unattractive to many burglars, and that in circumstances such as those described, only a certain proportion would be prepared radically to alter their *modus operandi*, the result being a real decrease in crime:

> They [burglars] would be unlikely, for example, to start raiding banks ... or to start robbing people in the street (which involves personal confrontation with victims—something housebreakers are traditionally thought to avoid).

We now consider a more fundamental question about target-hardening: one which, if not answered satisfactorily, casts a shadow over the whole of the foregoing discussion. This is, quite simply, whether locks and bolts within the price range that it is reasonable to ask most people to pay really are effective in keeping burglars out. Winchester and Jackson (in preparation) have produced some important findings which raise the depressing possibility that in fitting good security devices to their homes many householders are not significantly lowering their chances of being burgled. Overall, a higher proportion of victims (5.1 per cent) than of non-victims (1.8 per cent) had had the 'good security' of mortice deadlocks on all doors and window-locks on all downstairs windows; and there was virtually no difference between victims and non-victims where 'partial security' was concerned. Moreover, the percentage of victims who had failed to lock up on the day that they were burgled was precisely the same (22 per cent) as that of non-victims who said that the last time they had left the house they had failed to lock up. The former results may be partly explained by the fact that the victim sample contained a higher proportion of houses with high rateable value than the non-victim sample. However, they help to demonstrate the crucial point that neither the level of 'security' nor the extent of carelessness by residents is a primary factor in deciding who is burgled and who is not. As explained earlier (chapters II and III), Winchester and Jackson found '*environmental risk*' (defined mainly by ease of access and surveillability) to be the most important determinant of victimisation, with *occupancy* and *rateable value* also significant. It was only within certain categories of housing—most importantly, local authority estate housing—that level of security proved to have any significant independent effect as a predictor of victimisation.

These authors' analysis, although not complete at the time of writing, appears to support many of our own conclusions. The study gives some credence to the assertion made by nearly all the persistent offenders we interviewed, no matter where they stood in the hierarchy of burglars, that entering almost any house presented them with little difficulty. The results may also throw some doubt upon the relevance of research into 'displacement', inasmuch as they confirm our impression that not many burglars, particularly among those who burgle high-value property, are persuaded into going elsewhere on finding that a house is fitted with security devices. As reported in chapter III, we found some evidence of displacement in the statements of burglars that they would in some circumstances avoid alarms, 'Chubb' locks and aluminium framed windows, but we also noted their insistence that if other conditions were favourable—for example, if the garden offered enough cover to allow them time to beat the security measures or if the house seemed to offer particularly good rewards—they would not be deflected. This is not to say that the locks described are themselves ineffective. In many cases, either householders do not use the security devices they have, or else they heavily protect some possible entry points but neglect others. It is also not uncommon for good locks to be fitted to weak doors or window frames, and hence easily bypassed by the use of force. In our view, one of the central problems is that (as we have argued in chapter III) the 'burglar population' is not made up of a tiny set of skilled professionals and a mass of unskilled amateurs. Most people who have any experience in housebreaking, including groups of young

teenagers, quickly learn to spot weaknesses in the bricks, wood and glass of which houses are made. As Parker (1974:52-3) has illustrated, many very young boys in delinquent areas easily pick up sophisticated techniques of car theft, and housebreaking techniques are child's play by comparison (cf. also Phillips 1979.) Moreover, we have argued that burglary is usually a preplanned crime in the sense that offenders set out to find a house to burgle rather than stumble upon an opportunity. Where opportunities are *actively sought* by burglars rather than passively presented to them, security measures have to be exceptionally good to prevent an entry.

In sum, for persistent adult offenders at least, and we suspect for many younger burglars too, the choice of individual target within a given area seems to be influenced mainly by the presence or absence of potential witnesses and only marginally, if at all, by the supposed 'security' of the dwelling. Our findings and, it appears, those of Winchester and Jackson, set a challenge to conventional thinking about crime prevention. They not only bring into question the value of a purely 'target-hardening' approach, but offer little immediate encouragement to the idea of reducing burglary through other means of opportunity-reduction, as most of the factors found to influence the choice of· target cannot be changed: obviously, houses cannot be moved to safer locations or their surroundings radically altered. To some extent they support the contentions of Newman (1972) and his followers, who have stressed the importance of surveillance by neighbours in preventing burglary, and have suggested means of building 'defensible space' into new housing projects. But again, such ideas are relevant only to a small proportion of total dwellings.

The most constructive conclusion that may be drawn from our discussion is that a more imaginative approach towards crime prevention is needed. Much more attention should be paid to specific local patterns of crime and to the individual character of each small residential area. Above all, attempts should be made to see through a potential offender's eyes: does the street or block hold particular attractions for a burglar? If he chose a particular property to burgle, would he be likely to be seen approaching it? could he easily obtain access to the rear? would he be able to escape easily if disturbed? and so on.

If such questions were regularly asked in conjunction with detailed past information about criminal activity in the area in question, individual residents, perhaps guided by crime prevention officers, would be able to gain a much more realistic picture of their chances of being victimised and would be in a good position to decide for themselves how available crime prevention strategies (including, but not only, methods of target-hardening) could be tailored to their own particular situation. The 'Crime Specific' project in California described earlier (p. 159) made a similar recommendation as a result of observing the apathetic public reaction to house-to-house visits by police officers giving standard 'target-hardening' advice.[6] It is our belief, too, that most householders would be far more interested on such a visit to learn about crime in their own immediate neighbourhood, and hence more likely to take some action.

As examples of more imaginative efforts at crime prevention, we end on a note of optimism by describing first a project which, among many inconclusive American experiments in crime prevention, stands out as almost undeniably successful, and then a British project which demonstrates an unusual degree of constructive imagination. The first is the Seattle Community Crime Prevention Project (Cirel *et al.* 1977). The central core of this project is 'Operation Blockwatch', a scheme by which residents are encouraged by the police to form groups of 10 to 15 neighbouring households, meeting regularly in each other's homes. At the meetings the groups are provided with current information about crime in their area, tell each other when they will be out or on holiday, and organise rotas for tasks such as cutting grass or collecting papers in order to reduce the signs that houses are unoccupied. They are encouraged to keep an eye on each other's homes and to inform the police if strangers are seen near them. Each house displays a window sticker stating that the occupants are in the scheme and that their valuable property is marked with a number so that it can be identified if stolen and sold elsewhere. The residents are also encouraged to use 'occupancy proxy' techniques, such as time-switches on lights or radios, which give the impression to outsiders that somebody is at home.[7] Evaluations have shown that members of the scheme are much less likely to be burgled than others in the area who have not joined. Their rates of burglary (measured by victimisation surveys) have fallen by 50–60 per cent, and the overall rate of burglary in the area has also fallen, apparently to some extent overcoming the problem of displacement.

Of course, there are difficulties in maintaining enthusiasm (Cirel suggests that interest flags after about 18 months and new inputs are then needed to rekindle it), and the scheme is expensive and takes up a lot of police time. It is also clearly much more suitable for some areas and types of housing than for others. Nevertheless, the project has been greeted with local support and optimism, and remains one of the few clear successes in the field of burglary prevention.

The British experiment also deserves particular attention. This is the Cunningham Road project in Widnes, reported by Hedges *et al.*

(1980). A council-housing estate with a severe crime problem was the object of a considerable investment of expertise and resources, aimed not so much at increasing vigilance against thieves as at improving the general 'quality of life' in the area. Residents were surveyed and asked what they would like to see done to improve life on the estate. The answers included the repair of buildings, improvement of lighting, removal of graffiti, clearing of rubbish, mending of fencing and the provision of more youth facilities, as well as the institution of beat policemen, dog wardens and job creation schemes. Many of these requests were answered in a co-ordinated effort by police, local council, social services, voluntary groups and others. The next year saw a clear drop in the extent of vandalism, and the number of burglaries revealed by a victim survey fell by almost 60 per cent. Although, again, the long-term consequences may not be so dramatic, the scheme gives grounds for optimism, and once again supports the point that crime prevention entails much more than locks and bolts.

Finally, it is worth noting that this is the thrust of the argument behind the introduction of 'community policing' (cf. Alderson 1977), whereby crime is said ·to be more effectively discouraged by the improvement of social relations than by other more conventional methods of policing. The results of community policing schemes have not been convincingly assessed, and there is, as yet, little indication that the level of burglary has been reduced in areas in which it has been tried. (For example, neither Skelmersdale nor Myrtle Gardens in Liverpool showed any lowering in rates of reported burglary.) However, the idea has many supporters who believe that as a long-term strategy it is the best hope available. Certainly, in 'problem estates', where most burglary appears to be committed by local offenders, it offers a chance of encouraging residents to take more interest in 'policing' their own communities.

*   *   *   *   *

Summary and concluding remarks

Burglary of private houses conjures up many frightening and disturbing images—of violent strangers in the night, ransacked rooms, fouling of property and sexual assault. Previous research has shown that a considerable proportion of the population fear or frequently worry about the prospect of being burgled. We have confirmed that about one-quarter of those who actually become victims are, temporarily at least, badly shaken by the experience. Moreover, a small minority, mainly women, suffer long-lasting effects including fear, sleeplessness and a deep distrust of others.

Analysis of the actual circumstances of the offence has revealed that, although it is an all-too-common crime, burglary is rarely as objectively serious as people imagine. Confrontations between victim and offender are unusual, and physical contact or violence result in only a tiny proportion of cases. Research leaves us in no doubt that generally speaking, people who engage in burglary are 'sneak' thieves who will do what they can to avoid coming into contact with residents and, if disturbed, their first reaction is to run away. Roughly four out of every five burglaries occur during the day or evening in unoccupied houses, and the number of offenders prepared to engage in 'creeping' (entering homes at night while the residents are asleep) seems to be declining.

Deliberate violence to property, apart from force used to effect entry, is also less common than widely believed. Only five of the 322 victims we interviewed reported any gratuitous acts of vandalism and only one had the experience of finding a pile of faeces. Untidy searches were more common—45 (14 per cent) of victims reported property strewn extensively across the floors of rooms—but in the majority of cases very little had been moved.

The value of property stolen is often low. In 1979, over one-quarter of recorded burglaries in England and Wales resulted in a loss of under £5, and 65 per cent in under £100. Cash is the prime target, and is stolen in well over one-third of all cases. Roughly one in five cases involve pre-payment meters, a fact that suggests that serious thought should be given to the advisability of paying for gas and electricity in this way. Otherwise, burglars steal mainly electrical goods, silverware, jewellery, cigarettes, food and alcohol. However, there has in recent years been a rapid increase in the number of burglaries involving very valuable property, particularly high-quality jewellery and antiques. This is a particularly serious problem in London and the Home Counties. Here it seems that some high-level thieves have concluded that wealthy homes are an easier source of worthwhile hauls than raids on commercial targets, which have become increasingly well protected.

The distribution of burglaries both across the country and within smaller areas displays very uneven patterns. People living in large towns or cities are much more likely to become victims than are small-town or country-dwellers, unless the latter happen to be exceptionally wealthy and live within easy reach of a large urban area. Within sizeable towns, those living in or near to council estates or poorer housing areas, especially if these are situated close to the town centre, are the most vulnerable. However, pockets of particularly affluent middle-class housing on the outskirts of towns sometimes receive a disproportionate amount of attention from burglars. Middle-class housing located on or very close to main roads is also more likely to be burgled than similar housing which is less directly accessible to passers-by.

The burglar's selection of a specific house rather than others nearby is determined by a number of complex factors and is difficult to analyse precisely. The evidence suggests that both small and large detached houses are generally more vulnerable than semi-detached or terraced houses. Burglars also seem to prefer properties near the ends of streets (which give them more options for escape), those with ready access to the rear, those bordered by alleys, wasteland or fields, those whose gardens offer cover in the shape of walls, fences or shrubbery, and those not overlooked directly from the street or from neighbours' windows. Occupancy is also a very important factor. Burglars will avoid houses that are clearly occupied, and American experiments with time-switches and other techniques that simulate occupancy have had some success. On the other hand, it is not certain that either care in locking up or the fitting of good locks and bolts greatly influences burglars' choice of targets. If the house offers sufficient rewards and the entry-point is not easily visible from the road or from other buildings, offenders are both capable of and willing to spend time in defeating all but the most sophisticated crime-prevention devices. The most important exception seems to be burglary in council-housing estates, where Winchester and Jackson, who are generally sceptical of the effectiveness of physical security measures, found that the basic security precautions of closing windows and locking doors may play a significant part in determining which houses are and are not burgled.

Entry to houses is often a simple matter, the most common point of entry being a rear downstairs window. In nearly one-third of all recorded cases glass is broken, and in roughly the same number entry is through doors or windows left insecure. Few burglars carry tools any more sophisticated than a long screwdriver, jemmy or steel comb.

Data on known offenders suggest that on the whole they operate relatively close to home. Known burglars come overwhelmingly from deprived urban areas and the majority of offences for which they are convicted occur within two miles of where they live. All but a tiny proportion of cases cleared up in Reading and Banbury had been committed by residents of these towns; burglars from elsewhere may be under-represented among those arrested by virtue of being harder to catch, but there is no reason to believe that the picture is seriously distorted. Within the poorest council-housing estates, which generally suffer high rates of victimisation, our analysis of both detected and undetected offences has indicated that burglary is often an even more local affair, the houses attacked being previously known to the offender in a considerable proportion of cases. Children, particularly, who are known to commit many of the least serious burglaries, rarely travel outside their own immediate area to steal.

The major exception to these patterns is the kind of burglary that occurs frequently in Gerrards Cross. Very wealthy areas attract the most ambitious thieves who are prepared to travel much greater distances, and are interested mainly in silver, jewellery and antiques. These are not necessarily all sophisticated 'professional' criminals— older teenagers with ambitions to move into the world of serious crime sometimes try their hand at wealthy properties despite the difficulty in selling items profitably afterwards—but almost certainly form only a small proportion of all those who become involved in burglary. Finally, there is also some evidence of lower-level persistent offenders driving a few miles out of town in order to escape the attentions of policemen who know them, but once again, as in the Banbury examples, this can be seen as essentially 'local' offending.

In chapter III we concluded that, although there is a widespread tendency to think of thieves as falling into one of two categories—'professional' or 'amateur'—the majority of frequent offenders are best thought of as 'middle-range' thieves, people who have before them an image of successful professional crime but who fail to display the caution, self-discipline and organisation that this requires. Many take a short-sighted view of criminal behaviour, taking risks which virtually ensure their arrest at least once every one or two years. Despite periods in which they may make a considerable amount of money, very few could be described as having 'made crime pay' over the long term. Those living in small or medium-sized towns quickly become known to the local police, who are usually able to gain a fair knowledge of what they are doing. 'Sightings' of known offenders are filed by collators, detectives mingle with groups of thieves, some regular informers are paid, suspects are questioned about the movements of acquaintances, and so on. Being a persistent thief in a small town was described by one interviewee as 'like living in a goldfish bowl'. Although he almost certainly overestimated the extent of police knowledge about his movements, there is little doubt that to become a successful thief in Reading, for example, is much more difficult than in London, where anonymity is easier to achieve. In these circumstances it is crucial to a man's chances of avoiding arrest to be able to restrict precise knowledge of his activities to a small clique of associates whom he can trust. As we have seen, the attractions of excitement, companionship, exhibitionism, and admiration from others often work against this aim, and many thieves are deflected from the businesslike approach they know they should adopt by falling into a fast-living, hedonistic lifestyle. Moreover, once things go wrong, many partnerships are not sufficiently solidly based to prevent one partner betraying his associates in the hope of reducing his own discomfort or punishment.

We showed in chapter IV that it is possible for an individual in a small town to 'work his way up the ladder' into high-level burglary, but that, apart from sufficient skill and experience, he requires connections with receivers who deal in valuable property. Such people will deal only with thieves they think they can rely on, and even then, as Peter Hudson's account shows, are always ready to cheat the burglar by pretending that expensive items are worthless. Very few burglars ever reach the 'ideal' in their 'profession'—help and co-operation from a small group of trustworthy associates, a relationship of equality with an important receiver, and sufficient knowledge about, for example, jewellery or antiques to select the most profitable targets—but the small number who do can make enormous sums of money and are very difficult to catch. At present, the 'target' method of surveillance seems to be the only effective way of combatting them, although this has certain drawbacks, as pointed out on page 150. A final but most important point to remember about the above findings is that our research was concentrated upon the activities of persistent offenders over the age of seventeen. We have estimated that perhaps two in every five burglaries are committed by juvenile offenders. There is a pressing need for further research into patterns of burglary by juveniles, which would provide a more balanced picture of the phenomenon as a whole.

The findings concerning the reactions of victims to burglary, reported in chapter V, raise several policy issues. It was found that about 40 per cent of all female victims interviewed had suffered considerable shock or distress following the discovery of the burglary, and that almost two-thirds of all victims were still to some extent affected by the event over a month later. Widows and divorcees seemed to be particularly susceptible to serious and lasting aftereffects. Victim support schemes have for some time been aware of the degree of upset that burglary can cause, and these are now expanding considerably. Even so, they still only reach a tiny minority of the total number of victims, and the main source of immediate help remains the police.

Although the majority of victims we interviewed were satisfied with the service the police provided, more than one in six expressed clear dissatisfaction, and 30 per cent mentioned some form of criticism. CID officers were the targets of criticism much more frequently than uniformed officers. The main complaints were that detectives showed little interest in the case, treated the victims as 'unimportant', and that once they had left, nothing more was heard. It seemed that people were less interested in the offender being caught than in seeing a set of expected procedures carried out (fingerprinting, questioning, sympathetic listening), a finding that we interpreted as part of the victim's need to regain a lost sense of security. The feeling that 'the police are handling everything'—greatly aided by the appearance of a 'fingerprint man' or by a telephone call to explain the stage investigations have reached—seems to provide a crutch to help people regain a sense of normality. It becomes easier for the victim to see the burglary as an experience that many others go through and to which there is a standard yet caring official response.

One of the main conclusions that can be drawn from chapter V is that, although burglary is often relatively trivial in terms of value stolen and often holds out little hope of an arrest, the police can do a great deal for the welfare of victims (and, incidentally, for improving police-public relations) by some very straightforward procedures. They can listen sympathetically to victims' concerns, reassure them with basic facts about burglary (that the chances of a burglar returning are small, or that most burglars are non-violent and relatively young), and carry out initial investigations at the scene of the crime in a thorough manner, even though these may be clearly fruitless. The burden upon police time would not necessarily be greatly increased if a special effort were made to remind junior CID officers that what presents itself to a policeman as minor, routine offence may have a vastly different impact on a person who is experiencing victimisation for the first time. In addition, it could be made standard practice to inform every victim by letter or telephone about progress in their case at perhaps four to six weeks after the event.

Ultimately, of course, the question of finances and resources may decide the issue: whether or not public funds can be spared to develop victim support schemes and whether police administrators believe that too much time is already allocated to visiting scenes of minor crimes are factors in such decisions. Nevertheless, the damage done to victims over the long-term by the insecurity and mistrust of others that burglary fosters, and by the sense of having been 'short-changed' by a casual or unsympathetic response from the police seems, from the results of our study, to deserve some serious consideration.

Questions about the attitudes of victims towards burglary produced some surprising results. Despite the upset and inconvenience caused, only 29 per cent expressed a desire to see the offender in their case sent to prison. Many looked for more constructive solutions and regarded imprisonment as a last resort.[8]

Research into the effectiveness of efforts to prevent burglary has generally been disheartening. Not only is it a daunting task to persuade people to fit better locks or even to lock up when going out, but Winchester and Jackson's research (in preparation), taken together with the comments of our burglar interviewees, suggests that physical crime-prevention measures are often of little or no help in keeping burglars out. We have argued that most offences are not committed in an 'opportunistic' manner (in the sense of a person seeing a window open and thus being stimulated to break in), but by offenders who have decided well in advance to commit a burglary and who are thus actively seeking an opportunity to put their intention into practice. Their main concern is to find an unobserved access-point to an unoccupied house, and once this is done, physical barriers to entry have to be exceptionally strong to make them give up and look elsewhere. There seems to be more hope in wider strategies of opportunity reduction than in simple target-hardening, as evidenced in the success of the Seattle Community Project (see p. 163), and in the strategy of improving the 'quality of life', illustrated by the Cunningham Road project (p. 164).

As most researchers have discovered, burglary in a dwelling remains one of the most intractable crime problems of all. It is a crime which, despite heavy penalties, has flourished for many centuries; which is extremely difficult to detect or prevent; and which is committed by the most persistent adult criminals as well as by an exceptionally high proportion of children. No 'solution' to the problem is in sight, a situation which has led several North American writers on the subject to conclude that we must learn to 'live with' burglary, publicising what Waller and Okihiro (1978) call the 'peace-ful' nature of the offence in order to reduce unnecessary fear, and improving insurance arrangements to compensate victims. In a situation of limited police resources, it has been argued, the public must take more responsibility for protecting their own homes and not nearly so much should be expected of the police as is presently the case. While we would accept the spirit of these conclusions, we would emphasise that they should not lead us to take any less seriously the impact of burglary upon its victims. On the contrary, this is the one area in which a simple remedy—the provision of attention and a sympathetic ear—can have immediate beneficial effects.

Finally, although we would support, mainly on the pragmatic grounds of the gross overcrowding of prisons, a policy of shorter sentences and increased use of non-custodial alternatives for burglars as well as other non-violent property offenders, we emphasize that this does not imply a weakening of *moral* condemnation of burglary. On the contrary, increased attention to the plight of victims would highlight the psychological damage which is the worst aspect of the offence. It might even cause some offenders to see their own behaviour in a less rosy light.[9]

Psychol effect

Notes

I. Introduction

1 The public in the United States seem to put a particularly high emphasis upon crime among all social problems. For example, in 1974 a statewide survey in Maryland (see White *et al.* 1975:4) asked respondents to name the most important problems facing the community. The most frequently mentioned was crime and related problems (49 per cent), followed by economy (24 per cent), and then provision of social services (13 per cent). Respondents were also asked how much they feared specific types of crime. The most feared was vandalism (50 per cent said they were 'very' or 'somewhat' fearful of this offence), then burglary (47 per cent), robbery (46 per cent), and assault (42 per cent). When asked what 'priority' they attached to different crimes, rape (44 per cent) and murder/manslaughter (36 per cent) preceded burglary (30 per cent). A survey in Seattle (Cirel *et al.* 1977:1) placed burglary as the crime causing most concern. On the other hand, Waller and Okihiro (1978:80) found much lower levels of public concern in Toronto. They pointed out (cf. also Furstenberg 1972) that such surveys tend not to distinguish between concern and genuine fear, and that the way questions are worded has considerable influence on the results. It is hoped that the national victim survey soon to be conducted in Great Britain will produce more reliable information. (See n.2, p. 173).

II. Patterns of burglary

1 Burden (1980:140) quotes the results of a survey conducted by AGB in which it was found that for every 100 burglaries reported to the police there were a further 37 successful burglaries not reported. In addition there were 58 unsuccessful attempts for every 100 reported successful burglaries. Just over half the unsuccessful attempts were reported to the police. We interpret these figures to mean that there was a reporting rate of 73 per cent for successful burglaries and just over 50 per cent for attempts. The General Household Survey 1979, which included both theft and burglary in a dwelling, produced a reporting rate of

approximately 75 per cent and estimated that about 50 per cent of those offences known to victims were eventually recorded (cf. *Criminal Statistics* 1979:42).

2 It was, however, encouraging to learn shortly before going to press that the Home Office Research Unit have received permission and funding to undertake the first national crime survey in Great Britain. At present this is planned as a 'one off' survey, but it is possible that, if successful, it may be repeated to allow some longitudinal study of trends.

3 This is undoubtedly an underestimated total value for goods stolen in recorded offences. It is not uncommon for victims to discover that further items are missing when a more thorough check is made after the police have left. We compared the values given to us by victims we interviewed with the official values the police had recorded in the same cases. For 254 victims, the police figures produced a total value of £65,415, while the victims' estimates given to us added up to £96,305, a difference of 50 per cent (see Appendix 1, Table A3).

The latest insurance figures we have show that payments for thefts from private houses in the first half of 1981 reached £47 million, which is almost double the total for 1979.

4 It was noticeable that villages on or close to major roads suffered more burglaries than those accessible only by small country lanes. This phenomenon can be compared with the tendency for burglaries of middle-class housing within towns to occur near main roads, and suggests a reluctance of thieves to venture too deeply into completely unknown territory without quick escape routes (see also p. 85).

5 As explained in Appendix 2, we attempted to interview the victim of every third burglary recorded and, although the response rate was only 62 per cent, from a variety of tests those interviewed seemed to be representative of the total victimised population. In 36 per cent of cases the occupation of the head of household put the residents in the Registrar-General's social class categories 1 or 2, although only 17 per cent of households in the study were classified in these categories by the 1971 census returns. Categories 3N, 3M and 4 were under-represented among victims, but 17 per cent of victims interviewed fell into category 5, that is, double the proportion shown by the census.

6 Over two-thirds of the burglaries recorded within this area of Reading, which is made up predominantly of semi-detached council houses, involved the theft of cash, above all from pre-payment meters. This was the highest proportion of cash

burglaries among all the areas studied. It also had the lowest proportion of thefts of silver or jewellery. Four of the five offenders convicted for offences within the area lived within a few streets of their victims. When interviewed victims in this area were asked who they thought responsible for their burglaries, they usually replied 'local kids' or 'local teenagers'.

7 It may be, for example, that with fewer women tied to the house, homes are more likely to be unoccupied during the day thus making daytime burglary easier. Older burglars and policemen also commented that 'creeping'—night burglary—is a dying skill which is being replaced by cruder methods as the average age of burglars falls. This may, however, be an opinion formed on the basis of nostalgia rather than fact.

8 Hampshire Constabulary (1978:20) found windows to be the entry-point in 52 per cent of cases, over two-thirds of these being rear windows.

9 Waller and Okihiro (1978:20) refer to 'extensive disarrangement of contents' in 14 per cent of cases, a figure similar to our own findings.

10 Chappell (1965:37) found no damage in 48 per cent of cases and damage costing £25 or more to repair in only 1.6 per cent of cases (although here inflation must be taken into account). Scarr (1973:134) found no damage in 66 per cent of cases and damage costing more than $50 in eight per cent.

III. Persistent burglars

1 One of the authors also had considerable experience in interviewing thieves both in custodial and non-custodial settings, having worked as a research assistant upon a previous project (Webster and Maguire 1973) which was concerned with the social organisation of persistent offenders.

2 Similar divisions can be found in Keogh and Koster (1977: 'professionals' and 'amateurs'), Erez (1980: 'planned' and 'impulsive' offenders) and the US Task Force Report (1967: 'professional' and 'non-professional' offenders).

3 In fact, almost all our interviewees received lower proportions of the normal market value of goods than we had expected. The widely quoted figure of one-third of the market value (cf. Lees and Chiplin 1975) is in our experience far too high: it was comparatively rare for burglars of any kind to receive more than 25 per cent, and the majority received considerably less.

4 We had among our victim sample two cases of clumsy burglaries by offenders who were almost totally inebriated and who had

attempted burglaries soon after leaving public houses. They were quickly and easily arrested. We also have an exact copy of a young teenager's explanation of how he came to commit a burglary, taken from his statement to the police, which is reproduced here exactly as it was written:

> When i was playing with some of my mates i saw a shed that i wanted to have a look at so i smashed one of the windows and went in and had a look at it the i went home and said i have been playing with some of my mates i did not take anything out of the shed i Just look arond. one day i wanted a dringk of water so i went to and little house to ask if i could have a drink and there was no one in and one of the windows were open so i got in and had a look around and there was some fags and some mony so i took them my brother was with me so we went and smoked the fags and spent the mony the mony added up to six pound and two cans of double dimond.

The series of 'so I . . . ' links between seeing an opportunity and taking advantage of it seem to provide a good example of a 'stimulus-response' mechanism. It is possible that if the window had not been left open the boy would not have entered the house. Yet, as he had already smashed the shed window, even this is not certain.

V. The victims

1 There were no significant differences in terms of class, value stolen, method of entry or untidiness of search between respondents and non-respondents (see Appendix 2).

2 This was more frequently the case in housing estates or in streets close to housing areas perceived as containing 'problem families'. Residents of the predominantly middle-class towns we looked at were more likely to envisage the culprit as a travelling stranger.

3 The results described find some confirmation in data collected in 1974 by the Bristol Victims Support Scheme. The original questionnaires were kindly lent to us by the researcher, Chris Holtom, and our re-analysis revealed that 10 of the 12 female victims of burglary who had been most upset were separated, widowed or divorced.

4 Preliminary research by John Howley in a study of North London has produced similar findings (personal communication).

5 Sixteen (40 per cent) of the 40 victims of ransacking favoured prison. Waller and Okihiro (1978:39) also found that 'trashing' behaviour affected the victim's desire to see the offender imprisoned.

6 Twenty-three (31 per cent) of 75 who described their offender as a 'professional' desired a custodial sentence, compared with 27 (22 per cent) of 123 who thought he was an 'amateur', and 28 (45 per cent) of 62 who placed him between the two categories.

VI. Prevention, detection and sentencing

1 Sir Robert Mark: speech to AGB Conference Services seminar for security experts, October 17th, 1978.

2 As shown in Table 16 (p. 144), only 1.3 per cent of burglaries recorded in the Thames Valley in 1975 came to light as a result of police patrols. American research has also concluded that routine car patrols are of minimal value in the fight against burglars (cf. Pope 1977a:26, White *et al*. 1975:32). The most well-known study is that by Kelling *et al*. (1974), in which it was found that reducing or increasing the level of preventive patrol in Kansas City had no noticeable effect on burglary rates. Although these findings have been questioned, even the critics (e.g. Zimring 1978) admit that any success is only of a minimal order.

3 The importance of 'TIC's in detection rates is underlined by a passage in Burden (1980:92-5), where he describes how the clear-up rate for burglaries in the MPD in 1979 was improved by 20 per cent. This came mainly as the result of a top-level policy decision to keep all arrested offenders in police stations overnight and to subject each one to systematic CID questioning in order to elicit a higher number of confessions.

4 Unfortunately, most other figures available about levels of security refer, like ours, only to samples of victims, and are anyway couched in very general terms. These are gleaned mainly from police records. For example, Chappell (1965) reported that 52 per cent of victimised houses in his sample were 'insecure'. More recently, Walsh (1980:108) gives the equivalent figure for burglaries in Exeter as 44 per cent and Hampshire Constabulary (1978:18) quote theirs at 30 per cent.

5 The research is being conducted by the Department of Social Work Studies at Newcastle-upon-Tyne Polytechnic, and is funded by the Home Office Research Unit. A report is expected around March, 1982.

6 The researchers point out that many people had concluded that, in purely financial terms, expenditure on locks and bolts was simply not worthwhile. They also argue that in many cases the residents may be right: the average loss through burglary per house per annum was calculated at $12, so that any expenditure above that figure was not cost effective. On the other hand, they

suggest, some types of household are statistically at greater ris[ ] than others, and they recommend the provision of highly localise[ ] information about risk to help people make a more rationa[ ] decision. (It might also be pointed out that the psychological damage of burglary should also be considered in any such calculation.)

Many of the victims in our sample also commented upon the high expense of effective security. Only 56 (virtually all in the higher socio-economic groups) were referred to a Crime Prevention Officer by the police. Of these, 42 received a visit, but only 21 followed the advice offered, the remainder finding the costs prohibitive.

7 Waller (1979:16), in an evaluation of the Seattle scheme, compared with results from his own research, concludes that 'Occupancy Proxy' is the most successful element of the scheme, and advocates this as the first type of initiative to encourage in any anti-burglary programme.

Property-marking is relatively untried in England, but *Crime Prevention News* (1, 1982) reports an apparently successful experiment in Badsworth, Pontefract, where no burglaries at all were reported in the first weeks following a combined marking and sticker display exercise.

8 There is little other published research relevant to this issue, but Smale and Spickenheuer (*Victimology* vol. 4, No. 1, 1979) found that over 50 per cent of a sample of victims of serious property crime in Amsterdam stated that they would have pronounced a sentence on 'their' offender not exceeding three months.

9 Dermot Walsh recently made the point, seized upon light-heartedly by the Press, that burglars are as upset as anybody else when they discover that they have been burgled. One or two of our interviewees described similar experiences, and admitted that, more than anything else, these events had 'made them think' about what they had been doing.

Appendix 1 Tables

Table A1 *Reporting and recording of burglary: estimated proportion of 'true'*
number of burglaries (a) reported to police, (b) recorded by police

Source:	Dutch National Survey 1977		US National Survey 1973–7		US cities surveys		London survey 1972–3		General Household Surveys 1972–9		'Best guess'
	(a)	(b)	(a)	(b)	(a)	(b)	(a)	(b)	(a)	(b)	(b)
	83%	50%	46%	—	51%–67%	13%–49%	50%	25%	75%	50%	50%
Reference:	Van Dijk and Steinmetz (1980)		Department of Justice (1979)		Skogan (1976)		Sparks *et al.* (1977)		Criminal Statistics (1979)		Home Office Research Unit (1981)

Note   Based on a table submitted by the Home Office Research Unit to a conference discussing the possibilities of setting up a National Crime Survey in England and Wales, Cambridge, April 1981. By kind permission of Mike Hough, Home Office Research Unit.

Source *Criminal Statistics.*

Table A2 *Value of property stolen, burglary in a dwelling, England and Wales, 1973–79*

	Nil	under £5	£5 and under £25	£25 and under £100	£100 & under £500	£500 & under £1,000	£1,000 and over	Total
1973	35,064	25,835	50,156	37,745	23,528	3,645	2,442	178,415
1974	42,797	26,834	54,679	46,903	33,571	5,471	3,901	214,156
1975	47,823	24,898	54,753	54,156	42,565	8,153	5,424	237,772
1976	45,768	20,305	48,060	52,710	46,334	10,065	7,398	230,640
1977	52,066	20,318	48,732	59,059	57,694	13,889	10,848	262,606
1978	50,299	17,577	43,793	57,458	59,735	15,415	12,920	257,287
1979	48,217	14,218	40,228	56,322	61,252	17,311	15,314	252,772
per cent increase 1973–79	+ 37.5	− 45.0	− 19.8	+ 49.2	+ 160.3	+ 374.9	+ 527.1	+ 41.7

Table A3   Police and victim estimates of value stolen: interviewed victims, Reading, Banbury and Gerrards Cross: covering in each a one-year period between 1977 and 1979

Area		Police estimates (A)	Victim estimates[1] (B)	Victim estimates[2] (C)	B as percentage of A	B + C as percentage of A
Banbury	Number of cases	68	68	12	108.8	119.7
	Total value	£14,888	£16,191	£1,633		
	Mean value	£218.9	£238.1	£136.1		
	Median value	£15	£25	£42		
Gerrards Cross	Number of cases	57	57	25	162	297.4
	Total value	£30,562	£49,525	£41,366		
	Mean value	£536.2	£868.9	£1,654		
	Median value	£200	£500	£1,000		
Reading	Number of cases	129	129	31	153.2	177.8
	Total value	£19,965	£30,592	£4,904		
	Mean value	£154.8	£237.1	£158.2		
	Median value	£28	£40	£20		

Notes   [1] Where the police also recorded value stolen.
        [2] Where no value was recorded by the police.

Table A4   Type of property stolen, all offences of burglary in a dwelling recorded by Thames Valley police, 1975 (N = 6,484)

Type of property stolen	Percentage of cases
Cash	45
Jewellery/silver, etc.	14
Cigarettes/alcohol/food	13
Radio/stereo/tape-recorder	11
Handbag/wallet/purse	8
TV	6
Clothing	4
Nil stolen	19

Table A5   Property recovered by value stolen in cases involving any financial loss, all offences of burglary in a dwelling recorded by Thames Valley police 1975

Value stolen	Under £10	£10 & under £50	£50 & under £100	£100 & under £500	£500 & under £1,000	£1,000 & under £5,000	£5,000 & over	Total
Some property recovered	68 (10.5%)	178 (10.5%)	92 (13.5%)	122 (12.8%)	32 (13.1%)	28 (13.5%)	4 (21.1%)	524 (11.8%)
No property recovered	577	1,510	592	830	213	180	15	3,917
Total	645	1,688	684	953	245	208	19	4,441

Table A6   Juvenile involvement and value stolen, detected cases, burglary in a dwelling, Thames Valley, 1975   (N = 1,880)

Value stolen	Total cases	Number with juveniles involved	Percentage with juveniles involved
Not recorded	304	169	55.6
Nil	430	213	52.9
Under £10	232	132	56.9
£10 & under £50	425	216	50.8
£50 & under £100	145	58	40.0
£100 & under £500	220	43	19.5
£500 and over	124	9	7.3
All detected offences	1,880	840	44.7

Table A7   Value stolen by darkness and light,   Thames Valley, 1975 (only cases where this information is known[1])

Dark or Light	Nil	£1–£49	£50–£499	£500 +	Total
Dark	391 (44.2%)	345 (34.2%)	212 (32.1%)	40 (22.5%)	988 (36.2%)
Light	493 (55.8%)	664 (65.8%)	449 (67.9%)	138 (77.5%)	1,744 (63.8%)
Total	884 (100%)	1,009 (100%)	661 (100%)	178 (100%)	2,732 (100%)

Note   [1] In a further 3,752 cases, this information was not obtainable. However, there is no reason to believe that there is any systematic bias, as far as value is concerned, between the knowns and unknowns.

Table A8   Detection rates by value stolen, Thames Valley, 1975

Value stolen	Not recorded	Nil	Under £10	£10 & under £50	£50 & under £100	£100 & under £500	£500 & over	Total
Number reported	814	1,229	645	1,688	684	952	472	6,484
Percentage cleared up	37.3	35.0	36.0	25.2	21.2	23.1	26.3	29.0

Table A9   Burglaries recorded in three areas by period of day

	Reading	Banbury	Gerrards Cross
Day	36.4%	39.3%	41.2%
Evening	11.8%	16.7%	6.8%
Overnight	22.6%	14.0%	14.9%
Not known	29.1%	30.0%	37.2%
Total	100.0%	100.0%	100.0%
	(N = 797)	(N = 150)	(N = 357)

Table A10   'Overnight'[1] burglaries by month of year, Thames Valley, 1975

Month offence committed	Number of burglaries recorded by police	'Overnight' burglaries as a percentage of all burglaries recorded by police
January	518	13.1
February	463	13.4
March	512	20.3
April	485	21.4
May	485	25.8
June	412	22.6
July	449	22.3
August	421	23.3
September	470	14.5
October	497	13.3
November	468	12.0
December	565	12.9
Not known	58	—
Total	5,803	

Note   [1] Overnight burglaries are defined as those known to have taken place after 10 p.m. but not discovered until 2 a.m.–9 a.m. the following morning.

Table A11   Position of entry, burglary in a dwelling (excluding flats), three areas, Thames Valley: covering in each a one-year period between 1977 and 1979

	Rear	Front	Side	Other/ not known	Total
Window	440	64	52	107	663
	(40.6%)	(5.9%)	(4.8%)	(9.8%)	(61.1%)
Door	147	178	17	14	356
	(13.5%)	(16.4%)	(1.6%)	(1.3%)	(32.8%)
Other/not known	3	—	1	62	66
	(0.3%)		(0.1%)	(5.7%)	(6.1%)
Total	590	242	70	183	1,085
	(54.5%)	(22.3%)	(6.5%)	(16.9%)	(100.0%)

Table A12   Selected categories of victims interviewed showing percentage seriously affected

	Number in sample	Rated as seriously affected:	
		Number	*Percentage*
All victims	322	43	13.4
Women	159	34	21.4
Working-class women	65	16	24.5
Women living alone	60	17	28.3
Women over 60	35	12	34.3
Divorcees	25	10	40.0
Widows	24	11	45.8
Widows living alone	18	9	50.0
Working-class widows	10	6	60.0
Working-class widows over 60	8	5	62.5

Table A13   First reaction on discovering burglary, by sex and class

		Anger %	Shock %	Upset/ tears/ confusion %	Fear %	Surprise/ disbelief %	No strong reaction %	Total %
	Male	36	16	25	2	9	11	100 (N = 44)
Working-class	Female	15	26	26	14	5	14	100 (N = 65)
	All	24	22	26	9	6	13	100 (N = 109)
	Male	42	7	9	5	12	25	100 (N = 119)
Middle-class	Female	21	31	16	13	7	12	100 (N = 94)
	All	33	17	12	8	10	19	100 (N = 213)
All respondents		30	19	17	9	9	17	100 (N = 322)

Table A14   Effects on female victims, by disturbance of possessions

	No serious disturbance of property	Ransacking/ vandalism	Total
Serious effects on victim	26	8	34
Less serious effects on victim	115	10	125
Total	141	18	159

$(x^2 = 5.0, p < .05)$

Note   The 'ransacking' factor was even more important in its effects on male victims, although the smaller figures make the result statistically unreliable: four of the nine most upset had suffered ransacking.

Table A15   Detected cases of burglary, showing numbers of offenders held responsible in each case, by sex of offender(s), Thames Valley, 1975

Offenders arrested:	Male	Female	Mixed	Not recorded	Total	
Alone	1,190	44	—	—	1,234	(65.6%)
Pair	449	17	9	—	475	(25.3%)
3 or more	147	2	14	—	163	(8.7%)
Not recorded	—	—	—	8	8	(0.4%)
Total	1,786	63	23	8	1,880	(100.0%)

Table A16   Detected cases of burglary, showing number of offenders held responsible in each case. For two age groups, Thames Valley, 1975

	Alone	Pair	Group	Not recorded	Total
Adult	77.3%	18.1%	3.9%	0.7%	100.0% (N = 1,040)
Juvenile/child	50.4%	34.6%	14.8%	0.1%	100.0% (N = 840)

Table A17   Persons convicted of burglary in a dwelling by a court in the Thames Valley Police Force Area, by sex, age and sentence, 1976

Sentence	Total convicted No.	Total convicted %	10-under 17 %	Age: 17-under 21 %	21 and over %
MALES					
Absolute or conditional discharge	52	8.0	14.6	4.5	3.2
Fine	102	15.8	20.9	16.4	9.3
Supervision order or probation order	88	13.6	19.3	15.2	5.6
Attendance centre	30	4.6	11.8	—	—
Care order	36	5.6	14.2	—	—
Community service order	18	2.8	—	6.2	3.2
Detention centre	52	8.0	13.4	10.2	—
Borstal training	59	9.1	5.9	24.9	—
Suspended sentence	59	9.1	—	4.0	24.1
Immediate imprisonment	148	22.9	—	18.1	53.7
Other	3	0.5	—	0.6	0.9
Total	647	100.0	100.0	100.0	100.0
FEMALES					
Absolute or conditional discharge	5	13.2	17.6	8.3	11.1
Fine	8	21.1	23.5	25.0	11.1
Supervision order or probation order	14	36.8	35.3	50.0	22.2
Care order	3	7.9	17.6	—	—
Community service order	1	2.6	—	—	11.1
Borstal training	3	7.9	5.9	16.7	—
Suspended sentence	3	7.9	—	—	33.3
Immediate imprisonment	1	2.6	—	—	11.1
Total	38	100.0	100.0	100.0	100.0

Table A18   *Ages of offenders cautioned or sentenced for burglary in a dwelling, England and Wales, 1977*

	under 14	14 and under 17	17 and under 21	21 and over	Total *percentage*	*(number)*
Cautioned	5.9%	4.5%	0.2%	0.3%	10.9	(2,630)
Magistrates' Court	9.4%	25.0%	6.3%	9.2%	49.9	(11,982)
Crown Court	0.0%	3.7%	15.8%	19.7%	39.2	(9,420)
Total	15.3%	33.2%	22.4%	29.2%	100.0	(24,032)

Source: *Criminal Statistics*

Table A19   *Lengths of prison sentence passed at Crown Courts for burglary in a dwelling and all other indictable offences, England and Wales, 1977*

	6 months & under	over 6 months up to & including 2 years	over 2 years up to & including 4 years	over 4 years	Total
Burglary in a dwelling:					
Number	567	2,117	443	91	3,218
Percentage	17.6	65.8	13.8	2.8	100.0
All other offences:					
Number	5,782	10,306	2,655	984	19,727
Percentage	29.3	52.2	13.5	5.0	100.0

Table A20 Burglary in a dwelling, by Police Division and rate per 100,000 population, Thames Valley, 1975

Police Div.	Two largest towns: approx. population	Brief description of area	Approximate population in Division	Number of offences	Approximate rate of burglaries per 100,000 population
H	Oxford (110,000) Abingdon (20,000)	Smallest division geographically: includes university city and largest factory complex in area; wealthy satellite villages.	190,000	1,091	570
E	Reading (130,000) Wokingham (25,000)	Largest town in area, with extensive light industry and wealthy commuter country surrounding. M4 passes through Division.	320,000	1,528	480
C	Slough (90,000) Maidenhead (50,000)	Sprawling urban area Slough-Maidenhead-New Windsor: light industry. Exclusive stockbroker belt in south. M4 passes through.	350,000	1,600	460
B	High Wycombe (60,000) Chesham (20,000)	Wycombe, a sprawling town linked to London by M40: light industry here and in Chesham. Otherwise wealthy residential areas such as Gerrards Cross.	240,000	824	340
F	Newbury (25,000) Wantage (10,000)	Large area, sparsely populated on Downs. Borders of Division close to Reading and Oxford. M4 passes through.	170,000	575	340
A	Aylesbury (40,000) Thame (7,000)	Only one town of any size (Aylesbury), isolated from other urban areas: rest largely agricultural.	130,000	292	220
G	Banbury (30,000) Bicester (15,000)	Largely rural area: light industry in Banbury and Witney. No large towns. No motorways.	180,000	339	190
D	Bletchley (30,000) Wolverton (15,000)	Rural area now being developed to accommodate a new city: previously only Bletchley of any size.	140,000	235	170
	Total		1,720,000	6,484	380

Appendix 2 The Interview Samples

As explained in the text (pp. 5–6), victims for interview were drawn from three separate police sectors. The total number of cases recorded in these three areas was 1,304. As we were interested mainly in reactions to an intrusion into living space, the sample for interview was first reduced by omitting all cases of attempted burglaries, cases in which the property attacked did not constitute a regular dwelling (for example, garages, hotel rooms, holiday cottages), and offences which came to light only through other inquiries. In the Banbury area, the total remaining—130—was small enough to allow us to attempt to interview all victims. In Reading, which produced about six times as many offences, we decided to include every third case as it was recorded, which gave us a sample of 259. In the Gerrards Cross area we concentrated upon victims with an address in either Gerrards Cross itself, or in the adjoining village of Chalfont St Peter, two of the most prosperous parts of the sector. The total here was 134 burglaries.

Our final population for interview thus comprised 523 victims. In each case a letter requesting an interview was sent to the person named as the aggrieved on the police report. In most cases, this was the individual finally interviewed as the 'victim' of the case, although in 15 cases the spouse of the aggrieved was interviewed in the absence of the latter.

About 40 per cent of victims replied to our initial letters. If no reply

Table A21   Population for interview and proportions interviewed in the three study areas

	Banbury		Gerrards Cross		Reading		Total	
Interviewed	80	(61.5%)	82	(61.2%)	160	(61.8%)	322	(61.6%)
Refused	8	(6.2%)	10	(7.5%)	11	(4.2%)	29	(5.5%)
Ill, died, left area	9	(6.9%)	4	(3.0%)	7	(2.7%)	20	(3.8%)
Failed to contact	33	(25.4%)	38	(28.4%)	81	(31.3%)	152	(29.1%)
Total in sample	130	(100.0%)	134	(100.0%)	259	(100.0%)	523	(100.0%)

Table A22 *Social characteristics of victims interviewed in the three areas*

		Gerrards Cross Percentage (N = 82)	Reading Percentage (N = 160)	Banbury Percentage (N = 80)	Total Number	Total Percentage
1 Age	Under 40	23.2	43.1	35.0	116	36.0
	40 & under 60	53.7	33.7	48.7	137	42.5
	60 & over	23.2	23.1	16.2	69	21.4
2 Sex	Male	62.2	46.9	46.2	163	50.6
	Female	37.8	53.1	53.8	159	49.4
3 Class*	Working-class	4.9	44.4	42.5	109	33.9
	Middle-class	95.1	55.6	57.5	213	66.1
4 Marital status	Married	81.7	50.0	60.0	195	60.6
	Single	4.9	25.6	17.5	59	18.3
	Divorced/widowed/separated	13.4	24.3	22.5	68	21.1
5 Composition of household	Single adult	15.9	36.2	26.2	92	28.6
	Single adult with children	—	6.3	8.8	17	5.3
	Adults—no children	34.1	31.2	25.0	98	30.4
	Adults & children	50.0	26.2	40.0	115	35.7
6 Type of house	Detached	92.7	18.7	43.7	141	43.8
	Semi-detached	3.7	27.5	27.5	69	21.4
	Terraced	—	25.6	18.7	56	17.4
	Flats, lodgings etc.	3.7	28.1	10.0	56	17.4
7 Ownership	Owner-occupied	95.1	48.7	57.5	202	62.7
	Rented (private landlord)	1.2	31.3	22.5	69	21.4
	Rented (Council)	3.7	20.0	20.0	51	15.8

Note: * Registrar-General's categories 1, 2 and 3a are defined as middle-class.

was received, a follow-up letter was sent, and if this still produced no response, the house was visited or a telephone call made to the victim. The final response rate was 62 per cent. Five per cent refused to take part in the study, four per cent were ill, had left the area or died, and we failed to contact the remaining 29 per cent in three or more attempts. Table A21 shows details for the three areas.

In order to discover whether any bias was caused by non-response, we compared all available information about victims and offences for which we failed to secure an interview with that in which an interview was successfully concluded. No significant differences emerged. For example, 40.4 per cent of all those interviewed had been burgled during the day, compared with 38.3 per cent of those not inter-viewed. (The equivalent figures for overnight burglaries were 17.4 per cent and 18.9 per cent respectively.) Of victims interviewed 15.8 per cent had had nothing stolen, compared with 11.4 per cent of the remainder. (For burglaries of £500 and above, the figures were 11.2 per cent and 10.9 per cent respectively.) Where social class, probably the most important variable, was concerned, it was more difficult to ascertain information about non-respondents. However, some indications were obtained by looking at response rates for different areas where a particular social class dominated. In Area 1 in Reading (see Fig. 2, p. 38), which contains mainly large owner-occupied houses, the response rate was 51.4 per cent, while in Area 8, made up chiefly of local authority housing, the response rate was 56.8 per cent. In Banbury, there were similarly no significant differences between the response rate in Area 'A' (see Fig. 1, p. 29) and the remainder of the town. We are thus as confident as we can be that there is little problem with interview bias.

Table A22 shows the social characteristics of victims interviewed in each of the three areas.

Appendix 3 A Comparison of Data Recorded in Police Crime Reports and the Statements made by Victims

As a means of checking the accuracy of information received from police files it was possible in the 322 cases where the victim was interviewed to compare what the police recorded with what was said by the victim. Appendix 3 thus comprises three tables which contrast the data received from police initial crime reports and the statements made by victims for: the method of entry, the period of day the offence occurred and the type of goods stolen. A comparison of police and victims' estimates of the value of goods stolen is included in Appendix 1 (Table A3).

There are more unknowns in the police data, but otherwise there is sufficient agreement between the two sources to promote confidence that little inaccurate information is recorded in crime reports about burglary.

Table A23 Method of entry, taken from police crime reports and from victims' statements for the same sample of offences

Means of Entry	Banbury		Reading		Gerrards Cross		Total	
	Police	Victim	Police	Victim	Police	Victim	Police	Victim
Forced								
Window	14	10	23	23	20	20	57	53
Door	6	5	25	27	11	8	42	40
Sub-total	20	15	48	50	31	28	99	93
Glass smashed/removed:								
Window	18	17	28	38	28	35	74	90
Door	5	6	9	12	11	8	25	26
Sub-total	23	23	37	50	39	43	99	116
Insecure:								
Window	10	15	30	23	6	5	46	43
Door	18	18	25	29	–	4	43	51
Sub-total	28	33	55	52	6	9	89	94
Other/not known	9	9	20	8	6	2	35	19
Total	80	80	160	160	82	82	322	322

Table A24   Period of day in which burglaries were committed, taken from police crime reports and from victims' statements for the same sample of offences

Period of Day	Banbury		Reading		Gerrards Cross		Total	
	Police	Victim	Police	Victim	Police	Victim	Police	Victim
Morning	5	10	11	8	3	5	19	23
Afternoon	15	26	25	31	14	23	54	80
Morning/afternoon	16	8	21	26	20	14	57	48
Sub-total: Day	36	44	57	65	37	42	130	151
Evening	13	14	16	26	7	6	36	46
Overnight	12	13	36	33	8	7	56	53
Other/not known	19	9	51	36	30	27	100	72
Total	80	80	160	160	82	82	322	322

Table A25 Six selected categories of goods stolen, taken from police crime reports and from victims' statements for the same sample of offences

Goods Stolen	Banbury		Reading		Gerrards Cross		Total	
	Police	Victim	Police	Victim	Police	Victim	Police	Victim
Cash	27	28	47	54	7	17	81	99
Meter cash	8	10	26	28	1	2	35	40
Jewellery	7	7	18	27	28	44	53	78
Silver	6	7	5	7	14	22	25	36
Television	5	6	11	14	16	16	32	36
Stereo/other electrical equipment	6	10	19	27	9	7	34	44

References

ALDERSON, J. C. (1977), *Communal Policing*. Exeter, Devon and Cornwall Constabulary.

BALDWIN, J. and BOTTOMS, A. (1976), *The Urban Criminal*. London: Tavistock.

BARNES, R. E. (1971), *Are you Safe from Burglars?* New York: Doubleday.

BELSON, W. A. (1968), 'The extent of stealing by London boys and some of its origins', *Advancement of Science*, vol. 25, (124).

BLACK, S. (1963), 'A reporter at large: Burglary 1'. *New Yorker*, December 7th 1963, 63–128.

BLACKSTONE, Sir W. (1830), *Commentaries on the Law of England*, 4 vols. London: Christian.

BOGGS, S. (1970), 'Urban crime patterns' in D. Glaser (ed.), *Crime in the City*. New York: Harper & Row.

BOTTOMLEY, K. and COLEMAN, C. (1981), *Understanding Crime Rates*. Farnborough: Gower.

BOTTOMS, A. E. (1977), 'Reflections on the renaissance of dangerousness', *Howard Journal*, vol. 16 (22), 70–96.

BRANTINGHAM, P. and BRANTINGHAM, P. (1975), 'The spatial patterning of burglary', *Howard Journal*, vol 14 (2), 11–23.

BRANTINGHAM, P. and BRANTINGHAM, P. (eds.) (1981), *Urban Crime and Environmental Criminology*. Beverly Hills: Sage.

BRODY, S. (1976), *The Effectiveness of Sentencing*, Home Office Research Study (35). London: HMSO.

BRYANT, G. and CIREL, P. (1977), *Community Response to Rape: Exemplary Project*. LEAA, US Dept. of Justice, Washington DC: Government Printing Office.

BURDEN, P. (1980), *The Burglary Business and You*. London: Macmillan.

BVSS (1975), 'Summary of first six months' work of Bristol Victims Support Scheme' (mimeo).

CHAPPELL, D. (1965), 'The development and administration of the English criminal law relating to offences of breaking and entering'. Doctoral dissertation, University of Cambridge.

CHATTERTON, M. (1976), 'Police in social control' in King, J. F. S. and Young, W. (eds.), *Control without Custody?* University of Cambridge.

CHIMBOS, P. (1973), 'A study of breaking and entering offences in Northern City, Ontario', *Canadian Journal of Criminology and Corrections,* vol. 15, 316–25.

CHRISTIE, N., ANDENAES, J. and SKIRBEKK, S. (1965), 'A study of self-reported crime' in Christiansen (ed.), *Scandinavian Studies in Criminology*, vol. 1. London: Tavistock.

CIREL, P., EVANS, P., McGILLIS, D. and WHITCOMB, D. (1977), *Community Crime Prevention, Seattle, Washington: An Exemplary Project*. LEAA, US Dept. of Justice, Washington DC: Government Printing Office.

CLARKE, R. V. G. and HOUGH, J. M. (eds.) (1980). *The Effectiveness of Policing*. Farnborough: Gower.

CLINARD, M. D. (1978), *Cities with Little Crime*. New York: CUP.

COKE, Sir E. (1797), *Institutes of the Laws of England*, 4 vols. London.

CONKLIN, J. and BITTNER, E. (1973), 'Burglary in a suburb', *Criminology*, vol. 11, 206–31.

CRIMINAL LAW REVISION COMMITTEE (1966), Eighth Report: *Theft and Related Offences*, Cmnd 2977. London: HMSO.

DAVID, P. R. (ed.) (1974), *The World of the Burglar*. Albuquerque: University of Mexico Press.

DENTLER, R. A. and MONROE, L. J. (1961), 'Social correlates of early adolescent theft', *American Sociological Review*, vol. 26, 733–43.

DEPARTMENT OF JUSTICE (1973a), *Deterrence of Crime In and Around Residences*. LEAA. Washington DC: Government Printing Office.

DEPARTMENT OF JUSTICE (1973b), *Residential Security*. LEAA. Washington DC: Government Printing Office.

DEPARTMENT OF JUSTICE (1974), *Crimes and Victims: A Report on the Dayton-San José Survey of Victimisation*. LEAA. Washington DC: Government Printing Office.

DEPARTMENT OF JUSTICE (1977), *Criminal Victimisation in the United States 1975*. LEAA. Washington DC: Government Printing Office.

DEPARTMENT OF JUSTICE (1979), *Criminal Victimisation in the United States: A Description of Trends from 1973–1977*. LEAA. Washington DC: Government Printing Office.

DURANT, M., THOMAS, M. and WILLCOCK, H. D. (1972), *Crime, Criminals and the Law*, Office of Population Censuses and Surveys. London: HMSO.

EINSTADTER, W. J. (1969), 'The social organisation of armed robbery', *Social Problems*, vol. 17, 64–82, New York.

ENGSTAD, P. and EVANS, J. L. (1980), 'Responsibility, competence and police effectiveness in crime control' in J. V. G. Clarke and J. M. Hough (eds.), *The Effectiveness of Policing*. Farnborough: Gower.

ENNIS, P. H. (1967), *Criminal Victimization in the United States: A Report of a National Survey*, The President's Commission on Law Enforcement and Criminal Administration, Field Surveys II. Washington DC: Government Printing Office.

EREZ, E. (1980), 'Planning of crime and the criminal career: official and hidden offenses', *Journal of Criminal Law and Criminology*, vol. 71 (1), 73–6.

ERICSON, R. V. (1975), *Young Offenders and their Social Work*, Farnborough: Saxon House.

FRIEDMAN, A. B. (1968), 'The scatological rites of burglars', *Western Folklore*, July 27, 171–9.

FURSTENBERG, G. (1972), *Fear of Crime and its Effect on Citizen Behavior*. Washington DC: Bureau of Social Science Research.

GAROFALO, J. (1977), *Public Opinion about Crime*. LEAA, US Dept. of Justice. Washington DC: Government Printing Office.

GAROFALO, J. and LAUB, J. (1978), 'The fear of crime: broadening our perspectives', *Victimology*, vol. 3, 242–53.

GLADSTONE, F. J. (1980), *Co-ordinating Crime Prevention Efforts*. Home Office Research Unit Report (62). London: HMSO.

GREENBERG, B., YU, O. S. and LANG, K. I. (1973), *Enhancement of the Investigative Function Volume III*. Stanford Research Institute, Menlo Park, California.

GREENBERG, B., ELLIOT, C. V., KRAFT, L. P. and PROCTER, H. S. (1977), *Felony Investigation Decision Model*. LEAA, US Dept. of Justice. Washington DC: Government Printing Office.

GREENWOOD, P. W. (1970), *An Analysis of the Apprehension Activities of the New York City Police Department*. New York: Rand Institute.

GREENWOOD, P. W., CHAIKEN, J. M. and PETERSILIA, J. (1977), *The Criminal Investigation Process*. Lexington: Heath.

HALE, Sir M. (1682), *Pleas of the Crown*. 2 vols. London.

HALPERN, S. (1978), *Rape: Helping the Victim*. New Jersey: Medical Economics Company.

HAMMOND, W. H. and CHAYEN, E. (1963), *Persistent Criminals*, Home Office Research Unit Report. London: HMSO.

HAMPSHIRE CONSTABULARY CRIME PREVENTION DEPARTMENT (1978), *A Study of the Crime of Housebreaking in Hampshire*. Hampshire Police Crime Prevention Department.

HAWARD, L. R. C. (1981), 'Psychological consequences of being the victim of a crime' in S. Lloyd-Bostock (ed.), *Law and Psychology*. Oxford: SSRC Centre for Socio-Legal Studies.

HEDGES, A., BLABER, A. and MOSTYN, B. (1980), *Community Planning Project: Cunningham Road Improvement Scheme*. London: Institute of Social and Community Planning Research.

HENRY, S. (1978), *The Hidden Economy*. London: Robertson.

HOOD, R. and SPARKS, R. (1970), *Key Issues in Criminology*. London: Weidenfeld & Nicolson.

HOOD, R. (1974), *Tolerance and the Tariff: Some Reflections on Fixing the Time Prisoners Serve in Custody*. London: NACRO.

IANNI, A. J. (1972), *A Family Business*. London: Routledge & Kegan Paul.

IRVING, B. and HILGENDORF, L. (1980), *Police Interrogation: The Psychological Approach*, Research Study (1), Royal Commission on Criminal Procedure. London: HMSO.

IRWIN, J. (1970), *The Felon*. New Jersey: Prentice-Hall.

JACKSON, B. (1969), *A Thief's Primer*. London: Macmillan.

JEFFREY, C. R. (1971), *Crime Prevention through Environmental Design*. London: Sage.

KALTON, G. and LEWIS, S. M. (1975), *The General Household Survey 1972*. London: HMSO.

KELLING, G. L., PATE, T., DIECKMANN, D. and BROWN, C. E. (1974), *The Kansas City Patrol Experiment*. Washington DC: Police Foundation.

KEOGH, J. E. and KOSTER, J. (1977), *Burglarproof*. New York: McGraw-Hill.

KLOCKARS, K. B. (1974), *The Professional Fence*. London: Tavistock.

LEES, D. and CHIPLIN, B. (1975), 'Does crime pay?', *Lloyds Bank Review* (116), April 1975.

LETKEMANN, P. (1973), *Crime as Work*. New Jersey: Prentice-Hall.

LORENZ, K. (1966), *On Aggression*. London: Methuen.

MCCABE, S. and SUTCLIFFE, F. (1978), *Defining Crime*. Oxford University Centre for Criminological Research Occasional Paper No. 9. Oxford: Basil Blackwell.

MCCLINTOCK, F. H. and AVISON, H. N. (1968), *Crime in England and Wales*. London: Heinemann.

MCDONALD, W. F. (ed.) (1976), *Criminal Justice and the Victim*. Beverly Hills: Sage.

McINTOSH, M. (1975), *The Organisation of Crime*. London: Macmillan.

MACK, J. (1975), *The Crime Industry*, Farnborough: Saxon House.

McKAY, B. (1978), letter in *Liaison*, vol. 4 (11), 4 in reply to article by I. Waller.

MAGUIRE, M. (1980), 'The impact of burglary upon victims', *British Journal of Criminology*, vol. 20 (3), 261-75.

MAGUIRE, M. (1980b), 'Burglary as opportunity', *Home Office Research Bulletin* (10), 6-10.

MARCUS, M., TRIDEL, R. J. and WHEATON, R. J. (1975), *Victim Compensation and Offender Restitution—A Selected Bibliography*. LEAA, US Dept. of Justice. Washington DC: Government Printing Office.

MATZA, D. (1969), *Becoming Deviant*. New Jersey: Prentice-Hall.

MAWBY, R. (1979), *Policing the City*. Farnborough: Saxon House.

MAYHEW, P., CLARKE, R. V. G., STURMAN, A. and HOUGH, J. M. (1976), *Crime as Opportunity*. Home Office Research Study (34). London: HMSO.

MAYHEW, P., CLARKE, R. V. G., BURROWS, J. N., HOUGH, J. M. and WINCHESTER, S. W. C. (1979), *Crime in Public View*. Home Office Research Study (49). London: HMSO.

MIERS, D. (1978), *Responses to Victimization*. Abingdon: Professional Books.

NACRO (1977), *Guidelines for Developing a Victims Support Scheme*. London: NACRO.

NEWMAN, O. (1972), *Defensible Space: People and Design in the Violent City*. London: Architectural Press.

PARKER, H. (1974), *View from the Boys*, Newton Abbot: David and Charles.

PEASE, K. (1979), 'Incapacitation studies: a review and commentary', *Howard Journal*, vol. 18 (3), 160-7.

PERKS COMMITTEE (1967), *Report of the Departmental Committee on Criminal Statistics*, Cmnd 3448. London: HMSO.

PHILLIPS, B. (1979), *Patterns of Juvenile Crime*. London: Police Review Publishing Co.

PHILLPOTTS, G. J. O. and LANCUCKI, L. B. (1979), *Previous Convictions, Sentence and Reconviction*. Home Office Research Study (53). London: HMSO.

POPE, C. E. (1977a), *Crime Specific Analysis: The Characteristics of Burglary Incidents*. Analytic Report SD-AR-10, LEAA, US Dept. of Justice. Washington DC: Government Printing Office.

POPE, C. E. (1977b), *Crime Specific Analysis: An Empirical Examination of Burglary Offense and Offender Characteristics*. Analytic Report SD-AR-10, LEAA, US Dept. of Justice. Washington DC: Government Printing Office.

RADZINOWICZ, L. (1948), *A History of English Criminal Law*, vol. 1. London: Stevens.

RAYNOR, P. (1977), 'Services to victims of crime in Port Talbot' (mimeo).

REPPETTO, T. A. (1974), *Residential Crime*. Cambridge Mass.: Ballinger.

REYNOLDS, P. D. (1973), *Victimisation in a Metropolitan Region*. Minneapolis: Department of Sociology, University of Minnesota.

RILEY, D. and MAYHEW, P. (1980), *Crime Prevention Publicity: An Assessment*. Home Office Research Study (63). London: HMSO.

SCARR, H. A. (1973), *Patterns of Burglary*. National Institute of Law Enforcement and Criminal Justice. Washington DC: Government Printing Office.

SCHNEIDER, A. L. (1978), *Portland Forward Records Check of Crime Victims*.

LEAA, US Dept. of Justice. Washington DC: Government Printing Office.

SHAW, C. and MCKAY, H. (1969), *Juvenile Delinquency and Urban Areas*. Chicago: University of Chicago Press.

SHOVER, N. (1971), 'Burglary as an occupation'. Ph.D. thesis, University of Illinois.

SHOVER, N. (1972), 'Structures and careers in burglary', *Journal of Criminal Law, Criminology and Police Science*, vol. 63, 540–49.

SHOVER, N. (1973), 'The social organisation of burglary', *Social Problems*, vol. 20, 499–513.

SKOGAN, W. G. (1978), *Victimisation Surveys and Criminal Justice Planning*. US Dept. of Justice. Washington DC: Government Printing Office.

SMITH, L. J. F. and MARSHALL, T. F. (1981), 'Who gets away with crime? A study of unsolved burglaries', *Police Review*, Vol. LIV, No. 2, April.

SPARKS, R. F., GENN, H. and DODD, D. (1977), *Surveying Victims*. London: Wiley.

STANLEY, P. R. A. (1976), *Crime Prevention Through Environmental Design: A Review*. Ottawa: Solicitor-General of Canada, Research Division.

STEER, D. (1980), *Uncovering Crime: The Police Role*. Royal Commission on Criminal Procedure, Research Study (7). London: HMSO.

SUTHERLAND, E. H. (1937), *The Professional Thief*. Chicago: University of Chicago Press.

SYKES, G. and MATZA, D. (1957), 'Techniques of neutralization: a theory of delinquency', *American Sociological Review*, vol. 22, 664–70.

SZABO, D. (ed.) (1970), *The Cost of Crime and Crime Control*. Quebec: Second International Symposium in Comparative Criminology.

Task Force Report: Organized Crime (1967). US President's Commission on Law Enforcement and Administration of Justice. Washington DC: Government Printing Office.

THOMAS, D. A. (1979), *Principles of Sentencing* (2nd edn.). London: Heinemann.

THOMAS, D. A. (ed.) (1979b), *The Criminal Appeal Reports (Sentencing)*. Vol. 1. London: Sweet & Maxwell.

THOMAS, D. A. (ed.) (1980), *The Criminal Appeal Reports (Sentencing)*. Vol. 2 Part 1. London: Sweet & Maxwell.

TITTLE, C. R. (1980), *Sanctions and Social Deviance*. New York: Praeger.

VAN DIJK, J. J. M. and STEIMETZ, C. H. D. (1980), *The RDC Victim Survey 1974–79*. The Hague: Ministry of Justice.

VAN DIJK, J. J. M. and STEINMETZ, C. H. D. (1981), *Crime Prevention: An Evaluation of the National Publicity Schemes*. The Hague: Ministry of Justice.

VAN DIJK, J. J. M. and VIANEN, A. C. (1978), *Criminal Victimisation in the Netherlands*. The Hague: Ministry of Justice.

WALLER, I. and OKIHIRO, N. (1978), *Burglary: The Victim and the Public*. Toronto: University of Toronto Press.

WALLER, I. (1978b), 'Minor burglary', *Liaison*, vol. 4 (11), 1–4.

WALLER, I. (1979), 'What reduces residential burglary: action and research in Seattle and Toronto'. Paper given to Third International Symposium on Victimology, Muenster, W. Germany.

WALSH, D. (1980), *Break-ins. Burglary from Private Houses*. London: Constable.

WALSH, D. (1980b), 'Why do burglars crap on the carpet?' *New Society*, vol. 54 (993).

WALSH, M. E. (1977), *The Fence*. Connecticut: Greenwood Press.

WEBSTER, D. and MAGUIRE, M. (1973), 'Why can't you guys get organised like that?' Paper (unpublished) delivered to Fifth National Conference on Teaching and Research in Criminology, Cambridge.

WEST, D. J. (1963), *The Habitual Prisoner*. London: Macmillan.

WEST, D. J. and FARRINGTON, D. P. (1973), *Who Becomes Delinquent?* London: Heinemann.

WEST, D. J. and FARRINGTON, D. P. (1977), *The Delinquent Way of Life*. London: Heinemann.

WHITE, T. W., REGAN, K. J., WALLER, J. D. and WHOLEY, J. S. (1975), *Police Burglary Prevention Programs*. US Dept. of Justice. Washington DC: Government Printing Office.

WILLIAMS, K. M. and LUCIANOVIC, J. (1979), *Robbery and Burglary*. Washington DC: Institute for Law and Social Research.

WINCHESTER, S. W. C. and JACKSON, H. M. (in preparation) *Residential Burglary—The Limits of Prevention*. Home Office Research Study.

WRIGHT, M. (1977), 'Nobody came: criminal justice and the needs of victims', *Howard Journal*, vol. 16 (1), 22-31.

YIN, R. K., VOGEL, M. E., CHAIKEN, J. M. and BOTH, D. R. (1977), *Citizen Patrol Projects*. National Evaluation Program, Phase 1, Summary Report. LEAA, US Dept. of Justice. Washington DC: Government Printing Office.

ZANDER, M. (1979), 'The investigation of crime: a study of cases tried at the Old Bailey', *Criminal Law Review*, 203-19.

ZIMRING, F. E. (1978), 'Police experiments in general deterrence' in J. Blumstein, J. Cohen and D. Nagin (ed.), *Deterrence and Incapacitation: Estimating the Effects of Criminal Sanctions on Crime Rates*. Washington DC: National Academy of Sciences.

Author Index

Subject Index